# CRITIQUE AND CONVICTION

European Perspectives

EUROPEAN PERSPECTIVES

## A Series in Social Thought and Cultural Criticism

### Lawrence D. Kritzman, Editor

*European Perspectives* presents English translations of books by leading European thinkers. With both classic and outstanding contemporary works, the series aims to shape the major intellectual controversies of our day and to facilitate the tasks of historical understanding.

# CRITIQUE AND CONVICTION

## Conversations with François Azouvi and Marc de Launay

### Paul Ricoeur

*Translated by Kathleen Blamey*

Columbia University Press
New York

Columbia University Press
Publishers Since 1893
New York    Chichester, West Sussex

English translation © Polity Press 1998
First published in France as *La Critique et la Conviction* © Calmann-Lévy 1995
This translation first published 1998 by Polity Press in association with
Blackwell Publishers Ltd.

Published with the assistance of the French Ministry of Culture.

**Library of Congress Cataloging-in-Publication Data**

Ricœur, Paul.
    [La Critique et la conviction. English]
    Critique and conviction : conversations with François Azouvi and
Marc de Launay / Paul Ricœur.
        p.   cm.
    Includes bibliographical references.
    ISBN 0–231–10734–X
    1. Ricœur, Paul—Interviews.   2. Philosophers—France—Interviews.
I. Azouvi, François, 1945–   . II. Launay, Marc B. de.   III. Title.
B2430.R553C   1998
194—dc21                                                            97–27567
                                                                        CIP

Casebound editions of Columbia University Press books
are printed on permanent and durable acid-free paper.

Printed in Great Britain

c 10 9 8 7 6 5 4 3 2 1

*To the memory of Mikel Dufrenne, my friend*

# Contents

# Note to the Reader

The conversations that make up the present book took place in October–November 1994, in May and September 1995 at Châtenay-Malabry, in Paul Ricoeur's study. The recording was transcribed and submitted to Paul Ricoeur, who read it over and completed it. We have added bibliographical notes when this seemed necessary for the intelligibility of the text. However, we did not think it advisable to eliminate all the overlaps inherent in the conversational form; weaving from one topic to another, they also form a kind of guiding thread.

F. A. and M. de L.

# Chapter 1

# From Valence to Nanterre

• *Paul Ricoeur, you are above all a man of writing. Nevertheless, you were kind enough to accept the principle of a series of conversations. What does this represent for you?*

• I wish to say first that this is a form of language use that I fear a great deal, because I am indeed a person who writes but also someone who rewrites, who crosses out. I am usually, therefore, mistrustful of improvisation. And yet I have accepted your offer – for two reasons.

First because you belong to the generation of my best friends, a generation that is half-way between the old age in to which I am advancing and the youth I no longer engage with in the face-to-face contact of teaching. You are in the middle of life and you provide me with a closeness, a companionship, and, I might say, the grace of friendship. I would not have agreed to enter into this discussion with anyone other than yourselves.

The second reason has to do with the very nature of the conversations. I want to take the risk once in my life of precisely what dialogue allows, that is a language that is less controlled. I spoke a moment ago of *crossing-out*; now this crossing out is a kind of self-censure. Besides, I have always refrained from revealing confidences. The level to which we shall confine ourselves will be half-way between self-censure and personal confidence; a way of letting out what, alone with myself and the blank page, I might have crossed out, but especially what I would not have written. Here we are, between speech and writing, in a genre that affords us great freedom because vast expanses of language can be left, if not in their raw state, at least in their native, spontaneous state, while others, on the contrary, will be rewritten; in this way, the reader will be offered a variety of levels of speech and writing.

The freedom, the very boldness that this tone implies will enable me to speak off the cuff, as it were, on themes I have not written about, precisely because my thought had not yet attained the level of formulation, of sufficient rigour which I generally insist upon in my writings; this is the case, in particular, for the reflections on aesthetic experience. This will perhaps be the benefit – the reader will decide – of a less tightly controlled discussion.

Along the same lines, I should also like to say that we are going to play, in alternation, not only with the broader range but also with comparisons that I have not made previously. I am thinking, for example, of the religious and philosophical domains, which I have staunchly kept separate from one another for reasons I have always sought to justify. But here, in this more open conversation, I shall be more concerned with the problems arising from the interferences, the overlaps of the religious and the philosophical. In writing, I can separate these domains more explicitly and in a more concerted manner; on the other hand, in the exchanges we are going to have, where the man will speak more than the author, I shall have less justification for cultivating the sort of controlled schizophrenia that has always been my rule of thought. Here the rule of life will overtake the rule of thought.

• *On the whole, you are taking the risk of linking together, more closely than you have done in your writings, the two poles that have provided the title of this book: critique and conviction?*

• Right now, I shall say that critique is no longer on one side and conviction on the other; in each of the fields that are traversed or touched upon I shall attempt to show that there is, to different degrees, a subtle blending of conviction and critique.

• *You have devoted several important works to the theme of subjectivity; your most recent work is entitled* Oneself as Another. *But about you yourself, your life, your intellectual background, very little is known. Where did you spend your early childhood?*

• I was born in 1913 in Valence, where my father was an English teacher. The crucial fact of my childhood was being a *pupille de la nation*, that is, the son of a victim of the First World War, of a father who himself had been widowed several months before he was killed in September 1915, at the Battle of the Marne.

I have a memory, whether it is actually a recollection or whether it is a reconstruction on the basis of what I was told, I don't know: November 11, 1918 was not a day of victory and joy in our household.

I seem to remember having seen a trainload of noisy and joyful soldiers, while at home we were in mourning. Because we did not know if my father was actually dead: we had received only a notice of his disappearance. It was only much later, in 1932, that someone discovered his body while ploughing a field; he was identified by his dogtag. So the war came to a close in the mourning for my father; and this is why I have no memory of a joyous armistice, still less the memory of a victory.

I have a photograph of him, taken during his only leave, at the beginning of 1915; my sister and I are on his knees. Ever since, this image has never shifted; but I myself have grown older and little by little I have had to get used to the idea of a father who is younger than I, whereas at first I had the image of a man without age, situated above me. I have had to assimilate it as the figure of a young man whom I have gone beyond in life. Even today, I have difficulty dealing with my relation to this image, set for all eternity as that of a young man. I feel the same way in the presence of monuments to the dead, before the evocation of "Our children," wondering: but who are these children? Strangely, the monument speaks of a child who is my father, to another child who, himself, will not stop growing older. I have just read, moreover, a similar discussion in *The First Man* by Camus.

This relation to the figure of my father was extremely important because of the reversal to which it was subjected in the following circumstances. His image had been used as a means of educating me in a manner I disapprove of now. I was always told: "What if your father could see you!" I had to satisfy an absent viewer, who, what is more, was a hero. Then, around the age of ten or twelve, I was influenced by a man – our landlord, a Catholic pacifist of the Marc Sangnier tendency[1] – who turned me around completely by "demonstrating" to me that in the "Great War" France had been the aggressor, that the continuation of hostilities after Verdun had been a disgrace, that the Treaty of Versailles was a shame for which all of Europe was paying the price. And it was from this perspective that I viewed the rise of Hitlerism. This image has remained very sharp, and I have not entirely given up the idea that France bears considerable responsibility in this respect. In my eyes, then, my father had died for nothing; and when he had ceased to be a figure of moral censure, I had to struggle with this new vision of the war and of him.

- *What happened when your father died?*

- My sister and I were taken in by our paternal grandparents and we lived in Rennes, where my grandfather was a civil servant. I was therefore cut off from a large part of my family, mainly from those in

Savoie and Geneva on my mother's side. So in addition to being an orphan and a *pupille de la nation*, a good part of my family was unknown to me. From a very early age I found myself solely in the presence of my paternal grandparents. I did, of course, have an unmarried aunt who devoted herself to our upbringing, but she was herself under the hand of my grandparents until the death of my grandmother, when I was fourteen years old.

There is no doubt that this genealogical configuration was at once very formative – because the upbringing I received exerted a very strong influence – and at the same time very traumatic, since the maternal side was hidden, the young woman who raised me was herself under the tutelage of an ancestral figure, and in addition the paternal figure – a heroic figure and unattainable model, questioned quite early on – was absent. From time to time, I met cousins, but the maternal place was never occupied. Actually, I only understood the figure of the mother through the way my wife was perceived by her children. The word "mama" was a word pronounced by my children but never by me.

- *You mentioned your sister.*

- Yes, that touches something very deep, something that, many years later, would be reawakened by another death. My sister Alice became infected with tuberculosis at the age of seventeen. Born in 1911, she was about two years older than I. She died at twenty-one, but her youth was in a sense eclipsed by mine. I have regretted this all my life, with the impression that she received less than her due, while I received more than mine; I still struggle with the feeling of an unpaid debt, with the feeling that she suffered an injustice from which I benefited. This must have played an important role in my life: the "unpaid debt" is a persistant theme, turning up frequently in my work.

- *Why do you say that your youth eclipsed hers?*

- I was a very good student, whereas she encountered many difficulties in her studies. Everyone sang my praises, while she received little attention. She was a sweet girl who asked for nothing for herself and who ungrudgingly accepted that I was the one who reaped the acclaim.

- *And the aunt who devoted herself to raising you?*

- She was my father's sister, eleven years his junior: she was just a girl when she took charge of us, my sister and me. She died in 1968; she lived with us the last ten years of her life.

So I spent my childhood and my early adolescence in a household of older people, where reading played a dominant role: few games, a great amount of reading, to the point that school became more a form of recreation to me than a discipline. Even before the school year began, over extremely austere vacations, I had in a very short time covered all the school books: going to class was more of an entertainment, and I was, moreover, most inattentive in the classroom.

● *How did you acquire a taste for reading? Did you get it from grandparents?*

● No, I discovered reading by myself. I spent a lot of time in book-stores. It was the period when one could read in bookstores despite the difficulty of the uncut pages of the books. One would skip pages, read diagonally . . .

● *Do you remember the books that marked you in the course of your discoveries?*

● Between twelve and fifteen, I read a lot of Jules Verne, Walter Scott, then Dickens in *seconde*, Rabelais, Montaigne, Pascal; in *première* and then in the final year, in *terminale*, the philosophy class, Stendhal, Flaubert, Tolstoy and, especially, Dostoyevsky, who has always fascinated me!

● *You have never made a mystery of your Protestantism. Was the milieu in which you lived in Rennes strongly religious?*

● My paternal grandparents came from two very ancient pockets of Protestantism, going back to the Reformation: my grandmother coming from the Béarn region and my grandfather from Normandy, from a village by the name of Luneray, a sort of *boutonnière* where the tradition of the Reformation had been continuous since the sixteenth century, hardly affected by emigration or forced conversions. My great-grandfather was an artisan who wove cloth, which he then sold at the market in Dieppe. When hand-weaving was destroyed by the industrial mills, part of the family became factory workers, another opted for public service. My paternal grandfather began his career as a teacher in a Protestant school. And when the Protestant churches gave their schools to the state, he was taken in hand by a departmental treasurer, managing the office. This strong Huguenot tradition was deeply rooted in history. On my grandfather's side, there was an evolution towards liberal Protestantism, whereas, on my grandmother's side, the direction was that of Pietist Protestantism. I even think that there was a heavy dose of what was called Darbyism,[2] which was quite sectarian. My memories are not very precise. In fact, my parish environment was certainly more open than the family environment; the latter being a haven for me, safe and secure.

● *You had a religious education that, from the outset, included reading the Bible.*

● Yes, reading the Bible was central to this milieu. My grandmother read it regularly, a practice I inherited and have continued, during my youth and after. This reading was not undertaken in a literal-minded spirit but instead followed a conception I would call pneumatological: it indeed inspired everyday life; the Psalms, the writings of Wisdom and the Beatitudes occupied a more important place than dogma. Not being an intellectual milieu, it was quite undogmatic and gave preference to the private practice of reading, of prayer, and the examination of conscience. I have always moved back and forth between these two poles: a Biblical pole and a rational and critical pole, a duality that, finally, has lasted through my entire life.

● *And you spontaneously saw this as a kind of bipolarity?*

● Absolutely. After all, it is a position no more tormented than that of Levinas, who has moved back and forth between Judaism and Dostoyevsky . . .
I have been concerned – living a kind of double allegiance – not to confuse the two spheres, to acknowledge continuous negotiation within a well-established bipolarity. The philosophy class was a hard test in this regard, all the more so as at the same time the influence of Karl Barth was beginning to influence French Protestantism, directing it towards a radical and, one would have to admit, antiphilosophical return to the Biblical text. In my undergraduate years I was passionately drawn to Bergson, in particular to the Bergson of *Two Sources of Morality and Religion*: I was caught then between a religious philosophy of the Bergsonian type and Barthian radicalism. At that time, I experienced an inner conflict which was exacerbated to the point of threatening to rupture the double allegiance to which, ultimately, I remained faithful.

● *Let us talk for a moment about your year in the philosophy class at the Rennes secondary school.*

• The philosophy class and my meeting Roland Dalbiez, who taught it, figure as the high point of my schooling; I was dazzled, a vast new world opened. I had read a lot of classics – literature but also those called "philosophes": Diderot, Voltaire, Rousseau – and it was these "philosophes" that I had read in *première*, the year before, more than Corneille, Racine or Molière. Rousseau, in particular, had made a strong impression on me, and this naturally placed me in a position to begin the year of philosophy.

Roland Dalbiez was an extraordinary individual: a former naval officer, he had discovered philosophy later in life through Jacques Maritain. He was a scholastic, and all of his teaching was governed by rational psychology and, in philosophy, by realism. He had the greatest aversion to what he called "idealism," of which he gave a caricaturish, even pathological, portrait. I don't know if it is a memory I constructed after the fact, but I believe I can still see him depicting idealism as a huge pincer stretching out in space, and grasping nothing, turning back upon itself. Idealism was presented in this way as pathological "derealism," which he compared to schizophrenia, which was beginning to be widely discussed in psychiatry.

The second aspect of his teaching, one which was of real benefit to me, was a concern with argumentation. This did not prevent him from quickly shutting us up with a few Latin formulas worthy of a great scholastic – our Latin was not advanced enough to contradict him, or even to understand him. His course followed the prescribed program (perception, memory, habit, and so on) and always from the perspective of a progression that, starting with the philosophy of nature, would lead to a philosophy of the soul. But what I fundamentally owe to him is a precept. As he saw that I was hesitant about committing myself to a career in philosophy, for fear of losing a number of certainties, he said to me: when an obstacle presents itself, you have to confront it, not slip around it; never be afraid to go and see. This kind of philosophical intrepidness has sustained me throughout my life.

I should add that he was one of the first to attempt a philosophical reading of Freud[3] – which would prove very important to me in my future philosophical path. His Freud was the "biological" Freud; he stressed the realist conception of the unconscious which he used to refute the "Cartesian illusion" of self-consciousness, and the alleged reduction of the world to my representation.

I recently had the opportunity to sketch his portrait in a little book entitled *Honneur aux maîtres*, put together by Marguerite Léna, in which each contributor speaks of his or her first master. I was able in this way to pay homage to Roland Dalbiez.[4]

• *Rennes was a Catholic stronghold. Did you have the feeling of belonging to a minority?*

• At that time I was indeed very conscious of this, and the woman who was to become my wife, Simone Lejas, was even more keenly aware of it, probably because girls were much more affected by the Catholic religion than boys were. For me, the Catholic universe was completely foreign, and it is only quite recently that I was invited to give a talk at a private Catholic school in Rennes; I thought I would never even penetrate that world. It was elsewhere, and much later, that I became acquainted with Catholicism, but in Rennes Protestants were perceived as belonging to a minority and they lived without any close ties to the Catholic sphere of the vast majority – a situation perhaps comparable to that of Jews in a Christian milieu. I had the feeling of being considered a heretic by the majority. That is probably why the surrounding urban environment did not influence me much. I found only limited freedom there, and there was little point in hoping that it would recognize me fully. But I did not really suffer from this for I was busy reading. The outside world was instead a matter of curiosity.

• *Did you have Catholic friends?*

• Yes, in secondary school. The secondary schools in Brittany – which I knew later as an instructor, as I taught in three of them, Saint-Brieuc, Lorient and Rennes – were attended in particular by the children of schoolteachers and professors. Because Catholic secondary education, which was very strong in this region, siphoned off a large number of students, whose families were opposed to public education. Only the resolutely republican and secular families – above all the teachers – made it a point of honor to defend the public system and to send their children to these schools.

But it was nonetheless secondary school that served as an intermediary for me between the rather closed environment in which I was raised and the somewhat foreign Catholic environment that I contemplated from the outside; for not all the Catholic families were wealthy enough to afford private schools or hostile enough to secular instruction to deprive their children of the high level of teaching current in those days. I felt more comfortable in the secular environment than among the Catholics, even if some of them were very good schoolmates of mine.

• *Did you make up your mind quickly to study philosophy?*

• No, at first I resisted. I tried to do a degree in letters, but since all my papers were criticized as being "too philosophical," I shifted direction after a semester. I had tried to enter the École Normale Supérieure but Dalbiez, in fact, did not prepare us for this type of test; I received a pitiful score of 7/20 on the entrance examination, on the theme: "The soul is easier to know than the body." I must have been the only candidate not to know that this was a quotation from Descartes. Of course, I had argued that it was the body that was better known. I was obviously not on my way to the Rue d'Ulm. As a *pupille de la nation* I was under an obligation to complete my studies quickly – this was very constraining – and, at twenty years old, as soon as I had my degree (*licence*), I had to teach. So I was not able to prepare any longer for the Rue d'Ulm – this would have meant entering a Parisian preparatory class (*khâgne*). I was very good in Latin and in Greek but I was not up to standard in either philosophy or French. This is how I happened to find myself in October 1933 at the Saint-Brieuc secondary school – both boys' and girls' sections – with a teaching load of eighteen hours a week, while at the same time writing my master's thesis with Léon Brunschvicg in Paris on Lachelier and Lagneau.[5]

● *When you started teaching, you were almost the same age as your students. What do you remember about this?*

● I was two or three years older than they were. It was decisive for me to be "thrown" so quickly into teaching, and this was to remain a constant: my work in philosophy has always been tied to teaching. I had to give a framework to my personal reflections – insofar as I had any by then – that was compatible with the content of my teaching. After Saint-Brieuc, in 1933–4, I benefited from a scholarship to prepare the *agrégation*, still as a *pupille de la nation*, thanks to Georges Davy.[6] As a result, I had the good fortune of being a student at the Sorbonne for a year and then the good luck to pass the examination on the first try, carrying off second place, in 1935. The year of the *agrégation* was incredibly intense for me. I had the impression of having to fill a huge gap in one fell swoop. In a year I had covered the ground, as it were, filling in what Dalbiez had not taught me, although he had equipped me intellectually to be in a position to acquire all this: the Stoics – whom Léon Robin had us read that year and whom I did not know at all – but also Descartes, Spinoza, Leibniz. I read, besides, everything that Gabriel Marcel had written.

● *Gabriel Marcel?*

● Yes, every Friday I went to his house; his Socratic teaching helped me a great deal. He set a single rule: never quote authors, always start from examples and reflect by oneself.

In reading two articles by him that same year I discovered Karl Jaspers. And it was also during this period that I began to read Husserl's *Ideas for Pure Phenomenology*, in English translation.

● *And after the* agrégation?

● I was married just after, in 1935, to a childhood friend from the same Protestant community in Rennes. Then I went to teach in Colmar, where we spent our first year of married life.

The following year, I did my military service with the infantry. This I did grudgingly, nourishing profound hostility with respect to the military, first because I was older than the other soldiers, then because this meant an interruption in my intellectual work. This is where I discovered that France was still basically a rural country. Very few of the conscripts had university degrees. Having lived in an urban setting, it was the first time I had encountered this rural environment. The months I spent in training at Saint-Cyr (I was a reserve officer) were unpleasant: I was poorly treated by the training officers because I was perceived as unruly, which I probably was. That was the year when, out of a spirit of contradiction, I read Marx all the time, in counterpoint to Henri de Man. Then I returned to Brittany, where I taught at the secondary school in Lorient from 1937 to 1939.

The year in Colmar was important to me because I already knew that I would turn towards German philosophy; this was actually the reason why I had chosen that town. I took German lessons with a colleague at school (I had not previously studied German). Then I went to summer school in Munich, where I took intensive classes, and this ended in 1939 with the declaration of war. I shall always remember how the signature of the German-Soviet pact was hailed. When the French Consul told us, "Now, it is war," I left the following day.

● *What is your memory of the atmosphere in Munich at that time?*

● I remember perfectly the Feldherrnhalle: two Nazi giants mounted the guard, and we made a detour so we would not have to give the Hitler salute, which was obligatory. My wife and I were lodged with a Catholic family, and the wife, who was very much against Hitler, used to say, "Hitler has taken our children from us." I noted at that time, among certain Catholics, a reticence concerning Nazism, which Pius XI had, moreover, explicitly condemned in 1937 in his encyclical "Mit brennender Sorge." As for the Germans of my age, they were either enthusiastic Hitler supporters or people who preferred to remain silent. I was also struck by the fact that the Romanian and Hungarian students who were there all supported Hitler. Everyone admitted to the university had been carefully screened.

In France, no one thought that study in Germany should be avoided. Those who were first in the *agrégation* continued to go to Berlin until 1939.

• *In the early 1930s, did you follow events? Were people discussing them around you?*

• Yes, I was actually involved in the socialist youth movements early on. I was quite militant when I was in Saint-Brieuc, and a little later in Lorient, and also in Colmar. I remember that I took part in the marches of the Popular Front on July 14, 1936. I deeply supported the socialist cause, under the influence of a man who played a certain postwar role: André Philip. He was also a Protestant, influenced by Barth; he was trying to combine Protestantism and socialism without falling prey to the mistaken assumption to which many Christian socialists are prone, proclaiming that socialism is already entirely contained within Christianity. This is a mistake I have never made, thanks precisely to André Philip. Here again, I am assuming a double allegiance, with two orientations which are rather flexibly linked. There are, of course, in the Gospels certain maxims for action – all the duties implied by the particular respect owed to the poor, for instance – but in order to provide a rational basis for socialist commitment, an economic argument is required – Marxian or other – of a different nature than moral impulse alone, one that could not be deduced directly from love of one's neighbor. There has never been, in my eyes, reason for any confusion of these two orders.

• *How did you meet André Philip?*

• He was a professor at the law school in Lyons when I was in Saint-Brieuc, and I met him in the Protestant youth movements. When he attended socialist congresses, he used to preach on Sunday in the towns where the meetings were held. It was a way of countering the somewhat summary anticlericalism of the socialist party in those days.

• *So you went on to extend your Protestant religious education and your participation in the youth movements into participation in student movements?*

• Yes, and I spent a great deal of time during this period on Marx and the libertarian socialists. André Philip also had me read Henri de Man. Philip advocated a humanist socialism before the writings of the young Marx, the *1844 Manuscripts* in particular, were translated. But two earlier events had already played a decisive role, albeit on the periphery of politics: the death sentence given to Sacco and Vanzetti in the United States in 1927, which aroused my profound indignation, and then the Seznec affair.[7] So early on I experienced a sort of physical revulsion that made me extremely sensitive to certain singular injustices which I later came to think were symptoms of more general phenomena. It was this kind of indignation that was in a certain way moralized, intellectualized by doctrine, the doctrine of a socialism compatible with a moral vision of the world. My friends and my wife's family included anarcho-syndicalists: one of Simone's uncles, a very fine typesetter for *Ouest-Éclair* (which became *Ouest-France*), belonged to this "book" milieu, whose ideology suited me just fine. They were much closer to the anarchist tradition than to Marxism, with regard to which I myself never felt comfortable, intellectually speaking.

• *Did you participate in meetings?*

• I confined myself more to personal reflections and to readings because I do not think that there was any organized movement in Rennes. I really only became acquainted with the local groups of the Socialist Party in Saint-Brieuc, Colmar and Lorient, especially Lorient, in the years 1937–9, just after the Popular Front. And, looking back on it I understand better how the Socialist Party of that time got into the untenable position that split its practice from its doctrine. There were then two opportunities for choosing, which were alerts, so to speak: the Spanish civil war and Munich. And in both instances, the choice was ambiguous, because one had either to resort to force or risk having to do so. It found itself obliged to contend with its own antimilitarist basis. And until the declaration of war, it had not succeeded in freeing itself from this dilemma. All its choices were uncertain. Sometimes the majority went in one direction, sometimes in the other – Blum is entirely typical: he was torn between something like the desire to help those in danger – from the perspective of international solidarity – and a viceral antimilitarism, in which the military was itself the hated adversary. The war put the Socialist Party in the same situation when, in 1940, the majority of its *députés* voted for Pétain.

• *What were your own reactions to the war in Spain?*

• I myself was divided between these same tendencies and the choice was rather aleatory because there was no determinable product of these two forces, only a circumstantial one: in meetings, the votes of the members were split in an absolutely haphazard manner. What finally won out was nonintervention, in the manner of repeated retreats in the face of Hitler; but it was not perceived in this way. I would say that the negative fascination produced by the Croix-de-Feu,[8] by La Rocque (who himself ended up in the concentration camps), obliterated the international horizon. To be sure, one has to be careful not to project onto the past what is known to have occurred later, as if, in those days, people had before them two alternatives, with full knowledge of their consequences. We have to admit that certain choices were made in a kind of fog.

In this regard, the example of the Israeli historian Zeev Sternhell,[9] whom I recently met, is significant: in his books there is a vision of this period of history that is implicitly teleological and that falsifies perspectives. The facts he alleges are true, but not the light of finality through which he presents them. As though there had been only two histories for France: the Enlightenment on the one hand and, on the other, fascistic nationalism. Now some may well have belonged to both, at the moments when the paths were intertwined, blurred . . . I think that what he underestimates – perhaps more than others – is the extraordinary tumult of the prewar years, where, for instance, people who became Fascists were side by side with people who became Gaullists. It was a period of experimentation of all types, where the weaknesses of the institutions of the Third Republic were exposed. It is true that at the same time we made it even more fragile by our unbounded critiques – at any rate, this is what I understand in retrospect: the weaknesses for which we reproached the Republic were also the product of the actions we took against it.

• *All things considered, it was something like what happened, on the German side, with the Weimar Republic.*

• Absolutely. And it is also what would later take place with respect to the Fourth Republic, at least to a certain extent. But I think that people have been too harsh on it, for the admittedly weak, centrist governments that followed one another were constantly caught in the crossfire between the Gaullists and the Communists.

• *At what moment did you become aware of the true nature of Stalin's USSR?*

• It was really the Kravchenko affair in 1949 that was the decisive turning point. *Les Lettres Françaises*, the journal directed by Aragon, had brought a suit against the defector after the publication of his book, *I Chose Freedom*; the Communists had accused him of being a fraud and a CIA agent. Before the war, even the famous Moscow trials had not managed to tarnish the positive image that we had of Stalin's USSR

However, from my point of view, the fact of belonging to the Socialist Party also implied being in competition with the Communists and so helped to keep me from sharing in the enthusiasm so many intellectuals displayed for the "country of the workers." Being in the "old house," as it was called at the time, meant being on the other side. This immunized us against the fascination with communism. So both before the war and after it, I was sheltered from temptation.

What strikes me now is the fragility of the positions that were taken, even on the level of domestic politics: to have drawn up an entire economic plan on the basis of the "two hundred families" and the slogan "the wall of money" was really incredibly simplistic.[10] I recall having taken part in meetings in the Colmar bistros, in 1935-6, on the nationalization of the Bank of France: we were provided with a short list of arguments by the "old house" to show that a country was master of its economy only if it was master of its currency and that, in order for that to happen, the Bank of France had to be nationalized. We by no means perceived the Jacobin character of this reasoning, nor did we see the concentration of powers it necessarily implied, which was contrary to the libertarian, anarcho-syndicalist vision that was very strong then. I think that the friction within the SFIO[11] between the libertarian tendency and the Jacobin tendency has always produced the result that sometimes a majority emerged on one side, sometimes on the other of every issue, whether foreign or domestic. Indeed, the SFIO was itself the result of a merger between the anarcho-syndicalist libertarian strand and the strand promoting a centralized state. But this also produced some poisoned fruits, precisely in foreign policy, since it contributed to disarming us in the face of the real adversary: Hitler, who also drew on this anarcho-syndicalist source . . . What disarmed us in the face of Hitler is the very thing that protected us against Stalin.

• *In short, it was your pre-war political affiliation that did not permit you to see clearly the danger coming from Germany.*

• The error of people like me was first of all not to perceive the approach of war and then, when we knew it would occur, to continue to think of it in terms of the First. Because of the Treaty of Versailles, the reasons for adhering patriotically to the First World War had already been denounced; the fact of presenting the Second as a conflict between nations against the backdrop of patriotism produced exactly the same rejection. I think today that this extrapolation was wrongheaded inasmuch as the second conflict resulted from an entirely different set of circumstances. But I continue to think that the First World War was a monstrous error and a crime: bourgeoisies that were in fact quite similar perverted their own working classes. They broke up the Second International, which quickly gave rise to the Third.

One must always return to this; for it is in the feeling that the Treaty of Versailles was unjust that the pacifism of the socialist left found its justification, its cover. The argument consisted in saying that Hitler, after all, was doing no more than taking back what he had a right to. I still recall the headline of *Crapouillot* at the time of the occupation of the left bank of the Rhine: "Germany invades Germany." Basically, Hitler had to be ceded what the Germans had the right to take back. Nevertheless, I had been warned by André Philip, who himself had not made that choice: he was clearly opposed to Munich, while I was hesitant. I felt on the one hand that Czechoslovakia was suffering a great injustice and that it was even the victim of a crime, but on the other hand that the Sudetenland was despite everything a German territory. I was taken aback by the aggression against Poland.

We see this, moreover, in all the writings of Patočka: he says everywhere in them that it was the First World War that constituted the turning point; the First War was the "suicide of Europe." We did not understand that the Second stemmed from an entirely different set of problems, that it resulted from the rise to power of totalitarianisms. But what made it less possible for us to have a clear vision of things was that we had become the allies of one totalitarianism against the other.

- *Was your pacifism also fed by your reading of Alain? Was he a great figure for you?*

- No, not really. I had met him, but only when I was working on my master's thesis on Lagneau, since he had published the first series of *Célèbres Leçons*. I read his *Propos* only later in captivity under the influence of my new friend Mikel Dufrenne, who had been his student.

- *And what impression did he make on you?*

- Stimulating, but that was also because he had some strong anarchistic elements in him, especially in his opposition to the powers that be.

• *You came back from Munich in 1939, when war was declared. You must have been called up right away.*

• By September of 1939 I was assigned to a Brittany regiment from Saint Malo, remarkable people. I experienced the defeat in 1940 against the backdrop of personal guilt. I still keep the memory of the unbearable images of the flight of the armies in the North; I still see a sort of stereotypical soldier, wearing a bowler hat and pushing a baby carriage full of bottles of wine. I could not help but say to myself: "So here is what I have brought about through political mistakes, through passivity, for not having understood that, in the face of Hitlerism, France should not have been disarmed." This reproach has stayed with me and has led me always to be wary of my political judgment. Even though I have kept allegiances with socialism, and do not deny certain of its presuppositions, I think that political positions I took in those days were mistaken and even culpable.

In May of 1940 I found myself in a unit that had fought well and that, still fighting, had attempted to stem the flood of the army in retreat. I was then in a small unit which had been entirely isolated; I remember that the captain said to me, "Ricoeur, go east and west to liaison." For four or five kilometres, there was no one on either side. We were in a pocket, and we had attempted to prevent the Germans from passing. Through me, my section was awarded a citation for having held out. But we were taken prisoner; with the feeling that the choice was either dying or surrendering, I chose the second alternative. I remember clearly that after three days under the bombardment of the German Stukas, without artillery, without aircraft, crushed, we heard at 3 a.m. the German loudspeakers saying in French: "At six o'clock we will attack and you will all be killed." The chaplain and I made the decision to wake up the twenty-five or thirty unfortunate soldiers huddled in the trenches and to surrender, not without a certain feeling of guilt; my earlier political choice seemed to have led to this disaster, and I myself sanctioned it by a surrender.

I left for captivity in Pomerania, where I spent five years. I was in an *oflag*, a prison camp for officers. In all honesty I have to say that, until 1941, I was attracted, along with many others – the propaganda was intense – to certain aspects of Pétainism. It was probably that I held against the Republic the feeling of having participated in its weakness, the feeling that a new, stronger France had to be formed. This was the case so long as we had not received any news, had not heard the BBC, which, thanks to the Gaullists in the camp, we were able to listen to starting in the winter of 1941–2. A friend came to give us the BBC bulletin in the morning; he got it from someone else, but we never knew from whom. Later, we were the ones who announced the defeats to the Germans themselves. One day we arrived shaved and well turned out to the assembly, the Germans asked us what the occasion was for this change in our habits, and we announced to them the victory of the Russians at Stalingrad! At that moment the camps had been completely taken over by the communists and the Gaullists. But I regret my error in judgment during the first year.

● *What did you know in the camp about what was happening in France?*

● We knew that there was a legitimate government, that there was an American ambassador to Vichy – we watched that very closely – that a newly established educational system was based upon the values of virility, service, devotion. We were troubled when the general state of mind began to reflect no longer simply despondency but the desire to rebuild on the basis of what were practically feudal values. These were quite simply the principles followed by the Uriage school.[12] When I discovered after the war what had been done there, I realized that we were applying something similar spontaneously in the camps. The Uriage school was criticized by people like Sternhell under the pretext that the ideology of this school for cadres was fascist; yet the state of mind that characterized it was just the opposite of what had already become collaboration. It was a matter of putting France back on her feet, and we thought that this involved the Vichy conceptions as the government representatives presented them to us. The pamphlets they distributed to us revolved around this idea: the Republic had been weak, a strong France had to be remade, and this meant *with* the Germans. And yet I don't think any of us capitulated on the question of collaboration. The idea that guided us was more that of an inner renewal, along the lines of the youth movements, in a kind of continuity with what the Scouts had been before the war. And this is what we believed during the first year, when we were broken and cut off from the outside.

The manner in which we contributed, positively, to this renewal within the camp consisted in rapidly establishing an intellectual life so as not to continue to suffer from the defeat. With Mikel Dufrenne, Roger Ikor, Paul-André Lesort, and others who had set up a theater, we reconstructed an institutionalized cultural life – a somewhat curious phenomenon, one no doubt peculiar to life in captivity, which is to try to create a replica of free society within the camp. There was even a market with stock quotations: students and professors of economics had a stock market, where the prices were calculated on the basis of a standard unit, not gold, but the Russian or American cigarette!

We started by collecting all the books in the camp. Then we organized a facsimile of a university with programs, courses, hours, enrollments, examinations. We undertook to learn all the languages we possibly could: Russian, Chinese, Hebrew, Arabic . . . Five years is a long time!

It was in this camp that I began to translate Husserl's *Ideen I*,[13] in the margins of my copy, because there was no paper.

- *How did the books get there?*

- Some had been brought in the haversacks. I myself had two: poetry by Valéry and Claudel's *Five Great Odes*; these books really sustained me during the first year. And it was, moreover, thanks to them that I made the acquaintance of Mikel Dufrenne, who had given a lecture on these two authors, seldom presented together. Since there were between three and four thousand of us, we were able rapidly to put together a real lending library, one very carefully managed so that the works were not damaged and could circulate freely. Others came in the packages sent by the families and by the Red Cross – it was, I believe, through the latter that I was able to read Husserl and Jaspers. There was also a clandestine source: a few kind camp officers were willing to borrow books from the university library! In this way I got to read works from the Greifswald library (which is now in Poland) obtained in exchange for cigarettes, as I didn't smoke.

I was able to save my copy of *Ideen I* through a series of quite extraordinary circumstances. At the end of captivity, during the winter of 1944–5, our camp was moved further west, and the journey was made on foot – a difficult march for people who had received little food (to be sure, we were not in the state of destitution of those who had been deported) and were exhausted by the cold. We pulled our bags and the books we were trying to save over the ice on wooden sleds. After three days of walking, it started to thaw. We lost everything because we could no longer carry what we had more or less been able to pull. With a few friends such as Dufrenne, Ikor and Lesort, we told ourselves we would not go any further. We had wanted to save a certain number of things: our papers, in particular. As for myself, I had started to write my future dissertation on the will. We walked toward the east in the hope of being liberated by the Russians, and we found ourselves in a Polish farm where we were attacked by a Russian patrol that didn't know whom they were dealing with. Unfortunately, we had no map and we did not know where we were; in fact, we were not in the path of the Russians but in a space between two columns of the German army. The SS appeared: they had come to search the area and they found us. They wanted to execute us. Since we spoke German, we were able to make ourselves understood to a captain or a commander, and we were sent to a prison in Stettin, where I continued to work on the translation of Husserl's book for several weeks. Then we were put on a train and sent west; and so, the trip everyone else made on foot, we made by train. We ended up near Hanover in January of 1945. This new camp had not been made to hold the masses of prisoners that were packed in there; little by little, the guards disappeared, dressed in prisoners' clothes, or hiding, for their greatest fear was to be taken prisoner by the Russians. One fine day, no more guards! We continued our march towards the west and we ran into some Canadians. That is how we were "liberated!"

Once I returned to Paris, the first person I went to visit was Gabriel Marcel: he welcomed me with open arms like a son. Then I saw André Philip again who was now a member of the government. And he was the one who sent me to Chambon-sur-Lignon, which I had never heard of before – a Protestant school that had sheltered so many Jewish children that it was honored in Israel. I found myself in an environment of militant pacifism of nonviolent members of the Resistance, who had acted as runners to take foreigners and Jews over the border. The Protestant school, which was an essential part of this system of resistance, welcomed me warmly. It was during the first winter there that I met American Quakers, themselves nonviolent resisters who had come to help with the construction of a larger school. It was through this connection that, a few years later in 1954, I went to the United States for the first time, invited by a Quaker college on the east coast of the United States.

- *When did you learn of the death camps?*

- We witnessed the brutality inflicted on the Russian prisoners near our camp in Pomerania. But we had not discovered the horror of the deportation and extermination camps until the day we were liberated, because we found ourselves next to Bergen-Belsen. The English had emptied the village of Belsen as a reprisal, and we interrogated Germans who claimed not to know what was happening in the camp seven kilometres away. I saw the survivors coming out so haggard, many of them dying after taking their first steps, after eating jam or something. It was dreadful. All of a sudden, we had the feeling we had been incredibly spared. And those who felt this difference most strongly were our Jewish buddies, for the German army had always succeeded, against the SS, in retaining control of the prisoner-of-war camps. The SS never commanded these camps, and for this reason it was possible for Ikor and Levinas not to have to worry. I know that a certain number of Jews were sent into separate camps, sometimes with prisoners reputed to be subversive; but I have not read that these Jewish prisoners who were moved were made to suffer harsh treatment.

As for myself, I found escape from the accumulation of memories of captivity in intellectual work. I closed the door of the camp behind me when I left, and brought out with me the people who were to become my friends, to the end of their lives in the case of those who have died before me. Some of these friends wanted to revisit the places of our captivity; as for myself, I did not have any desire to return to what is now Polish Pomerania.

• *During your captivity, you did read a lot, especially German writers. In this way, what would become one of your strong points was taking shape: a thorough knowledge of the thinkers across the Rhine. Didn't these readings, in a prisoner-of-war camp, have a curative effect?*

• It was crucial for me to read Goethe, Schiller *there*, to make the circuit of great German literature over those five years. The first and the second *Faust*, among others, helped me to preserve a certain image of Germans and of Germany – the guards finally no longer existed, and I was living in books, somewhat as I had done as a child. The true Germany was there, the Germany of Husserl, of Jaspers. This enabled me, when I taught in Strasbourg in 1948, to help my students, most of whom had been soldiers in the German army and were coming late to their studies and believed that it was forbidden to speak German. I would say to them: imagine that you are in the company of Goethe, Schiller, Husserl . . .

• *What did you do right after the Liberation?*

• We lived in Chambon-sur-Lignon from 1945 to 1948. After a year I was appointed to the CNRS: I was allowed only five or six hours of teaching; so I taught part-time and continued meanwhile my translation of Husserl's *Ideen I*. I had a scare over it because someone else was also translating the same book on his own. Merleau-Ponty pleaded for my translation over the other one, which was never completed. I had finished my theses in 1948. But I was not able to defend them until 1950. In 1948, I received an appointment to the University of Strasbourg, where I wanted to go to be close to the German language. I stayed there for eight years. Eight very happy years, the best I have ever known. This had to do with the very harmonious relationships in our family life – my wife Simone, our sons Jean-Paul and Marc, born before the war, our daughter Noëlle, born during my captivity and whom I first met when she was five years old, Olivier whom we had in Chambon, and Étienne, in Strasbourg. This also had to do with the life we led in Strasbourg: the city was cordial, the university very engaging. The philosophy department had asked George Gusdorf and me to set up a philosophy circle promoting discussions and exchanges. Gusdorf had been appointed at the same time as I was: I succeeded Jean Hyppolite and Gusdorf, Georges Canguilhem.

From Strasbourg, I made frequent trips to Germany; this is how I went to see Karl Jaspers[14] in Heidelberg just before he left for exile in Switzerland. I was very struck by his almost Goethean nobility. He was a person who was very difficult to reach, shielded by his wife. It was learned later that Hannah Arendt had tried to reconcile Jaspers and Heidegger. She had succeeded as far as Jaspers, a very generous person, was concerned, but she ran up against the ferocious resistance of Heidegger, who thought – was this a pretext? – that there were no words adequate to say . . . that. Here too words are lacking . . .

Jaspers had expected a sort of conversion from Germany, a collective confession of sins, and he ended up convincing himself that Germany could not measure up to its guilt. He who had been able to endure Nazism could not manage to bear the new republic. I think that he lacked patience because Adenauer went as far as possible, given the circumstances of the disaster, in the reconstruction of a genuine republic.

I paid a second visit to Jaspers, after he had been called to the University of Basle, to present to him the book that Mikel Dufrenne and I had published together (our first book), *Karl Jaspers et la philosophie de l'existence.*[15] He had been kind enough to write a very friendly preface, although he did not particularly care for our book; he found our discussion too systematic. Jeanne Hersch who, like Hannah Arendt, has been one of the master's faithful, shared his reservations, I believe. In particular, she thought later that I betrayed Jaspers for Heidegger, that I like all the French succumbed, she said, to the pernicious charm of Heidegger; which is half true, but also half false.

- *Did you meet Heidegger?*

- At Cérisy in 1955, and I took away a bad memory of it. He was literally guarded by Axelos and Beaufret,[16] and he behaved like a schoolmaster. The central theme that had been chosen was the line from *The Critique of Pure Reason*: "existence is a position." He pointed his finger at us to read the next line and to put forward an explanation. But his comments were magnificent, especially on the poets. I believe it was the first time I paid attention to his relation to poetry. He had talked a lot about Stefan George, and it seems to me that it was later that I discovered Paul Celan.

It was only little by little that I was caught up in the Heideggerian wave, probably because of a kind of weariness with respect to the emphatic, repetitive and vague character of Jaspers's great books, published after the war. Heidegger's genius was more striking to me then than the great talent of Jaspers. There is nothing eye-catching in Jaspers; it is a well-constructed, moderate philosophy. I had liked enormously certain short texts by him, like the book on Strindberg and Van Gogh,[17] just as I had appreciated his famous statement: "We are not the exception, we think in the face of the exception." Now I am grateful to him not to have taken myself for the exception – which was probably not the case for Heidegger . . .

● *Do you recall what Heidelberg and Fribourg were like in those days?*

● In Fribourg I met Landgrebe and Fink[18] and, in Heidelberg, Gadamer. But there were no exchanges between the French and German universities, and I was very disappointed that Strasbourg at that time, and for obvious political reasons, did not serve as a bridge with Germany, but rather as a moat. If you wanted to look to the other side of the Rhine, you had to be willing to make the effort. The fundamental problem was the reintegration of Alsace into France. My colleagues at the university, like the people of Alsace themselves, did not understand very well why anyone would be interested in what was happening on the other side of the border, and I perceived in them something resembling the mistrust that the French had shown towards Germany before the war.

● *When you resumed "normal life" in 1945, did you renew your prewar political ties?*

● Yes, I did renew these ties beyond captivity – but after receiving the terrible lesson of the war, which had invalidated my earlier judgments and forced upon me a kind of political reeducation. I sometimes found myself holding positions very similar to those I had had in 1934–6, rapidly developing a hostility to the socialism of Guy Mollet. My friendship with André Philip never wavered, and this was true until his death. I went to Paris to participate in congresses, colloquia; and in the years 1947 to 1950 I discovered the *Esprit* group, which I had not known well before the war because I was then much more involved in militant socialism and I considered the people at *Esprit* too intellectual. I became much closer to this journal, and I published in it. My friendship with Emmanuel Mounier[19] grew deeper a short time before his death, which was a very great sorrow for me. I see myself, in 1950, in the garden of the "White Walls" in Châtenay-Malabry, not knowing that one day I would live here, and tears streaming down my face. The person of Mounier had truly won me over, not so much his ideas as himself. I had already been sufficiently shaped philosophically not to be one of his disciples; but I was nevertheless a companion of his. He himself was, moreover, in quest of a professional philosopher to lend him support; he had lost his "own" philosopher in the person of Landsberg[20] and then of Gosset, executed as a member of the Resistance in Brittany. Mounier would have wanted me to follow in their steps, which I willingly accepted. He was very aware of the fact that he lacked the conceptual structure, that he was sometimes forced to improvise. He had tried to remedy the situation by writing during his exile in Dieulefit the *Traité du caractère*, which is his most solid work. It is a good book, but it borrows too much from characterology and remains somewhat summary on the conceptual plane.

• *Among French philosophers, which one did you most feel the presence of?*

• Gabriel Marcel is by far the person with whom I maintained the deepest relationship, beginning in the year of my *agrégation*, 1934–5, and again later, visiting him periodically up to his death in 1973. During his famous "Friday evenings," which I began to attend in 1934, a theme for discussion was chosen and the rule was always to start from examples, to analyze them, and to resort to doctrines only as a means of supporting the positions defended. There I tasted a kind of discussion that was entirely lacking at the Sorbonne. At Marcel's one had the impression that thinking was alive, that it was doing the arguing. Moreover, when one reads Gabriel Marcel one often has the feeling not of effusiveness, far from it, but of a constant dynamic approximation, spurred by the concern with finding the right word. We argued in this way every week, for two or three hours, very actively, having the audacity to think for ourselves, which compensated in large measure for the historical culture that was dispensed at the Sorbonne.

I believe that this is what I fundamentally owe to him: to have dared to try to do philosophy and to do it in a situation assumed polemically – and this was, moreover, the kinship he saw between theater and philosophy. Many of his ideas are, in fact, expressed through characters on stage. His plays, whatever he may have thought of them, were not very good. He felt it unfair that Sartre was recognized but not him. Perhaps today I would be equally critical of Sartre's theater . . . I am thinking of a fine essay by Father Fessard entitled *Théâtre et philosophie*, that develops the idea that all the protagonists have a right to be heard – which does not mean that everyone is correct – since everyone can speak; this is what he calls "the superior justice of theater," which distinguishes, at least theoretically, didactic theater from true theater, where it is up to the spectator to draw a conclusion. Gabriel Marcel is half-way between these because he does put in the mouth of one of the characters the view he himself holds, but he also practices a sort of distribution of speech. The extreme attention that Gabriel Marcel paid to people was related to his experience in the First World War, where his work was to collect information about missing soldiers, to reconstruct individual destinies.

I possess a portrait of him: he looks like a cat. He was a very funny, caustic man, who liked to tell stories. But he had an enemy: Sartre, who despised him, while Gabriel Marcel admired Sartre, although he was scandalized by him. Sartre was a constant object of scandal not only because of his atheism but also because he claimed that man was the nothingness of things. Gabriel Marcel could by no means accept this. Perhaps my slight interest in Sartre owes something to Gabriel Marcel, although I attribute it instead to my preference for Merleau-Ponty. I never stopped meeting periodically with Gabriel Marcel, up to the program organized in his honor at Cérisy a short time before his death. He was the same as always, acting like one of the participants, one among others. If I have moved away from his philosophy, it is not because of his deep convictions, but because of a certain lack, in him, of conceptual structure. His is fundamentally an exploratory thinking that slips from one concept to another, an idea playing the role of a melodic frame for a series of variations; thinking by conceptual affinity, where one idea is specified by a neighboring idea. I would not go so far as to call it associationist thinking, but it does proceed by means of assonances and dissonances. In general, the intellectual distances taken from him by his closest acquaintances by no means diminished the affection he had for them. When I wrote my book on Freud, I have to say, however, that he disavowed me. He told me very clearly that I had given in to what he called the "spirit of abstraction." And I understand his judgment better to the extent that now I would reproach myself for having constructed everything on Freud's most theoretical texts (chapter 7 of *The Interpretation of Dreams*, the writings of the *Metapsychology*, along with *The Ego and the Id*) and not having sufficiently confronted the experience of analysis as such: the desire that comes to speech, the relation with another and with the primary others, the passage by way of narrative, the repetition compulsion, the work of mourning. Instead I discussed concepts, which Gabriel Marcel hated.

He used to say in particular: the *cogito* of Descartes guards the threshold of the valid against mystery. But I was always mistrustful of the idea of mystery when it would mean the prohibition of passing beyond a limit, in opposition to Kant's precept in *The Critique of Judgement* to "think more." It must not be forgotten, however, that Gabriel Marcel completed the opposition that he made between the mystery, which encompasses me, and the problem, which is before me, with a praise of second reflection, redoubling in a sense the first movement, which can only be a form of problematization. Anyway, that is what I insisted on emphasizing in him. Nevertheless, the fact that I moved from the problem of the symbol to the problem of metaphor to find a semiotic basis and an instrument of language that had been coded and known through the history of rhetoric, this amounted in his eyes to losing a certain thickness of the symbolic which was more important than its linguistic trace in the metaphorical. For myself, I thought that metaphor allowed me to treat the semantic core of the symbol. As for the systematic spirit Gabriel Marcel cautioned me about, I continue to claim it, even if it tends toward a certain didacticism, which is partially explained by the fact that all my work has been put to the test of my teaching. I confess that I have always needed order and, if I reject any form of totalizing system, I am not opposed to a certain systematicity.

Gabriel Marcel and Mircea Eliade – of whom we shall speak – are two examples of men who had a strong influence on me in our relations of friendship, but I never submitted to the intellectual constraints of being their disciple. These men made me free. Perhaps I might have known the same quality of exchange with Jean Nabert,[21] but he was not a man who maintained warm relationships. One year when he was in Brittany and I was as well, I decided to go and see him, and even to surprise him. I arrived mid-afternoon and found the garden open, the mail box filled with papers. I waited two hours, I even gathered some pansies that I replanted in my garden and which are still there. Then I learned in the newspaper that he had been taken to the hospital, where he died. I had never dared to go and see him, and it was the day of his death that I did so.

● *While you were in Strasbourg, what were your relations with the Parisian philosophers?*

● I became Parisian only later, and so I escaped a lot of things: I never knew the milieu of Saint-Germain-des-Près, I did not know Sartre personally. The only time I had a contact with him – in the years 1963–4, when I was working with the little philosophy group at *Esprit*

– it was after the publication of *Questions of Method*, a book to which Mikel Dufrenne and I had devoted a year of discussion within the group. So we had invited Sartre and prepared twelve questions. To reply to the first one, he spoke for two and a half hours, and we were therefore unable to ask the second! Simone de Beauvoir was there, watching to see that everyone was paying close attention. In the controversies that opposed him to Camus and then to Merleau-Ponty, I was on their side. I also had a correspondence with Sartre over one of his plays that had deeply affected and scandalized me: *The Devil and the Good Lord*. I had written an article, to which he replied in a cordial and generous manner. This article, which today seems to me a little naive, can be found in *Lectures 2*.[22]

• *Viewed from the provinces, how did the Paris of Saint-Germain-des-Près appear to you?*

• Like a superficial fable. This feeling also contained a strong anti-Parisian prejudice, reinforced by the intellectual climate of Chambon-sur-Lignon, then of Strasbourg. But this experience immunized me, so to speak, against the winds of fashion. As concerns Merleau-Ponty, I knew him when I was in Chambon-sur-Lignon in 1945–8; he was then teaching in Lyons and I met him there several times. I also ran into him in Louvain, at the home of Father van Breda, at the Husserl Archives in 1946–7, and at two colloquia: one of his lectures, "On the phenomenology of language" (1951),[23] had made a profound impression on me. Since he had, in my opinion, perfectly marked out the field of the phenomenological analysis of perception and of its mechanisms, all that remained open to me – at least this is what I thought at the time – was the field of practice. It was here that I undertook investigations that were to find their subsequent development when I turned to the problem of evil, of bad will – what, in theological terms, is called "sin." I had the impression that in the area of phenomenology only the representative side of intentionality had been studied, and that the entire practical field, the emotional field, that is the field of feeling and of suffering – although I had greatly admired Sartre's book on the emotions – had not really been explored.

My own choices appear to me today to have been determined in three ways: first of all, Merleau-Ponty had left open a field of investigation for which the tools of analysis were available; next, I had paid particular attention to the discussion between Descartes, Leibniz, Spinoza and Malebranche on the problem of freedom and determinism; finally, I had become involved with a problematic of Augustinian inspiration concerning evil and sin, which had led me to the symbolism of evil.

I came across some notes from captivity, written not by me but by someone who had taken down my courses almost word for word, and I was amazed to find to what extent I had anticipated what I would do later: they contained almost exactly the content of the *Philosophy of the Will*. The main structure had already been sketched out: the theme of the project and its motivation, then that of voluntary movement with the alternating cycle between habit and emotion, and finally the theme of consenting to necessity. In this way I was able to complete this dissertation very quickly, since I returned in 1945 and it was finished in 1948. There were, in truth, five years of reflections and teaching prior to this that formed its underpinnings.

The choice of my area had been sketched out even earlier, as witnessed by a lecture I gave in Rennes at the beginning of the war, while I was on leave: it was on *attention* considered as the voluntary orientation of the look. So I believe that my choice of the practical field dates back a long way: I had long admired Luther's treatise on the servile will, *On Christian Freedom*, as well as the great discussion in which he confronted Erasmus. Then the political context came to reinforce my orientation in the direction of these questions of freedom, evil, and responsibility. Even earlier, I believe that I felt great admiration for Greek tragedy, which puts the problem of destiny in the foreground. Nor would I deny the influence on me of my formative training in the Calvinist theology of predestination. The choice of my special area of study, the voluntary and the involuntary, is therefore strongly overdetermined.

• *In 1956 you were appointed to the Sorbonne and so you left Strasbourg.*

• I could have stayed there. But I belonged to that generation for whom the aim of a career was to reach Paris. I had been a candidate for the Sorbonne once before, presented by Hippolyte and the majority of the philosophy department, but the assembly elected Jean Guitton. The following year a chair came free and I was elected.

I was very ill at ease at the Sorbonne; this is why I later chose Nanterre. I did not find there the ties with students that had existed at Strasbourg. For me, the Sorbonne was something like the negative of Strasbourg.

It is true that the philosophy department of the Sorbonne was brilliant indeed: there was Raymond Aron, Georges Gurvitch, Vladimir Jankelevitch, Jean Wahl, Henri Gouhier, Georges Canguilhem, Gaston

Bachelard. And it is also true that I received great satisfaction from my teaching: the amphitheaters were full, the students were sitting on the windowsills to hear my courses on Husserl, Freud, Nietzsche, Spinoza in the years 1956–65. But, just because of their numbers, they were intangible; I did not know them and I was acutely aware that the university institution was entirely ill suited to this situation. In 1965 I took the initiative to put together an issue of the journal *Esprit* on the university, making a rather severe assessment that resulted in a number of proposals which resurfaced in 1968–9 (relating in particular to the appointment of professors by the college of the Sorbonne on the basis of criteria that were quite outmoded). You can still read these today, as I had them included at the end of *Lectures 1*, despite their predominently utopian character, for reasons of intellectual honesty, as I also have done in the same editorial framework for my notes on China and Israel.[24]

To return to my intellectual scruples, my disappointments and my projections concerning the university in the years before 1968, I had the impression that the task of creating a community of students and teachers was being entirely neglected. Nor did colleagues have any better relations among themselves. We merely crossed paths. There was no meeting place, outside of the occasions provided by the departmental meetings. We knew nothing of the life of our colleagues; we knew one another only as the author of one work or another. For example, I never met Mrs Aron, or Mrs Jankelevitch. There was no research conducted in common, no confrontations, no discussion. I had the impression of a sort of intellectual desert. What is more, not having been initiated into Parisian life, not being an alumnus of the Rue d'Ulm, I found myself in the midst of an environment where the dynamics had long been established. I felt like a foreign body there, working mostly for myself, although I did have the impression of enjoying a fair hearing from the students.

It is true, however, that my main preoccupation was, instead, of a personal nature: how was I to resolve the contradictions created by my situation at the crossroads of two currents of thought which were not reconciled – philosophical critique and religious hermeneutics? Even more sharply defined, my problem was to determine whether what I was doing within the philosophical field was not a form of eclecticism, were I really to articulate my multiple allegiances originally and honestly: Gabriel Marcel, Husserl, Nabert, not to mention Freud and the structuralists. This problem of intellectual honesty has always been agonizing for me: not to forget my debt to a given line of inspiration, or to any other.

• *In the name of this intellectual honesty, in the sixties you tackled the Freudian corpus, as a way of putting your reflections on consciousness to the test of psychoanalysis.*

• The first reason for this work was really the question of culpability, since I had devoted volumes 2 and 3 of the *Philosophy of the Will*[25] to human frailty – what I called "fallibility" in relation to culpability – and to the symbolism of evil, that is to say, to the passage from an analysis of the essence of the will to a symbolism of the myths expressing the figures and the genealogies of evil. I then found myself confronting a sort of residue, inaccessible to analysis and to the phenomenological method: infantile, archaic, pathological culpability. I was well aware that the entire field of culpability was not covered by the symbolism of evil illustrated by Greek tragedy, myths and biblical narratives, and that there was something else. The second reason was that I saw in psychoanalysis an alternative to phenomenology and, in a general manner, to the philosophies of consciousness. The fundamental limit of the Cartesian project, with its postulate of transparency, was always a problem for me. I finally took up again the motives that inspired Dalbiez, for whom psychoanalysis was a branch of the philosophy of nature: the philosophical study that takes nature into account in man. This involved a different perspective than that of the religious symbolism of evil – Christian or otherwise – and, moreover, an orientation unlike that developed by phenomenology.

In starting to work on it, I thought I was writing an article on morbid culpability. As I applied to Freud my habit of reading the whole of his work, and as I treated him like a philosopher, like a classic, I ended up with a big book,[26] which was also the occasion for a real internal debate, which today I would jokingly call a self-analysis on the cheap. This work did indeed help me to go beyond the somewhat obsessive and archaic side of the problem of culpability, which has been replaced in my work by the question of suffering, of excessive suffering that overwhelms the world.

• *When you decided to work on Freud long before he became fashionable, you must have been an isolated figure.*

• There were others though, Daniel Lagache, Didier Anzieu and Juliette Boutonier, who taught at the Sorbonne. But it is true that I was not influenced by them. My problematic was truly personal. Moreover, without being Popperian in any way, I have always been very attentive to the idea of "falsification," and I was asking myself what "falsifies" phenomenology. It is the main thrust of my investigation, whereas many people saw it as a sort of integration of psychoanalysis and phenomenology; on the contrary, I was confirming in my work that this could not be done, that something decidedly resisted it. Phenomenology does indeed have its other. In *The Voluntary and the Involuntary*[27] the problem of the unconscious was treated in the context of what I had termed the "absolute involuntary," that is to say, that which is completely resistant to analysis just as it is to conscious mastery. I considered three figures of this absolute involuntary: character, the unconscious, and life (I mean the fact of being alive). Already in my work in 1948 the unconscious acted as the blind spot of self-consciousness, the blind spot that cannot be assimilated into consciousness, that is not a lesser consciousness but the other of consciousness – in this sense, I have always been very Freudian.

● *Was it during this same period that you made the acquaintance of Mircea Eliade?*

● I knew Henri Puech and Georges Dumézil, and it was through them that I met Mircea Eliade. His insatiable curiosity and inexhaustible generosity were something astounding. He was a sort of Pic de La Mirandole.[28] At fourteen he had already written on coleoptera and he possessed quite amazing collections of rare stamps.

At the time I made his acquaintance he was teaching in Paris and giving a course under the direction of Puech and Dumézil. I had been struck by the singular nature of his first work, appearing under the title of *Traité d'histoire des religions*,[29] whereas it was actually a study of religious *patterns*. As Dumézil's preface points out, this is a typological, structural analysis. Instead of following a historicist schema in the old perspective of the comparative history of religions – in which religions are classified, from the most primitive to the most developed, from an evolutionist perspective – he restructured his investigations around dominant themes, essentially great cosmic polarities: the sky, the waters, rocks, the wind, and so on, borrowing examples from different bodies of writings, practices, and rites. It was this antihistoricist approach that struck me. But it was as if this structural conception was stifled by an almost ideological obsession: the opposition of the sacred and the profane. As a result, the diversity of the figures of the sacred was crushed by a sort of monotony of preference, regardless of the cultural context, for the notion of the sacred and the polarity of sacred/profane; what might have been a strength from a methodological point of view in the idea of a diversified symbolism was as if diminished by it. He ended up making shamanism a privileged structure, and this imposed itself on the historical plane as the dominant paradigm. Eliade thought he was resisting historicism by affirming what he understood to be the permanence of the sacred. I believe that one must genuinely understand the importance this antihistorical aspect had for him: basically, the sacred was to be everywhere identical to itself, but this was at the cost of conceptual vagueness.

The main problems that he finally encountered did not have to do with the content of his investigations but with the very evolution of the discipline: the idea of a science of religions that would be omniscient not only lost its prestige but became increasingly suspect. The specialists are unanimous in thinking that it is not possible to really know several religions at once, so that Eliade ended up being suspected of polymathy. And it was precisely to compensate for this accusation that he was led to reemphasize the organizing pole, that is to say, the polarity sacred/ profane. I was well aware of the profound difficulty he confronted, in that he had to master an ever more abundant body of knowledge – even if one considers the Hindu domain alone, he had to make himself familiar with a corpus of several tens of thousands of pages . . .

It is unfortunate that Puech and Dumézil were unable to keep him in Paris, because if he had had the choice Eliade would have remained in France. But the University of Chicago, as soon as it could, offered him a position and he took it. The language he spoke at home was Romanian, his cultural language was French and all his books were written in French, English being only the language in which he taught. I do believe that he never published anything in English that was not translated from the French. He had been introduced to Sanskrit by Petazzonni and his Hindu masters; in addition, he had lived for two years in a Tibetan monastery, where he got to know and in some respects practiced, as a Westerner could, the ascetic and meditative disciplines. In this way he had acquired, from the inside, a knowledge of the wisdom belonging to the religions of the Orient.

● *Was this a subject of discussion between you?*

● Yes, we talked especially about the possibility of inhabiting several different religious sites. For my part, I was rather reserved, having always had the feeling that just as one can have only very few friends, one cannot participate in several religions; I shared the mistrust of Merleau-Ponty, who, in another context, thought that one could not have an overview of the totality, and that one can therefore proceed only step by step. And what is more, I felt a great resistance to the opposition sacred/profane, linked to what I considered to be an abuse of symbolism; this had led me to prefer the notion of "metaphor" which presented a structure that seemed to me to be more manageable. There

were basically three lines of discussion between us: first the relevance
of the opposition between sacred and profane – I was more attentive to
the opposition between saint and sinner; next, the possibility of an
encompassing view – I had always been struck by the fact that the
religious exists only in structured ensembles, just as language exists
only in particular languages; finally, the role of the text, of writing. He
thought that I overvalued the role of textuality in the production of
meaning; for him, the textual level was if not superficial, at least a
surface phenomenon in comparison with the depth created by the oral
tradition and sentiment. Not without provoking resistance from the
specialists, he thought that the religious sphere possessed autonomy
and that it was autostructured by the predominance of the category of
the sacred. Eliade held closely to the hypothesis of the immanent
comprehension of the religious phenomenon: he defended the idea that
this phenomenon is to be understood on its own terms, the specialist
being obliged to inhabit the phenomenon under analysis, without
taking any distance. At the present time, we are witnessing instead the
revenge of the specialists. Even the chair of comparative history of
religion at the Sorbonne has been split into different branches.

- *Did he place himself within a religion?*

- He was originally Orthodox, and it is certain that the liturgical and
pneumatological aspects of Orthodoxy, in opposition to Roman Catholicism and to Lutheran Protestantism, brought him closer to the
thought of the Orient. He said to me very often: "Don't you see how the
history of the Reformation roots it within the West in the constant
forgetfulness of the Orient, and that it places itself in the wake of the
great schism?" He himself was a dandy as a young man, quite detached
from his religious roots; it was Hinduism that brought him back to his
Romanian and Orthodox Christian sources, but in a synchretic form.
The liturgical sense of Orthodoxy nevertheless allowed him to affirm
that before doctrine comes belief, before belief the rite, before the rite
the liturgy.

My friendship for Eliade was deep and faithful. He was one of the
Romanian trio in Paris, with Ionesco and Cioran. This trio is no more.
The friendship between Cioran, Eliade and Ionesco was not an empty
word, although their personalities were very different. They shared the
same destiny, were very close and saw one another often. At the party
in honor of Mircea's seventy-fifth birthday, I recall, Ionesco asked him:
"Do you remember when you were so much older than me at school?"
While Ionesco was a humorist, Cioran was rather cynical; he loved, for
example, to go to inaugurations because they were ridiculous. The last

time I saw him was at a ceremony in front of the house where Gabriel Marcel had lived, 23 rue de Tournon; someone had set up a little stand on the sidewalk; but it had more or less fallen down and people were picking up pieces of it, while someone was reading the praises of the philosopher; people were passing by laughing, while Cioran observed the scene, laughing derisively.

● *Among the other great philosophers you have known, which one has remained close to you?*

● Hans-Georg Gadamer, certainly, despite the geographical distance. I began as a reader of Gadamer, a great figure of the hermeneutic current. I had been involved in his old quarrel with the "first" Habermas, and I situated myself somewhat between the two of them, rejecting in particular the opposition between truth and method.[30] I have come to be more concerned with integrating in interpretation the moment of critique, that is, the human sciences, which Gadamer cast out in the direction of what he called method, but which in fact was a kind of methodicalism. Today, I give him greater credit, precisely, on the point of his hostility to Heidegger, who tended to treat him as a traitor to himself and to Husserl. As we see in his autobiography,[31] Gadamer is very hostile to Heidegger's reading of Plato, construing Platonism as a dogmatic theory – theory of ideas, the opposition of the intelligible and the sensible, and so on. Gadamer was much more attentive to the incessant movement of the dialogues, which he saw not as rhetorical clothing, but as the very movement of thought, as its play. At the period when I was engaged in a debate with structuralism, I was led to part ways with Gadamer in order to look for a kind of median position between critique and the hermeneutics of appropriation – since, for Gadamer, the hermeneutical enterprise consists essentially in attenuating, diminishing, if need be annihilating, distance, whether distance in time or distance in space; this is what I was resisting by holding that one does not know oneself, that one has to go by way of the detour of others, always valuing the detour of critique.

The man is rather astonishing. His mind is steeped in poetry: he knows by heart all the German poetry he evokes immediately in conversation: Goethe, Schiller, Grillparzer, Stefan George, Paul Celan. He also has profound knowledge of Greek tragedy. He actually lives in the texts, which he inhabits through recitation. There is in him something like a hermeneutics of the oral recitation of writing.

Our relations are friendly, but I have often had the impression that he retained certain reservations, thinking that I was on Habermas's side. We had a somewhat stormy evening when I presented the Gifford

Lectures[32] again in Munich in the autumn of 1986. He had come to hear me, and I was not really at ease because my German was not good enough for a discussion on equal terms with him; he himself gave a rather polemical turn to this meeting. Since then I have seen him again several times in Paris and in Germany. More recently I feel that my relationship with him has calmed down. And now that we are both moving off the world stage on tiptoe, we do so with a great amount of mutual affection. I had the great pleasure of participating in the celebration of his ninety-fifth birthday this year in Heidelberg and to give the "main address" at his invitation.

• *Let us return, if you will, to the chronology. We left you at the Sorbonne, dissatisfied with the relations among teachers and the relations with students. When you were given the opportunity to go to teach at Nanterre, you said that you did not hesitate for a minute.*

• I knew nothing of the dealings that had preceded the founding of this university, which was an annex of the Sorbonne and which had no autonomous status but just an administrative council. The proposal descended on me without my knowing the ins and outs of it, or the nature of the plan. One day at the Sorbonne the Dean informed the professors that a new university was being created. There were three of us who agreed to go there – Pierre Grapin, Jean Beaujeu and myself – and we were each of us Dean in turn, with the success that you know. Grapin, the German scholar, was the first to take on this function. I had made his acquaintance both professionally and politically at Strasbourg – he was a communist, or close to the Communist Party, and I recall having taken part in joint meetings organized more or less under the auspices of the Peace Movement; not a very good reference! Between us there was a sort of left-wing proximity and my admiration for his work as a German scholar, devoted to Heine, as well as for his intellectual probity.

As for myself, I especially wanted to leave the Sorbonne and to have an experience in which I could once again find a genuine contact with students. The first time I went to Nanterre, it was during the winter and the taxi driver refused to go all the way; there was so much mud the driver said to me: "Do you take my car for a landing craft?"

I remember the burlesque scene of laying the first stone. Pierre Grapin and I transported this celebrated stone in a taxi, but we didn't know what to do with it. We put it down in the mud and we left. It is very curious that I did not realize what a desolate place it was. Perhaps I was taken with a certain working-class fantasy that made me think it was not so bad after all to build a university in the middle of the shantytowns.

But in my eyes Nanterre represented a radical change from the Sorbonne and the Latin Quarter. I did not perceive its architectural ugliness, either. This completely astounds me today.

Nanterre was created with a few little pieces of the Sorbonne and some professors from the provinces, including Mikel Dufrenne. We formed a philosophy department, and I was particularly proud to have succeeded in bringing in three philosophers who had not taken the *agrégation*: Henri Duméry, with his ecclesiastical titles; Sylvain Zac, who had not been able to take the *agrégation* because he had been excluded, as early as 1935, by the first laws of "protection" against foreign Jews, the laws requiring five years of naturalization in order to be a candidate for the *agrégation*; Emmanuel Levinas, whom I had read, and who had been Mikel Dufrenne's colleague at Poitiers. In addition there was a kind of automatic recruitment: a certain number of colleagues who had been expelled from Algeria were appointed without having been elected. They were warmly welcomed. But we had no autonomy since the election of professors still depended on the Sorbonne.

I had two happy academic years: 1966–7 and 1967–8, very fruitful, very happy years. There were not many students, which allowed us to know them better and to follow them in their development. We remained longer at Nanterre than today and we willingly spent the entire day there. For me, it was a way of finding the atmosphere of Strasbourg in Paris. I had always had in my mind the idea of a community of teachers and students, which had led me, moreover, to support the plan of incorporating students in the university councils – I now believe that it was a serious mistake: being a student is not a profession. The Anglo-Saxon system is much better, where there are very solid student organizations but ones which negotiate from the outside and which, finally, have much greater weight than if they were lost in the administrative councils – where, anyway, nothing important is decided, at least not then, since everything was determined on the ministerial level.

● *In 1968 you were a professor and the head of the philosophy department. You were there when the "events," as we say, began.*

● The events started in Nanterre on the basis of questions outside the sphere of teaching, such as the right for the young men to visit the girls in their residences; at bottom, it was the "sexual revolution" that was its detonator. Nanterre suffered from two handicaps: the first had to do with the choice of disciplines presented – letters on the one hand, law and economics on the other, along with political science; since the students of letters included a strong leftist faction and the students of law an active right, their confrontation was inevitable. The second handicap had to do with the geography of student recruitment: on one side, bourgeois, from the residential suburbs of Neuilly and from the sixteenth and seventeenth arrondissements; on the other, working class, from Nanterre and the other, less wealthy suburbs. The sons and daughters of the bourgeois were leftists; the others, communists, were very attached to the proper functioning of the institution – for them, the university was still a traditional way of rising, offering knowledge and the prospect of social success. On the side of the bourgeois, however, it was felt that the university was no longer a privileged factor in social ascension. Since their parents had already conquered these positions, the young bourgeois could ally themselves with those who found themselves at the university without any real means of succeeding there and could dream only of destroying the instrument which was no longer, for them, a reliable means to future success. When I became Dean in March 1969, I benefited from two ideological supports, so to speak: the anti-leftist communists and the socially committed Catholics; my adversaries, paradoxically, were the traditionalist bourgeois and the leftist bourgeois.

- *What judgment did you make in 1968 on what was happening?*

- At the time, it was positive; I thought that the positive outweighed the negative; the experience of freedom of speech, the fact that everyone was talking with everyone else, all the aspects of conviviality seemed extraordinary to me. Today I wonder what really happened. Nothing or a great deal? Was it a sort of great waking, playful dream, as Raymond Aron thought, or did something important really happen which may have had no political results but which had profound cultural significance, bringing to light as it were everything that had been covered over, hidden, everything that had been held back – a sort of liberation, a social eruption? Why did this occur simultaneously throughout the world, in Paris, Tokyo, Berlin and on American campuses? The sole common element, it seems to me, is the rapid demographic growth, beyond the control of an institution that was elitist in its origin and which found itself very rapidly having to obey a more popular objective, incapable of readjusting its elitist structure to its new function of the general distribution of knowledge. This is the only factor I can see that is absolutely common to the four university systems most strongly affected. In addition to that, the changes in behavior, distinct yet convergent, manifested the massive rise of an age group whose dreams of emancipation were thwarted by a real economic and financial dependence, which was to worsen after this.

• *That is true. But in France the phenomenon went far beyond the universities.*

• Yes, because the students succeeded in mobilizing the labor unions. But, at the same time, I believe that they did not see that the unions controlled the situation much better than they did and knew when not to go too far. Incidentally, what was not understood at the time was the moderation of the police. It has been said that they were violent, whereas in reality they showed extraordinary tact; no one was killed, which is amazing, considering the number of people present in the demonstrations and the number of demonstrations.

• *When did you have the impression that things were escaping your jurisdiction?*

• After the return of General de Gaulle, May 31, 1968. Before that, there had been a political plan, a little crazy perhaps but not incoherent, which rested on the idea that institutions formed a chain, that the university formed the weak link in this chain, and that from the weak link to links that were not as weak all the dominoes would finally fall. Now the day General de Gaulle took things in hand again, there was no longer a viable political plan in opposition, there was only a plan to sabotage the institution. This is what I inherited in 1969 when I was elected Dean. I had before me a will to disorder that was no longer grounded in any political motivation, that was based only in a local motivation of disfunction – preventing the university from functioning. The margin for discussion was, therefore, extremely slim. In 1969 the situation had deteriorated, with no political plan except a purely ideological confrontation, where power was immediately identified with violence and denounced blatantly as such.

• *Was your election as Dean a unanimous one?*

• I was elected in a simply astonishing manner. I had participated with groups of professors, assistants, and students in many decisions, discussions, and more or less utopian projects for recreating the university. René Rémond and myself had been placed in competition without ever having been candidates, for the sole reason that he had left the independent union and I, the SNESUP (Syndicat National des Enseignants du Supérieur): for various reasons, neither of us accepted the discipline of the unions; I was elected by the provisional administrative council, which at that time included professors, assistants, and students. I had voting for me the quasi-unanimity of the students, the majority of the asssistants, and the minority of the professors. I considered that it was my duty to accept, but I did so on the condition of choosing my principal assistant, which was René Rémond. Those who had elected me were upset because René Rémond had had the majority of the professors for him. But we always acted in unison. René Rémond, moreover, wrote a very fine book[33] in which he recounts the entire history of Nanterre. He displayed absolute loyalty in regard to my choices, even when he disapproved of them, reproaching me, for example, for being overly patient with the leftists.

● *In sum, according to you, 1969 was very different from 1968, in that the aggressiveness of the students was resolutely focused on the professors.*

● The year 1969 saw something like a rejection of knowledge. I recall that once I was dragged into a large amphitheater to explain myself. "What do you have that we don't?" someone asked me. I answered, "I've read more books than you." This rejection made no distinction between knowledge and power, and power was reduced to violence, so that nothing that had anything to do with a vertical relation could be lived honestly.

● *You remained Dean about a year; then, in 1970, you resigned. The events that preceded your resignation have inspired many commentaries and legends. Could you tell us about the events and, in particular, the manner in which the police moved onto the campus?*

● I would very much like to correct a historical point concerning the arrival of the police at Nanterre, because the interpretation that has been given was shameful for me. I was summoned one evening by the Minister, Guichard, at the height of the crisis, after my administrative council had voted, in their distress, in favor of a text stating that order on campus could no longer be maintained and that we retained only the sovereign responsibility for the safety of the buildings. The very evening of this vote, the Minister said to me: "Order must be restored, this cannot continue." I returned home and at midnight his general secretary called me back: "Tomorrow morning at seven o'clock, the police will be on the campus." I answered that he could not do such a thing. "Yes," he said. "You voted yesterday to release the campus from your authority. You renounced your authority, so we are stepping in." And this is how I found the police on the site. I did not call them, they were already there.

Recently René Rémond said to me: "What is extraordinary is that all that was illegal. We had no right to vote on a text of that nature, and, what is more, it had not been ratified by any competent authority." That is to say, I was in fact, without being aware of it, still the person responsible for maintaining order on the campus, our vote of renunciation being invalid. I reacted by choosing the worst possible solution: forbidding the police to enter the buildings. The police did not go in, except on a few occasions against my will. It was the worst solution because the police surrounding the buildings were bombarded with typewriters, tables, and so on, and I genuinely feared that there would be deaths. Nanterre was sacked for three days. A week later, I resigned.

- *Looking back on it now, how do you interpret your resignation?*

- I would say that my failure at Nanterre was the failure of an impossible plan to reconcile self-management and the inherently hierarchical structure of any institution; or, in any case, the asymmetrical distribution of the distinct roles that it implies. But it is perhaps the basis of the question of democracy to manage to combine the vertical relation of domination (to use Max Weber's terminology) and the horizontal relation of shared lived experience – to reconcile Max Weber and Hannah Arendt. My fundamental failure is to have wanted to reconstitute the hierarchical relation on the basis of the horizontal relation. In this regard, the episode of the deanship has borne fruit in my subsequent reflections on politics.

At a deeper level, I believe that it produced in me – in a lasting way – an unstable mixture made up of a utopian dream of self-management and the very precise, very positive experience of the American university campus, to which would have to be added the German university, which formed an intermediary reality. I have always found myself caught between nonviolent utopia and the feeling that something irreducible subsists in the relation of commanding, of governing; this is what I rationalize now as being the difficulty of joining together an asymmetrical relation and a relation of reciprocity. When, by duty or by mandate, one is the bearer of the vertical relation, one continually seeks to give this a legitimacy drawn from the horizontal relation; this legitimation, in the end, is fully authentic only if it allows the asymmetry tied to the vertical institutional relation to disappear; yet this vertical relation cannot completely disappear because it is irreducible – the agency of decision can never perfectly correspond to the ideal representation of a direct democracy, where each and every person would actually participate in every decision. Do we not observe on the juridico-political level that the true problems of justice are not those of equal distribution but those posed by inegalitarian distributions? And the question finally amounts to determining what are the least unjust inequalities. Inegalitarian distributions are the daily bread of the governing of institutions of all sorts. This is the problem I find again today in Rawls and in the various theories of justice.

But it was a great apprenticeship to have tried this and failed. In trying to understand the reason for my failure, in making more specific the anatomy of the institution, I became better aware of the squaring of the circle proper to politics: the impossible dream of combining the hierarchical and the convivial; such is, for me, the labyrinth of politics.

# Chapter 2

# France/United States: Two Incomparable Histories

• *Two weeks after resigning from Nanterre, you left for Chicago. It has often been concluded that it was because you were disappointed with the experience of Nanterre that you went to teach in the United States.*

• That is sheer fiction. I had been teaching on a regular basis in the United States – for six weeks, a trimester, a semester, even for an entire year – since 1954.[1]

At the beginning, I did not speak English fluently; I became bilingual at the expense of the students I had the first year! Some still remember this . . .

My first stay, as I have already mentioned, was at the Quaker college of Haverford, near Philadelphia, where I had been introduced by American Quakers who had come to help out with the Protestant college at Chambon-sur-Lignon. Before speaking of my many years of teaching at Chicago, allow me to go back to this first American experience. In entering the American system through the Quaker side, I encountered it in its most tolerant form. Even the word "tolerant" is too weak to express the *systematically* pluralistic nature of the Quaker spirit, the credit each person is deliberately given regarding the capacity to find his or her truth, share of spirit or spark of meaning; tolerance is elevated here to the level of a genuine religious conviction. This spirit of conviviality, of fraternity, coloured not only the everyday relations between teachers and students, but also collegial relations, and relations among students.

My experience with the Quakers is clearly marked in my memory: I remember, for instance, the burial of a philosopher colleague and the incredible simplicity of the ceremony, in contrast with all the rituals of

American funerals: the man was wrapped in a shroud and placed directly in the earth, without a casket, and with perfect tranquility.

I also recall the Thursday meeting, which, although not mandatory, was nevertheless well attended by the students. It was a time of meditation; anyone could have the floor to say whatever occurred to them or to read a religious text; this was not necessarily a Biblical text, it could be an Eastern text, but it could also be a passage from a novel or lyrical work, all of this in accordance with the spirit of syncretic spirituality which they embodied.

● *How did you enter the University of Chicago?*

● I was made a doctor *honoris causa* at this university in 1967, along with Raymond Aron and Claude Lévi-Strauss, and the Divinity School had chosen me to succeed Paul Tillich[2] in the John Nuveen Chair. I was quickly coopted by the philosophy department and by the Committee on Social Thought, an interdepartmental institution founded by Hannah Arendt, whom I met at the home of Paul Tillich, to whom she was very close.

● *The change from the Quaker college to the New York Union Seminary and, especially, to Yale, where for the first time you were involved in postgraduate teaching, must have represented a complete transformation of your working conditions.*

● The Quaker university was only a four-year college, whereas Yale indeed included graduate school. The very prestigious universities in the United States are characterized by a small undergraduate college and a large graduate school that confers the Master of Arts (M.A.) and the Master of Science (M.Sc.), then the Ph.D. (Doctor of Philosophy, following a terminology inherited from the eighteenth century). In reality, the actual end of the system in these prestigious universities is the doctorate; and when a student cannot go that far, it happens that he or she is given the Masters as a consolation prize. This is not the case in the average university. The University of Chicago, for example, is a doctoral factory, flanked by a very small college, which serves it as a breeding ground, and this, in turn, is preceded by an experimental-type secondary school from which it draws a few of its students, groomed for its college.

● *Were the children of your colleagues among your students?*

● Most of the American university professors do not want their children to remain in their own university; they prefer to send them to the other side of the continent to finish their studies. This is, moreover, how the Americans avoid generational conflicts: at eighteen years of age, it is usual for a student to cross the entire country to go to college. This is part of the customary joke: they say that the student leaves with a refrigerator, a girlfriend or boyfriend, and a checkbook and returns home only at Thanksgiving, which is still the big family holiday.

• *You speak of the American college, but this has nothing to do with what we call the "collège" in France.*

• The college constitutes what, to my mind, is best in the American system. It is an institution of higher learning that spans four years; it takes young people from eighteen to twenty-two and corresponds more or less to what in France would be the end of secondary school and the beginning of higher education. When one thinks of the American educational system, one usually thinks of the great universities – of Harvard, Berkeley, Stanford – but its greatest strength is to have created the institution of the college.

College is necessary to make up for the relative weakness of secondary education, which in the United States is very uneven and, in any case, clearly inferior to European instruction. It allows the young Americans to make up for their delay in intellectual maturity in relation, for example, to French students. At eighteen they really begin to blossom and they display a thirst for learning that is incomparably greater than anything one finds in French students after they have taken the baccalauréat. I may add that the proportion of young people enrolled in college is considerable: up to the 1990s, a higher number of American twenty-year-olds were in school than among their French counterparts. A large number of secondary students go on to college and receive undergraduate training, while only one in four or five students continues to graduate studies.

• *What do you think are the advantages of this system?*

• Its superiority over ours involves two things. First, the student is left with a very wide freedom to choose direction. In the first year, one has to choose five courses – each course represents three hours of instruction – but one is able to select whatever combination one wants. In the third year, the program of studies has to include a major and a minor. In this way, many students, whatever their major may be, and even if it is far removed from letters, or as they say there, "humanities," choose philosophy as a minor. And this explains why philosophical studies are doing very well in the United States: the three associations of university professors of philosophy (Eastern, Central and Pacific divisions of the American Philosophical Association) include more than fifteen thousand members.

In second place, the institution of the seminar must be mentioned. Alongside the large introductory courses on different subjects, colleges organize seminars, and their numbers increase as the student advances through the curriculum and the choices become more specific. In high-quality colleges, there are fewer than twenty participants in the seminars; students are obliged to contribute to the work by giving an oral presentation and by writing papers, which are more or less the equivalent of what in France we call a *dissertation*. The choice of the paper topic is usually negotiated in terms of the common program or the subject profile of the seminar, but also in terms of the interests of the student and the contents of other courses or seminars chosen. In addition to the seminar, there is also a tutorial, following the British or Scottish model, in which the professor will give direct comment and guidance focused on a paper read by the student on an agreed subject; this reading is followed by an hour's discussion during which it is decided what the next step will be. In other words, the student completes a course which is settled in relation to the choice made at the beginning, but which is also adjusted step by step. From one meeting to the next, the professor gives the student numerous readings to cover, on which comment is then to be made. The reading capacity of certain students is absolutely astonishing: you give them dozens of pages of Hegel to read during the week; when they return, not only is the reading done, but it is done with unbelievable care.

- *Is the British heritage noticeable?*

- The memory of Oxford and Cambridge has remained very clear; but also that of the Scottish universities, whose mark is particularly felt in certain places, in Chicago, for instance. Don't forget that even after the Civil War the American patricians – whether the great Bostonian businessmen or the Southern plantation owners – continued to send their children to Oxford or Cambridge, and they returned imbued with a very classical culture. This is what explains, let me say in passing, why so many small American towns have Greek names: there are no fewer than six Athens in the United States, and just about the same number of Syracuses! New influences were felt in the 1930s, when Jewish refugees from Germany began to arrive; then a sort of synthesis occurred, especially on the East coast, between the Anglo-Scottish heritage and that of the German university, carrying the acknowledged stamp of the Jewish intelligentsia.

• *When you arrived in the United States and began to teach there, were you immediately won over?*

• To begin with I was dazzled by the teaching system and by the relations among colleagues, before reaching a more moderate, more critical view and seeing its shadows. It is true that the campuses are like a bubble within American society: the difficulties of real life, the struggle to find a position in society are very attenuated there; the university environment thus seems ultraprotected. The good side of this privileged condition is that it allows the development of a critical and speculative activity which a large number of students enter into with great pleasure. At first, I was more than a little surprised to see in them such a rapture of discovery, such an appetite for reading; the libraries are full until midnight, even later if that is possible. You have to understand that the campus offers the students a complete living environment; many of them visit their family only once or twice a semester or trimester.

For the professors, this system is a double-edged sword. On the one hand, much more is demanded of them than in France; they must show an effective presence on campus for a certain number of hours per week, in particular, several hours a week during which they meet with students. These are known as office hours: the professor posts the hours when he or she is available and the students sign up. Some, of course, require more guidance than others. Some are very jealous of their autonomy. But, anyway, you have to be there. Moreover, American university professors are in the habit of working on site. Professors have their office and their personal library at the university, not at home.

French professors often find it hard to conform to these rules, they are used to working at home. That is why they are sometimes considered less committed than their American colleagues. But the other side to this servitude lies in the quality and quantity of the services offered by the administration to the teachers, which, on the whole, frees up an appreciable number of hours from drudgery, and shelters them from material cares. Most of the professors have an assistant, a secretary or a share of secretarial support, to say nothing of the wealth of the libraries and the ease of access – so different from the library use to which French university professors are condemned and, alas, have grown accustomed!

• *Were you pleased with this way of life with the students, with this proximity to them?*

• I keep coming back to my myth of Strasbourg: after my departure, and I have to say, after my disappointment with the Sorbonne, I found there the practices I had known a little in Strasbourg. In particular, I have always been astonished by the very subtle mixture of familiarity and respect in the relations that the students have with their professors. Even in the 1970s, at a time when their relations with the institution were the most strained, they always maintained their sense of a vertical acknowledgment without forfeiting the horizontal dimension of conviviality. American students seem to me to have the consummate art of guiding themselves in these subtle, delicate relations. Of course, one always encounters certain extreme cases, students who want to share their problems with you and who talk to you about the boyfriend or girlfriend who left them: one then has to forestall the confessional mode somewhat and attempt to move the emotions to a more discursive level.

It is true that one often sees in young Americans of eighteen or twenty a marked discordance between their prolonged adolescence on the affective level and an astonishing intellectual vivacity, between their emotional immaturity and their extreme intellectual maturity. This discordance tends to come out in their style of writing: in the midst of perfectly constructed arguments, kinds of puffs of sentimentality suddenly appear; and this occurs all the way up to the predoctoral level.

• *What do you think causes this emotional immaturity?*

• First of all, the fact that during their secondary education they have not benefited from sufficient intellectual stimulation; all of a sudden, they have to make up for this lag. Then one must realize that a large majority of families are second- or even first-generation immigrants. In American society one does not find the features of the old French citizenship. So the students find themselves, at the end of adolescence, confronting the difficulty of working out a compromise between their new status of intellectual and their cultural heritage, which remains very strong, especially in the case of the Hispanic families and, even now – at least from the 1960s to the 1980s – of Italian or Irish families as well. To say nothing of the blacks – previously called Negroes, then colored people, and who now prefer to be called African-Americans.

• *Were you immediately aware of the magnitude of the problem for the blacks?*

• The middle of my years in America coincided with the great advances of civil liberties and with the struggle led by Martin Luther King Jr. In the North things were not experienced in the same way as in the South, where the taboos had to be shattered. One should not overlook this difference between the South and the North: historically, American blacks long remained slaves in the South, while this was not so in the North. But after this, the slaves from the South became the proletariat of the North, often even more destitute in this merciless society than they had been in the patriarchal system of the plantations, where on occasion they benefited from a benevolent order. In the industrial society of the North, they fell into the most total abandonment.

With regard to the universities and their policy concerning blacks, it is not an exaggeration to call it a disaster. The thirty or fifty greatest universities have never succeeded in integrating blacks in significant numbers. The reason is terribly simple: they suffer the worst primary and secondary education; they are the primary victims of the incredible inequalities in standards between schools. A large number of them live in lone-parent families and are raised by single mothers; onto the economic disaster is grafted a cultural one. To this is added the fact, which continues to worsen, that those blacks who achieve success immediately leave their original neighborhoods. In Washington and other large American cities, there is no lack of extremely rich black doctors or lawyers; but they do not live in black neighborhoods, they live in white neighborhoods. So what one finds is a community whose best and brightest are constantly skimmed off, a community that is unceasingly beheaded of the elements that could contribute to giving it a new physiognomy. Blacks who have succeeded rarely involve themselves in educational activities on behalf of their own people; in this way the black community is massively abandoned to its sad lot.

To give you an example, I do not recall having had a single black student at Haverford; perhaps a few at Yale, certainly many more at Columbia, if only because the university is located uptown, just south of Harlem. It wasn't until I went to Chicago, which has a huge black population, that I was able to measure the full extent of the problem.

• *The American secondary school does not play its role of integration.*

• It is certainly in this area that there is the most notable lag in the United States, because of the very fragmentation of the educational system. They have nothing comparable to the work that has been done in Europe, and especially in France, on the establishment of a national educational system. In the United States there is nothing equivalent to our Ministry of Education. Each state has the primary responsibility for education, despite the adjustments made by the federal system.

• *In addition, the American system is fee-paying; studies are very expensive, and this contributes to widening the disparities.*

• It is the lower-middle-class students who suffer most from this system because, being neither rich nor poor, they have difficulty obtaining scholarships and the cost of enrolling in the university inflicts a great hardship on them.

It is true that this constraint is relatively well ingrained in the American mentality; it is taken for granted that education is expensive for families; even in the state universities enrollment is expensive, far beyond anything we are used to in France. For this reason, as soon as a child is born, parents begin saving for the university education of their offspring.

It is also true that in order to offset this great handicap, there are many scholarships financed by private foundations and by industrial benefactors. I recall having a student at Chicago who had received a scholarship from an oil company. One may wonder why oil companies would be interested in a philosophy student. The answer is simple: by distributing lots of money, in a random manner, but to young people who show notable intellectual aptitudes, there is the chance that one of them one day may win a Nobel Prize. In any event, a poor student who has managed to show talent in secondary school is sure to find money to go all the way to the end of graduate studies. It would be unfair not to underscore this point.

Moreover, the United States offers the singular example of a society in which, at all levels, nonmarket relations to money coexist with the most implacable system of profitability. The most obvious example of this is the place of volunteer work in American society: Americans devote the most time to nonremunerative activities, in churches, in innumerable cultural associations – museums, concerts, British-style clubs, etc. – in hospitals, sports clubs. This is something the French have a hard time understanding; I myself continue to find it unfathomable that there is this juxtaposition in one and the same society of the most widespread generosity and the most rigorous economic calculation.

• *What was the content of your teaching in the United States?*

• At the university a professor can negotiate the theme of his teaching with the department head. In this way, I was invited to Chicago to give a voice to what in the United States is called "continental philosophy" and which goes from Kant and German idealism to Levinas and Derrida, passing by way of Nietzsche, Husserl, and Heidegger. I was also able to give courses on other periods in the history of philosophy, as I had done in Strasbourg. In addition, I had the luck to choose the subject of my courses, thanks to the liberalism of the university institution. As a result of this, from the 1960s and 1970s on, my books were almost always "tried out" on my American students in the form of seminar courses before being written; the other side of the coin is that these works have perhaps retained an overly didactic form.

At Chicago, the department of philosophy did not extend a very warm welcome to the type of philosophy I embodied; most of the teachers were logicians, representatives of logical positivism. I was rather the black sheep. But it was finally accepted that someone was needed to talk about Hegel . . . and to make the bridge with historians, political scientists, and legal scholars.

One of the interesting experiences I had at Chicago was teaching in pairs: the professors reply to one another in turn; or they share the same course, which they conduct as an open discussion. The students adore seeing two of their professors amicably opposing one another. I recall having taught the *Critique of Judgement* with an excellent Kantian who had an "analytical" orientation. I learned a lot, moreover, about how the history of philosophy is taught by analytical philosophers, with a constant concern to strengthen the arguments of the text to the point where they are invulnerable; if there is anything comparable to this approach in France, it would be the work of Martial Gueroult.[3]

At the Divinity School team teaching was almost the rule: there would be, on one hand, a theologian and, on the other, someone more speculative, or maybe a specialist in the history of religion.

- *How would you translate "Divinity School"?*

- I would say "school of religious sciences" since the instruction at the Divinity School includes several fields: biblical exegesis – Old and New Testament – comparative history of religions, Christian theology, Jewish studies, philosophy, psychology, and, finally, literature and religion – the latter forming a very flourishing field, in which two sorts of questions are examined: the influence of religion on literature, and the fact that literature potentially contains questions of an ethico-religious character. My own teaching was situated between philosophy and theology, and was bizarrely entitled "Philosophical Theology"; that was the name of Tillich's chair. What I say elsewhere about the way in which I conceive of the relations between philosophy and theology indeed contradicts the title of the chair. But no one attached any constraints to this title, which I found upon arriving at Chicago. Anyway, my other two affiliations, with the department of philosophy and with the Committee on Social Thought, authorized me to conduct my teaching as I saw fit.


● *Who were your students?*

● I had two kinds: on the one hand, the students enrolled in the Divinity School or in the philosophy department; on the other hand, students who had a double enrollment – for instance, attending my courses on epistemology or the philosophy of history, or on political philosophy, were students from the history department or the political science department. One of the most brilliant of these, Jeffrey Barash, has in the meantime become our colleague in France: he came from the history department, where he was the student of Leonard Krieger, the great specialist on Leopold Ranke and the German historical school, who had created in his own department a subsection of the history of ideas; it was here, and not in philosophy, that a student could hear of Hegel and Heidegger.


● *So your students knew nothing of the history of philosophy?*

● This was not so for the graduate students, the doctoral candidates. They often came from the better colleges, where they had received good instruction in the history of philosophy. I note in passing that the preparation for the doctorate in the great universities requires long and extensive study, covering several fields related to the topic of the dissertation; a series of examinations called "comprehensive" sanction these peregrinations into varied and sometimes distant territories.

To this one must add that despite the strong opposition between "analytical" philosophy and so-called "continental" (that is, European and not British) philosophy, one philosopher at any rate remains common to both traditions: Kant. But it is not exactly the same Kant. The "analytical" one is the philosopher of the categorial structure of the understanding, detached from the transcendental deduction, especially in the second version of the *Critique of Pure Reason*, the latter considered a "subjectivist" concession, even a fall into psychologism. In this way, one has a Kant stripped of the transcendental subject, a "depsychologized" Kant, to employ their terms. The Kant of P. F. Strawson[4] is a prime example of this.


● *The American students, you said, stay on the campus and leave it only now and then to visit their families. But when you were at Chicago, did you make excursions off campus?*

• I actually know very little of the heart of America; I know almost nothing of the worlds of lawyers or doctors; I do not know the business world, the world of the influential. Despite numerous trips, for meetings, lectures, or simply for pleasure, I never really knew much outside of the campus and its surroundings. The country is incredibly vast; it is an entire continent, soaking up its own news and, as a result, showing little interest in the rest of the world and, on the whole, not knowing it very well. I remember that someone once asked me – this was in the fifties – "Finally, who did they give Strasbourg to? To the Swiss? To Luxembourg?"

Having said this, you used the word "excursion." This is quite precisely the appropriate word to express what happens when one drives across even the city of Chicago. Chicago stretches along Lake Michigan for over forty kilometres from north to south. Crossing the city amounts to a taste of the exotic: from one neighborhood to the next, you visit the Italian district, the Polish district, the Slovak, the Ukrainian districts, and so on, not to mention Chinatown. The stores often display signs in two languages.

These phenomena of distinctive identity have become even more marked in recent years. Do they imply, at any rate in the North of the United States, a risk of dissolution? I don't think so. Because the factors of integration remain strong: I am thinking in particular of the practices of work and leisure that have an enormous power of equalizing the living conditions of individuals. This has to be stressed: American society is a merciless leveler. I recall the strong impression made on Tocqueville in his day by what he characterized as the "equality of conditions." On the other hand, when the demand for separate identity becomes a mass phenomenon, as in the case of the Hispanics in the South, then the threat of disintegration is serious. Miami is in the hands of the Cubans; the mayor of the city is himself Cuban. It is a bizarre reversal that takes me back fifteen years, when people used to say: "Cuba is an island that does not exist: its population is in Miami, its government in Moscow, its army in Angola." Many things have changed since then; what remains, unfortunately, is the destruction of the cities – often there is nothing at the heart of the cities but offices and . . . the poor!

• *People often say that the Hispanics have surpassed the blacks in social success.*

• And this has happened despite the disadvantage of language. Sociologists attach the greatest importance, and they are surely correct, to the fact that the fabric of the Hispanic family is very strong, while the black family has totally disintegrated. This is a consequence, it is said, of slavery: women and men were often separated on the plantations, and families had already been dislocated at the time of the transfer from Africa to the New World. So, when the blacks from the South emigrated towards the large industrial cities of the North, families were already shattered and were never truly reconstituted.

To this must be added the retreat of the ideology of integration. After the civil rights period, marked by the movement of whites in the direction of blacks, Americans are now in a phase of retrenchment, where the norm becomes once again group identification. And unfortunately, this state of affairs is now having grafted onto it all the ideologies of difference which have become so powerful, and which serve to consolidate the differences that already exist: "They are different, just as we are different; that is their culture and this is ours." This is the type of discourse that tends to predominate. I have witnessed this development at Chicago during the past few years: in the cafeterias on the campus, blacks congregate more and more often among themselves, without mixing with whites, who themselves accept this and seem to find it normal. From the melting-pot society, people are going back to a fragmented society, playing upon the cultural redefinition of minorities. It is probable that the Hispanic phenomenon accentuates this movement and this is equally true for other groups, including those of Slavic origin . . . In Chicago, every neighborhood has its national holiday: on these occasions you see Slovaks in Slovakian costumes, Poles in Polish costumes, and so on. The city is divided up into ethnic pieces.

I myself, as one who has always felt very cosmopolitan, always feeling at home in three cultures, French, German, Anglo-Saxon, was taken by surprise by this American phenomenon of magnifying ethnic differences. It is true that I am also speechless in the face of what is happening today in Europe: I cannot believe that we are in the process of giving in to these paroxysmic displays of ethno-cultural identity coming from another age.


• *Is this to say that you are opposed to what in the United States is called "multiculturalism?"*

• The question is not posed in the same way for all societies. With respect to American society, one has to remember that it is the only one made up of émigrés; if only for that reason it cannot be compared to any other. The fragmentation of the United States has nothing to do with that of the Balkans, where one returns to a situation prior to the three great factors of assimilation resulting from the Ottoman empire, the Austro-Hungarian empire, and the Soviet empire. Take the map of the Balkans: it is as though one had emptied out a little pack of Hungarians here, a little pack of Czechs here, a little pack of Croats there . . . The map of the United States presents nothing comparable: American emigration has been geographically dispersed with the movement westward. Moreover, until the competition of Spanish in recent years, English has been the common language of integration. And finally the three major religions to which Americans belong, Catholicism, Protestantism, and Judaism mix people together on a basis other than their ethnic origin. Islam, which has made a more recent breakthrough, poses an entirely new problem in this regard.

What is currently called "multiculturalism" consists in a positive reevaluation of the ethnic and familial past going back two or three generations.

● *Let us take things from the other side: where is the American melting pot found today?*

● First, you have to remember that professional affiliations are in no way marked by cultural origin; the market economy is based on this. In addition, the university, through the integrative character of campus life, also acts as a factor of homogenization. But it is especially the society of production, with its absolutely imperative models of consumption, and the almighty power of advertising that bring about integration. If I am sometimes tempted to evaluate the phenomena of multiculturalism in a positive light, it is in reaction to the merciless leveling of the society of production, consumption, and leisure that characterizes the United States.

I can think of another element of integration: sports, as it is practiced there in a way that has nothing to do with sports here. American football, baseball, and basketball are the occasion for great festivities on campus. Moreover, the great teams are university teams. There are even universities that can almost be said to specialize in sports: students enroll in them because they are good at sports, even if they are less well qualified in other subjects. The University of Notre Dame, which is an excellent Catholic university, has one of the finest football teams. An important game is a festive occasion for everyone: students, professors, inhabitants of the city, everyone comes. At New Haven, the small town next to Yale University, where there is a good deal of tension between the academics – students and professors – and the citizens – town and gown – everyone turns out for the games, in the midst of majorettes and an atmosphere of jubilation. One never sees scenes of violence there like those we know in Europe.

● *Did you witness the birth of "political correctness?"*

● I did actually see the beginning of it without really understanding the phenomenon. It seems to me that, here too, things are more complex than they seem.

One probably has to go back to McCarthyism, which was an attempt at intellectual terrorism on the part of the reactionary right: one had only to be the least bit critical to be accused of communism. It was the period when the distinction was made between liberals and radicals: liberals, in the political sense of the term, are what we would call "moderates"; they were – and are still – in favor of equality of the sexes and of the races, but on the basis of an individualist and contractualist philosophy, guarantor of the rights inscribed in the Constitution and its famous amendments. The radicals of that time professed the same philosophy but extended it by means of a militancy directed against the Establishment and all the institutional forms judged to be hypocritical and surreptitiously repressive. This form of radicalism, still close to the ideals of individualism – *my* rights in opposition to the encroachment of the institution – was replaced by a new form of radicalism that broke with the system at the very level of the principles that liberals and radicals, regardless of their differences, had still shared. In this way we see, formulated by feminist groups, associations of homosexuals, movements based on ethnic origin, demands grounded no longer in alleged wrongs inflicted on individuals in present circumstances, but in injustices committed in the past with respect to membership in a group. The fact of belonging to a category injured in the past, therefore, becomes a basis for demands. The new argument rests on what could be called a change in the principles of legitimation and of the justification for demands, in short, a paradigm shift at the level of political and juridical philosophy: to introduce considerations relating to group membership and to wrongs inflicted on one of these groups in the past is to go against juridical and political individualism and what could be termed the relation of contemporaneousness presupposed by contractualism.

Having said this – and I think that one has to go directly to the underlying principles – the actual behavior given the label of political correctness must be handled with caution. In my opinion, to be fair and precise, types of behavior should be put along a sliding scale depending on whether the new paradigm is confined to the role of adjusting the political and juridical philosophy inherited from the Founding Fathers or whether it is clearly substituted for the latter.

So, no one is undermining the classical foundations of life in society when they recommend, as is common practice in many universities – at Chicago, among others – the use of an inclusive language, which speaks of men in the sense of males and of women in the sense of females. One does not say "men" but "men and women," "he and she," or "humans." In other words, one does not use the word "men" in the generic sense. In the same way, people are strongly advised not to use language that explicitly or implicitly excludes women or African-Americans, homosexuals or lesbians, and so forth. This careful attention to language is not unbearable in itself, although the moderate expression of political correctness may signal the threat of a language police and hence an attack on freedom of expression.

One moves on to something more serious with the espousal by many institutions of what is termed "affirmative action": in the case of two candidates supposedly of equal rank with respect to the customary criteria for recruitment, themselves in keeping with classical, political, and juridical philosophy, the administration reserves the right to prefer, for example, a woman over a man, a black over a white, a Hispanic over an Anglo-Saxon, and so on, by reason of the wrong done in the past – and, it is true, also in the present – to the group to which the individuals in question belong. Inasmuch as this policy is declared openly and is supported by at least a tacit consensus of the community, it can be seen simply as the expression of a corrective justice attached to an abstractly egalitarian distributive justice. But even more so than in the case of inclusive language, one may fear that this preferential policy may come to explicitly contradict the principle of equal opportunity that is effectively based upon tests of qualifications for which individuals strive, as individuals, being judged in terms of their current performance. Two philosophies come into competition here, without any compromise being argued. One cannot but invoke Rawls's thesis here,[5] which holds that the first principle of justice, positing the equality of individuals before the law, is lexically prior to the second principle, requiring that in unequal distributions the law of maximizing the minimum should prevail, that is the protection of those worst off. Consequently, if one follows Rawls, who in this respect remains within the tradition of juridical individualism and contractualism, one cannot employ a social policy which, in order to remedy past injustices, would begin by violating the principle of the present equality of individuals before the law. Now this is what political correctness begins to do.

To my mind, a more radical stage of paradigm substitution is reached when attacks are made on the idea of universality underlying that of equality before the law. The threshold is crossed when the debatable but not scandalous idea of corrective justice is supported by an ideology of difference, directly applied to membership groups (sex, sexual orientation, ethnic group, social class, etc.). Ultimately, the "rights" inherent in these groups are themselves declared to arise from different principles and the mores proclaimed by these groups are held to be incomparable. Stemming from this explosive mixture of corrective justice and the ideology of difference, troubling practices begin to assert themselves on the public stage. Some are simply ridiculous: it will be said, for example, that only women can give seminars on women's studies, only blacks can direct black studies. More debatable is the attempt to introduce quotas of feminine authors or of ethnic minorities in drawing up a curriculum of studies, even of proscribing classical writers declared to be sexist, macho, colonialist, etc. The damage is still no doubt minimal, inasmuch as the most extreme demands meet solid resistance from the administration and the university community as a whole. It is, nevertheless, potentially devastating: the ideology of difference, by failing to differentiate among differences, destroys the critical spirit which rests on shared common rules of discussion and on the participation of communities of argumentation recruited on bases other than the historical constitution of different group affiliations. The paradox is indeed that the praise of difference ends up reinforcing the internal identities of the groups themselves.

The harm produced by political correctness becomes obvious when certain forms of discourse are forbidden; then it is freedom of expression, the formal condition of free discussion, that is threatened; and political correctness tends toward a sort of inverted McCarthyism. A strange paradox is taking shape before our eyes, namely the transformation of the libertarian ideals of the 1970s radicals into repressive pressures.

I would nevertheless like to retain from this serious dispute, on the one hand, the notion that the classical philosophy of individual rights is less and less apt for the demands that are supported by entire communities claiming an indivisible collective identity; and on the other hand, that the ideology of difference, if pressed to its extreme, takes too little account of the ideal of universality, which, rightly or wrongly, has classically been tied to juridical individualism. The idea of individual rights and that of universality are in the process of taking separate roads. This is why I am more interested in the debate between universalism and communitarianism, which permits a glimpse of more fruitful mediations.

• *How do you explain the importance this ideology of political correctness has acquired?*

• Don't lose sight of the place where it is trying to take hold: the campuses. I picture the American college campus as a vast archipelago, spread over the surface of the United States, cut off from the land of real life. When they leave it, after having spent five or seven years there, the students all of a sudden give up their habits of marginal or bohemian life and instantaneously take on the outward signs of social life: suit and tie. Political correctness belongs to a universe that is forgotten as soon as one steps out of it, the universe of professors and students; in other places outside of the campus it is much less in evidence, although one can point to lawsuits that have been brought concerning hiring or lodging, on the basis of a set of arguments involving political correctness.

The development of political correctness in the campus archipelago is also explained by the fact that in the rest of the country we are dealing with a system that is in no way Jacobinical and which, consequently, only reinforces the institutionalizing of customs. Wherever state laws are extremely weak, there is a greater tendency to engage in particularities, to follow historical traditions, and to self-regulation, which can either move toward centralization or greater dispersion; at the moment, Americans are moving more toward redispersion. Bill Clinton's failure to establish a health system on the national scale is a good indication of this. In the United States the universal does not operate at all in the same way as here. It is certainly not by chance that it is in the United States that the great debate has developed between Rawls, who holds to a kind of universalism in juridical and moral matters, and those who are termed "communitarians," who insist upon taking particularities into account; among these are people of high quality, such as Sandel or Walzer,[6] who have nothing to do with political correctness.

In addition, one must not underestimate the importance in the United States of associative life, which includes the dimension of volunteerism I was talking about. This is a form of self-governing relations which, outside the campus, involves large sectors of cultural life. There is no doubt that it represents a factor of fragility with respect to homogenization, a factor of the great susceptibility to fragmentation. This associative life forms a reticular fabric in which the pyramidal elements are much less important that the networks; Hannah Arendt was so struck by this that she introduced it on the speculative level in her work.

• *Is not the United States simply passing through a crisis of Puritanism?*

• I completely refuse to use this word with the connotation it has in France. We often forget that Puritanism was itself a high, clearly defined culture. Let us instead speak of "fundamentalism." But fundamentalism is not found on campus; in the world of the university there is only the expression of religious forms that have already integrated many critical elements. That outside of the universities, certain intellectuals – in particular, those whose culture is scientific and technological and who have no habit of critique – take the Biblical text literally and believe in the literal reality of the creation in seven days, the story of Adam and Eve, and so on, this is true; but this is inconceivable on campus. The culture of the archipelago is entirely at odds with that of the continent. Moreover, there is no doubt that the liberal forms of Catholicism, Protestantism, and Judaism that are found in the universities have been factors or accelerators for secularization. This is why the hard core of what Americans call "organized religion" is constituted by fundamentalism but this is for the most part outside of the university.

• *It remains that American democracy, unlike the French, is explicitly anchored in religion. Does this have a connection to the problem of multiculturalism?*

• The two phenomena are inseparable in the case of the United States, where there is nothing equivalent to the historical and political role played in France by the state in the formation of the nation, nor is there any equivalent to the revolutionary break which destroyed all the intermediary associations and placed in direct confrontation – almost short-circuited – the individual citizen and the state. In France, the state represents the universal at the very level of its political constitution. One must never forget that this is something that has no parallel in the United States, where the nation was constituted by the successive waves of emigrants, all bearing their traditions and their culture. The American nation, despite the features of universalism contained in its Constitution, was formed from the bottom up, unlike our own, and on the basis of strong communitarian experiences. The way in which it was written is significant: bit by bit. Seven or eight eastern states first grouped together, then an agreement was established between the Bostonians, who were merchants in the main, and the Southern planters. From the outset – this is something that Tocqueville saw clearly – the Federal government was defined with limited powers. While the powers of the different states were enumerated in an unlimited way, those belonging to the Federal state were enumerated in a limited and exhaustive manner. Even if a universal meaning is attached to the Federal, the latter is defined by the limits that are marked by the other authorities subordinate to it; there is a delegation of powers enumeratively limited. Once again, this is completely different from the French system.

American multiculturalism is, therefore, based on two factors: the constant generative force of associative life, and the priority of local powers over federal power. This is the reason why the American discussion between universalists and communitarians, which often seems abstract to us, has an entirely concrete basis in the United States. To our eyes as Europeans and as French, the universal possesses an abstract, trans-historical character, without reference to location or epoch, individual or group adherence. And, moreover, the historical has long been the province of the nation-state. When one enters into the American discussion between communitarians and universalists, one has to recognize that it is anchored in a historical context that is quite unlike our own. If one were to make a comparison with a European country, it would probably be with Germany after 1945, which went back before its totalitarian history and connected up again with the full, strong tradition of the debate between universalism and culturalism, the apex of which had been the period of romanticism. It is undoubtedly not by chance that our two points of reference for thinking in a more dialectical, less antinomic manner about the relations between the universal and the cultural in particular are the American and the German models. On our side, due to the lack of our associative, communitary experience, to define the citizen we have available to us only the face-to-face relation to the state.

• *You seem to deplore the absence of any intermediary level between the individual and the nation-state. Is this not the void that decentralization was supposed to fill?*

• Certainly, but this was done by fragmenting the state and creating a political regionalism, which is entirely different. In French-style decentralization, the state lost control over things that in fact are related to its sovereignty. The fragmentation of sovereignty creates political voids and for all that still does not offer the fullness of associative life. We are paying for this today in the spread of corruption at the local level and by the proliferation of "affaires."

But I deplore this void for another reason, which relates to the problem of representation in our democracy. Ideally, a Deputy is a fragment of myself projected into the political universe. But today, citizens no longer recognize themselves in the class of politicians: "my" Deputy, instead of being the same as me, as soon as he or she begins to circulate in what has been called the "microcosm," becomes other than me. The crisis of representation is essentially the result of the fact that, between the level of the individual and that of the state, there is nothing.

In political philosophy, this is the question many people are working on. I am thinking, for example, of Walzer's legal pluralism, as he strives to pluralize the very concept of "justice" in terms of the multiple "spheres" to which we belong. His enumeration is, moreover, very interesting: we have membership in a legal space but also in a system of needs; the civic sphere is itself only one of these spheres, caught up in a constellation, a network.

But I am also thinking of Jean-Marc Ferry's book, *Les Puissances de l'expérience* and of what he calls the "orders of recognition," which make up the various places in which we construct our identity.[7] His vocabulary is borrowed from what is most interesting in Hegel's political philosophy, the idea that practical morality resides in customs, mores, and consequently in institutional hierarchies found at every level: family, civil society with its system of needs, its jurisdiction, and its administration, then the state properly speaking. Don't forget that the Hegelian state crowns a hierarchy in which all levels are occupied. These "orders of recognition" are, in fact, our true allegiances.

I wonder whether it would not be a reasonable project, even if it could easily be labeled reactionary, to try to revive the idea of political representation for our different systems of allegiance. This was one of the aspects of General de Gaulle's 1969 referendum; he had thought that this reform had to be linked to that of the Senate, which no one was concerned about. In itself it was a perfectly legitimate idea, and I have the feeling that we will once again have to move in this direction. To what do we belong? What are our orders and places of recognition? How can we have a political representation of these places of social and civic recognition? For instance, for those of us who are students and professors, how can we bring it about that the university, with its obligations, its rights and its interactions, be represented as one of the components of the political realm? Could we not reconstitute the political by starting with all the intermediary organizations to which we are bound by our allegiances at the same time as they are, for us, the means of recognition? The term "recognition" seems to me much more important than that of "identity" which is the focus most of the time of the debate on multiculturalism. In the notion of identity there is only the idea of sameness; whereas recognition is a concept that directly integrates otherness and allows a dialectic of the same and the other. The demand of identity always involves something violent with respect to others. On the contrary, the search for recognition implies reciprocity.

And one can follow this dialectical schema of recognition from the biological level – where identity is defined by the conquest, on the part of the organism, of both difference and complementarity between the self and the nonself – up to the sociological, juridical, and political level. On the juridical plane, I found this in the penal system, when I adopted the idea that the problem is not solely, nor even fundamentally, that of punishment, but that of the recognition of each person in his or her proper place. It is a matter of saying who is the guilty party, who is the victim, of employing the language of the law that places each one at the proper distance; in other words, it is above all a matter of mutual recognition. And often it is much more important to have said who is the guilty one than to have punished that person: for punishing is causing more suffering, it is adding one suffering to another suffering, without lessening the former. However, the victim must be recognized as having truly been injured: the language that states this must in itself have a therapeutic role. The idea of recognition thus has a heuristic power starting with the biological level all the way to the political level, passing through the ranks or orders of recognition in the social dimension and through civil and penal law, civil law being the place where damage calls for reparation and most often for remuneration, and penal law that where imputability calls for penal sanctions.

• *By stressing the theme of recognition as you do and by underscoring the part of historicity that weighs on every political system, are you not in fact placing yourself on the side of the communitarians in the American debate?*

• In truth, I prefer to approach the problem in a different way; perhaps it is my obsession for reconciliation . . . I approach things on the basis of the ethical presuppositions of the discussion – in a Habermasian style – which assumes unlimited deliberation, without the constraints of time or participants, and I try to determine what is lacking in this approach that describes itself as transcendental pragmatics. The entire question is then whether one can contextualize the universal while keeping it as a regulative idea. This is very similar to the project of transcendental thought, which by definition functions only in conjunction with the empirical. The best example of this is provided in Kant's system by the example of the theory of law, which is the only case where one sees at work the actual integration of the transcendental and the empirical: the conditions for the functioning of society, in fact, are defined by conflict, by "unsocial sociability" (this is Kant's expression), and it is here that the project of the recognition of "mine" and "yours," which is the very basis of law for Kant, must be established. A project of distinguishing between "mine" and "yours" must be linked to the conditions of the exercise of "unsocial sociability"; we have in this an exemplary model.

In the opposite direction, if we start with communitarianism, we find that living communities, making explicit their shared understanding, to use Walzer's term, leave untouched the problem of the principles of the rules of the game, or, if you prefer, the principles of the rules of compromise. In order to ground *the* rule of justice which redistributes *the* spheres of justice in their rightful place and at their proper distance, there must be a regulative principle; and this is where we encounter the Habermasian or Rawlsian problem of the principle of justice.

It is this to-and-fro between communitarianism and universalism, on the basis of their recognized shortcomings, that interests me, much more than having to situate myself in relation to one of the two positions; it is their dialectic that seems fruitful to me.

• *Fruitful in the sense that it could be transposed outside of the United States?*

• I feel that it could be of great therapeutic value to us, to the extent that we lack the intermediary level between the individual and the universalist claims of the state. Specifically, we need to find in the self-structuring of the nation-state the elements of a communitary history, or a history of communities: communities that have been erased and obliterated by the censure placed on them for two hundred years.

This does not mean applying to France measures taken elsewhere: every system has its drawbacks and its advantages, and it is incumbent on it to reform itself in accordance with its internal capacities for improvement; this is true at all levels of social life, and this includes the university. We cannot imitate the American university in France: we start from the hypothesis of a free education and from diplomas that have a national character; all of this presents enormous drawbacks, as we well know, but we have to correct our system on the basis of its own characteristics.

Now it does happen that today in France we almost have an equivalent of the debate between universalism and communitarianism, with the discussions on the problem of the political void produced by the delegation of sovereignty by the citizen to the state. This delegation occurs by means of elections, but in France the only election that really counts takes place every seven years: the presidential election. If, as many people say, there is a deficit of democracy, it is certainly here that it is most visible. This deficiency is dangerously supplemented by the institution of public opinion polls – which I think deserve harsh words because they present themselves as a substitute for deliberation. The polls are not a form of deliberation: people are consulted one by one, and then their opinions are added up. At no time is there any debate; the figure that results from this is in no way the product of deliberation, as is implied in principle by an election. Moreover, quite often, the election itself is no longer the end product of a debate, but is itself only a full-scale opinion poll. What should never be more than a means of information about the state of opinion, for the use of politicians, is transformed into a sovereign authority that decides candidacies, their number, the identity of the candidates, etc.

• *In saying this, are you thinking of a sort of bicameralism?*

• It is true that the systems that function well are those that do indeed have a bicameral system: whether this is the United States, where the states have equal representation in the Senate – two per state, regardless of its size, the same for Arkansas as for New York – in Germany, with the Bundesrat and the Bundestag, or in England, and the system peculiar to it. In France we have reduced the role of the Senate too much, limiting its function to that of a chamber for reflection and discussion, the power of decision ultimately lying with the Chamber of Deputies, become once again the National Assembly.

How far will the crisis of representative democracy go in France, along with the discredit it brings to the political class? Will it be enough to reform the system by a mode of parallel representation or must the system of representation be entirely overhauled? This is certain in any event to be the problem of the coming decades.

• *You were saying that the question of communitarianism is inextricable, in America, from that of the anchoring of democracy in religion. Isn't this finally the starting point for all the differences between France and the United States?*

• Tocqueville had perfectly recognized that one of the singularities of the United States had to do with the fact that, unlike France, they had not experienced any radical, intractable conflict between the Enlightenment and religion. A conflict took place but it was played out within Christianity, between a democratic form of management of religious communities and a hierarchical conception of the episcopate. Consequently, an alliance in fact, which was also an alliance in thought, was established between forms of ecclesiastical practice that can be called antiauthoritarian and a conception of the state as being under the eyes of God.

The balance between the religious and the political, upon which the

United States was founded, is rooted, moreover, in a history of religion that is itself an antiauthoritarian and pluralistic history. From the beginning of American history, the famous Founding Fathers, the Pilgrims of whom Walzer has spoken so well,[8] had the idea that several sorts of denominations ought to be able to live in the same public space. From the outset, they held as self-evident a conviction that we were able to reach in Europe only painfully, and only in the territory of the Germanic Holy Roman Empire, at the end of the Thirty Years War. This was where the idea, as yet very restricted, was conceived that there was room in the same political space for two religions, on the condition that each of the component states was homogeneous; this was the principle *cujus regio ejus religio*, for each region, its own religion; this was a sort of multidenominational mosaic and not the genuine religious pluralism that, in the United States, was recognized from the start as a founding principle. It is particularly important that the idea of tolerance was from the outset a religious idea, unlike the use of the term current here, where "to tolerate" means to put up with what one cannot prevent. In the United States, tolerance has long rested on a genuine acceptance of diversity; the recognition, even from within the ecclesiastical theology characteristic of certain denominations, of the fact that there can be other bearers of a share of the truth; at the founding of the political history of the United States, there is the idea that the public space is the place of cohabitation of several religious traditions. For Tocqueville, it was just as important as not having any enemies, not to have to continually resolve the problem of war and peace.

This is how the Americans answer the problem of the foundation of democracy. For in a democracy there is always the question of knowing what the Constitution is founded on, what it is based on, if not on an implicit consensus, on a relation of mutual trust; lacking a consensus, we would be dealing with a sort of self-foundation on a void. Americans themselves have instead the strong feeling of a distant and indirect foundation – yet one that is still well anchored – in a fundamental religious pluralism.

This in no way prevents there being a complete separation between church and state on the institutional level. What one can say is that the way the political sees itself includes a religious dimension, which follows no institutional mold.

One must go even further and say that tolerance extends not only to non-Christian religions – American Jews have not suffered the forms of discrimination experienced by European Jews – but also to those who do not recognize the grounds for religion: agnostics and atheists. The political history of the United States has been marked by the integration of all parties in the sphere of public discussion.

• *Have you read Tocqueville extensively?*

• I have read him very often, I don't know how many times. What is absolutely astonishing is that he foresaw what would be the major drama of American society: namely, the problem of the blacks. In the final pages of *Democracy in America*, he posed the problem in its most radical form: either the United States would be a multiracial society, and this would finally be the reign of the *métis*, mixed-race, or else the blacks would be eliminated as the Jews had been from the Iberian peninsula by the Spanish and the Portuguese. Sooner or later, the United States would find itself confronting this alternative. And it is true that it has constantly oscillated ever since then between exclusion and assimilation.

In fact, most of the blacks you see in the street are of mixed race, quite simply because in the plantations the slave owners exercised the *droit de cuissage*. The mixing of the races was part of the mores and customs, and became a sort of social practice.

The history of America is a strange history: émigrés came to a territory which was already inhabited by people – the Indians – and exterminated many of them, pushed others onto reservations; but at the same time, these first immigrants brought along other émigrés, by force, who were their slaves. It is a singular history that has no equivalent in Europe.

This is why I always return to the idea of incomparable histories, and consequently to the specificity of ethnic and political problematics. This is also why the universal, in this domain, cannot be constitutive but regulative.


• *Can you give an example of a universal idea in a regulative sense?*

• One of those I am particularly keen on is found in Kant's "Perpetual Peace": it is the idea of "universal hospitality." The third definitive article reads: "The law of world citizenship shall be limited to conditions of universal hospitality. ... Hospitality means the right of a stranger not to be treated as an enemy when he arrives in the land of another. ... It is not the right to be a permanent visitor. ... It is only a right of temporary sojourn, a right to associate. They have it by virtue of their common possession of the surface of the earth, where, as a globe, they cannot infinitely disperse. . ."[9] Has anyone noticed that this is a Copernican-type argument, resting on the idea that we live in a finite space? Humans could always go elsewhere; but since we are obliged to live in a finite world, we then have to be able to live anywhere: "and hence must finally tolerate the presence of each other. Originally, no one had more right than another to a particular part of the earth."[10] As in the preceding articles, Kant insists that it is not a matter of philanthropy but of *right*. "Hospitality means the right of a stranger not to be treated as an enemy. . ."[11] This passage is truly astonishing, with the idea of invoking geographical finiteness: because the earth is round, its inhabitants must tolerate one another, that is, be able to live anywhere on the round ball. Hence it is the very principle of right – the coexistence of free wills in a finite space – that leads to hospitality. What a fabulous argument!

If you think about it, this goes against the idea of a promised land, since everyone in the world can by right live anywhere. This does not mean that everyone thereby becomes a citizen of anyplace at all; in other words, the argument does not attack sovereignty in any way, it attacks *xenophobia*. There is a space of jurisdiction which is the state; and Kant says only that every person has the right to live in this space of jurisdiction, to be received there.

- *Don't you see in this a reminiscence of the Bible?*

- Undoubtedly: the famous triad comes to mind: "The orphan, the widow, and the stranger at your door." The orphan is the one who has lost the support of an ancestral lineage, the widow the one who, having lost her husband, does not benefit from the levirate, and finally the stranger is the one who is without rights except precisely the right created by hospitality. Kant was imbued with Biblical culture; that ought to be self-evident.

An idea like this one has a value of regulative universality. I strongly stress this transcendental level in opposition to the idea that one could generate a principle of cohabitation of a political nature on the basis of specific spaces of mutual recognition. This is where, in my opinion, the weakness is to be found of communitarians such as Walzer in the United States or Boltanski and Thévenot in France.[12] For the political sphere continues to preserve its specificity in relation to this level of mutual recognition: it contains an element of power, of sovereignty, and therefore it poses the problem of its necessary limitation. A problem that cannot be deduced from any consideration that could be said to be geographical, cultural, ethnic, hence communitarian. With this problem of limitation, we are on the level of Kantian philosophy, where reason serves to limit the claims of this or that agency. In the social system, state sovereignty constitutes the principle of limitation regarding the claims of subordinate "spheres"; in its turn, political sovereignty encounters the question of its self-limitation on the occasion of its claims to legitimacy. This question immanent to sovereignty is so insistent that it reemerges at the heart of definitions of the State that make explicit reference to the use of violence as a last resort, as in Weber, compelled in his definition of the state to term this recourse *legitimate*. Now, precisely, what is it that ultimately gives the epithet *legitimate* this value of internal limitation on the ultimate exercise of violence if not a universal regulative idea? One could say that the communitarian principle is constitutive, whereas an idea like that of hospitality is regulative: it serves as a limitation on the claim that a power might have to elevate itself to the extreme.

- *But then the value of universality would have to be recognized by consensus. This is just what is contested today.*

- But as soon as one recognizes at least partial rules of play, even those of a gang, one can regressively determine the conditions of the possibility of a minimal recognition in a space of exchange. And there one will again always find a universal prior to the regional operations of the spheres of recognition. In other words, the most radical critique of my thesis, a critique that would lead to a sort of communitarian nihilism, would be the idea that one cannot recognize any kind of social tie; this would be the hypothesis of a wild creature, with no ties. I have to say that this hypothesis seems as abstract to me as the one which cultural relativism strives to combat, the hypothesis of a universal. This is why the distinction between a constitutive universal and a regulative universal offers a resource because it allows us to seek a point of intersection between founding on the basis of mutual recognition and the absence of an ultimate ground of this mutual play of recognition; starting from the absence of the ultimate character of a purely historical constitutive principle, the necessity arises of a universal that is solely regulative.

This is the way that I would argue, treading in the footsteps of Kant, and the way I would attempt to go beyond the debate between the universalists and the communitarians.

# Chapter 3

# *From Psychoanalysis to the Question of the Self, or Thirty Years of Philosophical Work*

• *In 1965, after three volumes of your* Philosophy of the Will, *where you had already touched on the problem of psychoanalysis, you published* Freud and Philosophy: An Essay on Interpretation. *The least that can be said is that this work was not received calmly in the psychoanalytic community . . .*

• The reception of this work in France was in large part dominated by its rejection by Lacan, a rejection expressed publicly in his seminar as well as in private. I was accused of silencing the understanding of Freud that I was supposed to owe to him.

I should like to say in this regard that there are several misunderstandings intertwined in this quarrel. I shall begin with the one that questions my good faith.

It has been remarked that I attended Lacan's seminar before the publication of my book, and the conclusion was drawn from this that I had borrowed my interpretation of Freud from him. There is the matter of dates here that I should like to clarify. I first presented this book on Freud in my teaching at the Sorbonne before I went to Lacan's seminar; this can be verified in the lists of course titles. In addition, in 1960 at the invitation of Dr Ey I gave a lecture at Bonneval, which was published only in 1966 and which can be found in *The Conflict of Interpretations*.[1] Jacques Lacan, colleague and friend of Dr Ey, attended this lecture, and publicly praised it, before accompanying me back to Paris and inviting me to his seminar. Now this lecture contains the essential elements of my interpretation of Freud, which had ripened over the course of my earlier teaching at the Sorbonne. My book, then, had for the most part already been composed; it had, at any rate, been thought out in its general lines before I attended Lacan's seminar.

This is, moreover, an example of an incredible lack of intellectual integrity on his part: for the discussion that took place after my lecture, in which he participated, was eliminated from the published volume of the Bonneval colloquium at his request. The other texts generally are followed by the discussion to which they gave rise, but not mine.

This text is a key text because it presents my overall interpretation of Freud's work, namely that the Freudian discourse is composite, and hence of great epistemological fragility, for it plays on two vocabularies: a vocabulary of energy, with terms like repression, energy, drive, and so on, and on the other hand, a vocabulary of sense and interpretation, present in the very title of *Traumdeutung*, *The Interpretation of Dreams*. I held that this composite character was to Freud's credit, moreover, without classifying it as a defect of conceptualization or of epistemological lucidity; I saw this as a deliberate use of a language appropriate to its object, which itself is situated precisely at the point of articulation of the domains of force and of language.

This misunderstanding, which cast doubt on my good faith, was found in Michel Tort's article, which appeared in *Les Temps Modernes* under the title, "La machine herméneutique"; this was a devastating article that blasted me and said in essence: Ricoeur spoke once of the unconscious in *The Voluntary and the Involuntary*, he speaks about it a second time in *Freud and Philosophy*. What was there between these two works? Nothing, except Lacan. But what there was between them was my own exploration of symbolic language in the framework of my book *The Symbolism of Evil*, and, consequently, the emphasis on the linguistic dimension of our relation to the unconscious. This dimension is in fact brought to the fore in Lacan, but I had coordinated it with the energetic, dynamic dimension, instead of opposing the former to the latter as he does.

- *What in your opinion did Lacan want from you? Why this cordiality directed toward you?*

- I think that at bottom he expected from me what he had wanted first from Hyppolite[2] and then from Merleau-Ponty: a sort of philosophical backing. I obviously disappointed him on this score.

- *And you yourself, what did you expect from his seminar?*

- I lived through those meetings as a sort of obligation, terrible drudgery and frustration, which I assiduously imposed on myself, because I always had the impression that he was *going to* say something important that had not yet been said, that this would be said the next time and so on; he had a consummate art of suspense, which I found absolutely intolerable. For me it was really an ordeal to go back time after time, feeling a kind of obligation but also an incredible disappointment. I remember going home one afternoon and saying to my wife, "I've just come from the seminar; I didn't understand a thing!" At that moment the phone rang; it was Lacan who aked me, "What did you think of my talk?" I told him, "I didn't understand a thing." He hung up on me.

With regard to Lacan, I felt very intimidated. In every sense of the word: I became timid but also I had the sentiment of being subjected to a constant threat of excommunication. Anyway the atmosphere of veneration that reigned at the seminar was stupifying! It was unimaginable that someone could stand up and say that he had not understood or that it was absurd . . . Here I experienced the inverse of the American seminar.

But the most "serious" thing remains to be said. I had written in the introduction to my book that I would speak of no one but Freud and that I would quote interpreters only on a given, specific Freudian theme. So I set aside from the outset all the other Freudians. I set aside those whom Lacan himself criticizes, and rightly so, especially in fact the American psychoanalysts – even if it is regrettable, let me say in passing, that he is unaware of the most interesting among them, those who developed the narrative aspect, the role of narrative in the reconquest of a coherent story through the cure; the latter I encountered in New York, where I participated for a year at Columbia in interesting seminars conducted by psychoanalysts. But I also set aside Anna Freud, Ernest Jones, Winnicott, Bion – whom I had discovered during the same period – and, finally, Lacan himself. This was the unpardonable mistake, to have placed Lacan under the same banner as the post-Freudians; this, for him, was a serious offense! Perhaps he expected a book that would have been a sort of reinterpretation of Freud on the basis of his own writings, which I had not begun to read before attending his seminar.

• *Later when you read Lacan's writings, what did you think of them?*

• Élisabeth Roudinesco made what, for me, is at once the most favorable and the most crushing statement on this topic:[3] Ricoeur could not have borrowed from Lacan because he has understood nothing of him. I have to say that this is true. I do not understand this form of articulation or of thinking; it is entirely foreign to me. I do not understand how this thinking works; at times I am dazzled, as if by flashes, but without being able to follow the thread of his discourse. I suspect that I must not be the only one . . . I have always been sorry about this and quite often have felt it was a kind of infirmity on my part. In a certain manner, as you see, I have remained a prisoner of that intimidation.

• *You have told us that, after the fact, you reproached yourself for having underplayed the clinical aspect in your book, and for having overplayed some of Freud's theoretical writings, in particular those on metapsychology. But you also devote a large part of your analyses to the Freudian interpretation of culture.*

• Concerning your last point, I in no way regret this. I continue to owe much to this theory of culture. *The Future of an Illusion, Civilization and its Discontents*, the correspondence with Einstein on war and peace, *Moses and Monotheism* are texts with which I continue to battle, and which I would place on an equal level with Nietzsche's texts on religion, corrosive as they are. I include them both in what at the time I called the "hermeneutics of suspicion."

As for my reproaching myself for having understated the clinical aspect and for having overemphasized Freud's theoretical writings, I have given a full account in an essay published in Belgium – and not in France! – in the volume in honor of Alphonse de Waelhens, *Qu'est-ce que l'homme?*[4] To give full credit to the conceptual resources offered by its practice, I tried to characterize psychoanalysis by three features. First, the fact that the unconscious speaks: psychoanalysis would not be possible if there were not a sort of proximity between human drives and language. This is another way of restating, in other than epistemological terms, the union of the dynamic and the interpretive. Second, the drive is *addressed to*: there is in it the feature of being addressed to the father, to the mother, and so on – the Oedipal complex would not be comprehensible if there were not at the very outset a sort of relation to the other which is genuinely constitutive. Third, the narrative component of the analytical experience: the fact, first of all, that the patient brings fragments of narrative, but of a shattered story, with twists and turns which the patient can neither tolerate nor understand; in a certain way, the task of psychoanalysis is to reestablish a story, rendering it intelligible and acceptable.

Today I would say that not only has theory in Freud perhaps been overvalued, but in addition it has not been seen that theory lags behind in relation to his main discovery, which is precisely in the area of narrative, far from biologism, far from scientism. This is not incompatible with Lacan, to the extent that I understand him.

It seems to me in any case that if one takes analytical practice seriously, and if one admits that it is in advance of theory, then one has to have a certain familiarity with what goes on in the course of a cure, and in particular with the episode of transference. I increasingly think that this is where it all happens. Moreover, Freud says as much in his writings that are collected under the title *Papers on Technique*. Later, I was led to reflect on the notion of *Behandlung*, of "handling" – a notion that cannot be captured in the nets of interpretation in a purely linguistic sense, and which designates a relation to instinctual drives, a handling of forces.

• *You have spoken of several misunderstandings concerning your book on Freud.*

• I was also thinking about an error made regarding what was supposed to be my intention – I have already alluded to this in the course of our discussions. People attributed to me the idea of attempting to include psychoanalysis within phenomenology, and beyond that, within its hermeneutical version. I have said quite the opposite, namely that there is something irreducible in it and that here phenomenology encounters its limit. With psychoanalysis, I was confronted with something that resists a theory of consciousness. It is true that I had not, at that time, taken seriously enough the aspects of phenomenology that are concerned with passivity: passive syntheses, in particular. There would probably be some bridges, some passages possible between phenomenology and psychoanalysis, but by some path other than that of a theory stubbornly centered on consciousness, of a phenomenology in its most idealist phase as this is found in Husserl's *Cartesian Meditations*.

• *In the years that followed the publication of your book on Freud, and after three years at the University of Louvain, you returned to your teaching at Nanterre. You had a seminar on phenomenology?*

• It was called "Phenomenology, hermeneutics." After a certain length of time we added "and the philosophy of language." It was the period when I was introducing themes of analytical philosophy (in the Anglo-Saxon sense) in the seminar; this was also the period when I introduced the theme of action.

• *In the debate in those years, marked by the famous opposition between explanation – which was held to be the task of the natural*

*sciences – and understanding – which was held to be the work of the*
*sciences of culture and the mind, what side did you take?*

• I do not think that hermeneutics and epistemology are distinguished
by two separate methodologies, two projects of intelligibility; these two
perspectives intersect over and over again, are in constant interference
with one another, first of all because the term "hermeneutics" subsumes
at least three things: precise methods containing rigorous rules – this is
the case of philology and the exegesis of the great classical texts, such
as those of jurisprudence; next, a reflection on the very nature of
understanding, its conditions and its operation; finally, a more ambi-
tious axis, a sort of "philosophy" that presents itself as another path of
intelligibility and that claims to understand scientific endeavors better
than they are able to understand themselves, fencing off these endeavors
within the limits of a sort of "methodologism." This is more or less the
position adopted by Gadamer, in relation to which I have taken a
certain distance. Now hermeneutics, even in the first sense, that of
exegesis, constitutes to my mind *an* epistemology, in which intelligibility is saturated by the notion of "sense."

What is more, when science is understood not through its objects, its
methods or its principles, but as a theoretical practice, it obeys an
intentionality proper to it which cannot help but raise the question of
its sense: the legitimacy of a hermeneutics in this sense is therefore
entirely well-founded here. This is, as a matter of fact, a hermeneutics
of scientificity as one practice among others.

This is what has led me to reject the opposition introduced by Dilthey
and developed by Rickert between "explaining" and "understanding."[5] In opposition to this I reaffirm the constant intersecting of
methods: linguistics and political economy, in particular, mix insepar-
ably together the explanatory mode and the comprehensive mode;
econometry, for example, obeys an explanatory method. The natural
and the human do not, therefore, constitute two fields where one would
have to be assigned to science and the other to hermeneutics.

In this regard, I owe a debt to Jean Ladrière,[6] who has made a
remarkable analysis of the different modes of explanation. He distinguishes four of these: explanation by subsumption, placing a fact under
a rule (exemplification of the principle); explanation by reduction,
explaining a phenomenon by the what lies beneath it (to a large extent
what human biology does when it notes the conditions necessary for the
appearance of a given organ, without thereby explaining the production of the phenomenon by what underlies it); genetic explanation, in
which a given phenomenon proceeds from another through a series of
ordered transformations; and, finally, explanation by the optimum,

attaining an optimum level of functioning of coordinated and convergent subsystems.

- *What do you think, then, of Heidegger's famous statement: "Science does not think."*

- If one conceives of science not as a theoretical practice but as an intellectual operation resembling a calculation, then one can affirm as he does that "science does not think." But this is provided thinking is restricted to the capacity of that being in the world that I am, as a concerned being, to grasp hold of itself in its self-understanding; the science of nature is not, in fact, this type of thinking. It could never think its object in the mode of human concern or, to use my own terms, in the mode of action. In the order of actions, in fact, it is always possible to find an agent behind the objective systems, the economic, political and other systems in which the agent has been engaged. The subject of thinking can always try to correct herself in her activity with respect to the products of that activity; on the side of nature, the concept that would be closest to that of action would be productivity, by which phenomena, facts, are placed under principles; and these explanatory procedures, whether they be causal, genetic, structural or the search for the optimum, allow us to account for the way in which a given set of facts are placed under certain principles. The autoproduction of nature, to borrow an idea already developed by Hegel, cannot be thought after the model of human thinking, that is to say, after the model of self-reflection capable of correcting itself with respect to what it produces.

I am genuinely committed to maintaining this distinction between thinking under the category of action – that is, thinking what human beings do – and thinking under the category of production – thinking the way in which facts are subsumed under principles. It is true that one could be tempted to believe that this subsumption depends essentially on models that we ourselves have worked out, and that this modeling does make the productions of nature resemble the products of human thought. But it remains nonetheless that the representative character of the model in relation to the domain it models remains a puzzle. This representativeness is presupposed, it is not produced in the sense in which an action is. So it is really impossible to consider as identical the production of nature and the self-understanding of the agent in his or her action. This is not a matter of returning to the nature/mind distinction: the mind itself knows through its forms of passivity (the biological base of life, all the mechanisms of mind that escape us, such as inventiveness, the production of ideas, and so on) a sort of autoproduction comparable to nature's, and just as puzzling. So that, here too, we control by our concerted action only a very small portion of the activity of the mind.

Once the intelligibility of nature and that of action have been clearly distinguished, it is possible to ask about the meaning of the intelligible whose production we find puzzling. From the very core of this intelligibility arises the question of the meaning of the scientific enterprise which then enters into the field of action: "doing science." Action thus defined is then in quest of its self-understanding. But neither is this a matter of reducing the specificity of science surreptitiously for one cannot understand the sense of the activity without doing it; it is in relation to its project – why do you want to understand nature? – that it has to be analyzed, and it is in unfolding its own project that science discovers, piece by piece, some fragments of its meaning. Theoretical practice is the practice of an action that understands itself in the search for intelligibility: the knowledge of nature as production which I cannot reduce to an action of wanting to know, which is not itself entirely transparent to itself. But the mind cannot grasp itself in its totality, and it knows itself, precisely, only in the scores it plays, formed by the different actions it undertakes. Science can think its own end only in the very process of the development of intelligibility that it produces; finality is, then, immanent in the very operation of science itself.

If one asks toward what goal this project is ultimately directed, and what distinguishes it from other projects that guide our actions in other domains, I would call upon Jean Nabert, for whom several fields of profound intentionality remained open, subsumed under the idea of the just, the idea of the true, and the idea of the beautiful, and forming as many centers of reflection. Science includes the idea of the just, if only in the necessary competition of concurrent hypotheses, where each one is bound by the obligation of listening to the other's reasoning and of taking it into account in the process of discussion. And perhaps science also conforms to the idea of the beautiful, if one thinks of the wonderment, the admiration it professes before the beauty of nature. Curiosity, in fact, is not enough to account for scientific activity, which cannot be determined simply by psychological motives, any more than it could be inspired solely by that other motive – the will for domination.

- *How did your phenomenology seminar function?*

- It was in the United States that I learned how to conduct a seminar. I have always thought of it as very demanding for the participants who were supposed to contribute actively to it. Thanks to the American model, I always resisted the tendency of many French research centers to become lecture machines. Moreover, even in France, I almost always had American students, and they were the ones who often set the tone. I tried to establish the same practice as on the other side of the Atlantic: at the first meeting, I proposed ten or so books and about twenty articles to be read by all, and I made it clear that I would strive to move among these texts, so they would be the common realm of experience for the instructors and the members of the seminar.

This practice of the seminar is the reason that, in my books, I always focused more on my students than on an outside public. So that I was rather well armed against criticism, except that of Lacan, who questioned my intellectual honesty. All the rest seemed perfectly normal to me; I never felt myself to be personally attacked by them. For, at bottom, one thing truly preoccupied me: the consistency of my discourse; for me, it mattered above all to resolve my own contradictions, the tensions between various influences. My problem was always to determine whether I was constructing false windows, whether what I was doing was merely a compromise, or if it was really the proposal of a third position capable of holding the road. These were my concerns. But I never felt what I later read about myself, that I had been "in seclusion" until recently – forgotten. On the contrary, I had always had the feeling of having the audience I deserved, neither more nor less; the great satisfactions of teaching and satisfactions I would call conceptual in my relation with myself.

This is how I traversed extremely varied philosophical landscapes from the existentialism of the 1950s. I paid relatively little attention to what the expectations of the public might have been, and so the idea of building a faithful readership never crossed my mind, perhaps mistakenly so.

When I have written a book on a topic, I don't speak about it after that, as though my duty has been done in its regard, leaving me free to continue on my way. It is in this way that I dropped the problem of psychoanalysis, but also that of metaphor after *The Rule of Metaphor*.

● *This is why people have sometimes had the feeling there was a kind of break in your course from one book to the next.*

● Yet it is often in the remainders from an earlier subject that I have seen the urgency of another theme. This is true of my relation to psychoanalysis, since it is truly from *The Symbolism of Evil* that *Freud and Philosophy* stems. Having adopted a line that was broadly speaking that of the phenomenology of religion, close to Eliade, I distinctly felt that in Freud, Marx, and Nietzsche there was an opposing thought that I had to come to terms with.

• *This was also the period when you crossed through the structuralist "landscape," to use your expression. The upshot of this journey was precisely, in 1975,* The Rule of Metaphor. *This was another way of testing the phenomenological method. Some may have believed that you had become a structuralist!*

• I have always made a clear distinction between a structuralist philosophy and a structural study of specific texts. I have considerable appreciation for the latter approach, because it is a manner of doing justice to the text and of extending it to the fullest dimension of its internal articulations, independent of the author's intentions, and hence of the author's subjectivity. This aspect of structuralism was not foreign to me as I had always espoused, under the title of the semantic autonomy of the text, the idea that the text escapes its author and signifies for itself. Now this semantic autonomy of the text opened it up to approaches that take into account its objectivity alone, as what is said, written, and so objectified. I take objectification in a very positive sense, as a necessary passage by way of explanation, with a view to a better understanding, before the return to the author.

I distinguish this from a structuralist philosophy, which draws from its practice a general doctrine in which the subject is eliminated from its position as the author of discourse. I am at one and the same time an habitué of structural practice and in a conflictual relation with structuralism, which seemed to me to attain its highest point in Lévi-Strauss, the member of the structuralist school whose work I most respect. We had, in the philosophical circle of *Esprit,* a very interesting confrontation, in which I introduced the expression "transcendentalism without a transcendental subject" to characterize his position. For me, he was an adversary against whom I strove to measure up as a worthy opponent, in my defense of the philosophy of the subject; I saw him as the one establishing the level of the discussion. In my eyes, he incarnates the model of a work conducted without the slightest concession.

• *It remains that his analysis of myths, deliberately stripped of the vertical dimension of transcendence, did not satisfy you. How far do you go along with Lévi-Strauss?*

• I am thinking in particular of the "finale" of *The Naked Man.*[7] In relation to this text I feel a sort of admiration at a distance; a reverence for an enterprise which is genuinely different, but which counts. For there are also many works by other authors that are very foreign to me but which do not count for me and of which I do not speak.

With Lévi-Strauss, I had tried to argue on the basis of his own theory, starting from the distinction he makes between a "cold society" and a "hot society." He defines the former as a society on which history has no hold, and in which myths and discourses are also to be taken as "cold" objects, resting in a conceptual empyrean; myths and discourses said by no one, addressed to no one – they *are*, possessing a sort of objectivity. But in other societies, with which he has not been concerned – to an initial degree the Greek world, but to a much greater extent the Semitic world – history is constitutive, not only of self-understanding, but of the very content of what is said. The fact, for example, that a large part of the theologies of ancient Israel consisted in placing certain stories in a selected order and that, consequently, this society invested them with meaning through narrative, implies that history is not just something that has an external hold on discourses, but that it is constitutive of them. It is not simply an object but an operative mode.

● *It is true that the Greek myths, the Judeo-Christian myths, but also Indian myths offer in relation to the Amerindian myths, to which Lévi-Strauss has always confined himself, the noteworthy difference that they present themselves as possessing a metaphysical – if this be the right word – significance.*

● I believe that Lévi-Strauss chose the object domain that reinforces his theory; I would say that one finds in him a sort of joint selection of doctrine and of field. What would he say about the myths you refer to? Perhaps he would reply that our own interest in the relation between the existential and the transcendent causes us to value them, but that if one were to approach them with a philosophy in which the structural constitution were the preferred manner of signifying, then it is easy to relate these productions to an imaginary realm, the source of illusions, after the manner of Spinoza.

What is dominant in his conception is certainly the idea of the homogeneous character of all structural systems, using the analogy of the brain with its neuronal structure: it is as though there were a neuronal man who was replicated in a man of myths. Although you would also have to eliminate the word "man" . . .

● *Others besides Lévi-Strauss actually did eliminate it. What was your feeling about Foucault's declaration of the death of man?*

● The idea that man is a recent invention seems to me sheer invention. I am thinking, for example, of the "Ode to Man" in Sophocles' *Antigone*, where we read: "There are indeed many marvels (*polla ta deina*) in this world, but nothing is more *deinon* than man" (lines

332–7). More marvelous? more terrible? more formidable, in the literal sense of the word? How could we forget the Stoic concern, the mastery of desires and passions, to which Foucault himself returns in his later texts, which I greatly admire, *The Use of Pleasure* and *Care of the Self.* But precisely, this is a philosophy quite different from the one he had developed in *The Order of Things.* I had many reservations about that book. The idea of *episteme* that replaced one another with random transitions not only seemed unintelligible to me, but more importantly, I found that it was not based on a wealth of content great enough for each of these *episteme.* How could one speak, in the seventeenth century, of the *episteme* of representation without taking into account mathematics, or the law, to say nothing of theology? Foucault seemed to me to take too limited a sample in each case to be convincing. To have placed under the category of *correspondences* everything that preceded the seventeenth century did not seem to me to do justice to the incredible variety of philosophies and thoughts from the Renaissance and the sixteenth century.

On the other hand, I devoted an entire section in the third volume of *Time and Narrative* (1985) to *The Archeology of Knowledge* concerning the concept of "discursive formation."[8] I discuss in great detail his idea that the continuity of memory, and hence of the history of the subject, is an idealist illusion. This was the period when I was beginning to discover the theme on which I am now working and which remains an enigma to me: the *Zusammenhang des Lebens,* or the "coherence of existence," which is located beneath consciousness and which, as a consequence, escapes the criticism that it would be an idealist claim on the part of the subject to demand it for itself.

It is to the extent that Foucault distanced himself from himself with his last two books that I felt closer to him; but I never had the opportunity to tell him so. That is a meeting that never took place. Certainly, he was expecting nothing of the sort, and I was on paths where I encountered him infrequently, except at very localized points of intersection.

• *Among the theorists of structuralism, you pay a lot of attention to Greimas.*

• With him, at first, I found myself in confrontation. I recall our first meeting: I had tried to explain that structuralism represented a stage in my own discourse, the passage through the objectivity of the text. He had answered: "In sum, you encompass me. But since you are speaking, I do the semiotics of what you have said, so I encompass you!" That is how we began. Little by little, we got beyond these conflictual relations, which were followed by years of deep friendship, mutual respect, and even affection. I did lengthy analyses of his book on Maupassant's novella *Two Friends*; I went quite far in my argument on behalf of Greimas, based on a genuine effort to understand his project.

I think, moreover, that this exercise is a good example of my critical relation to the structuralists. I have great respect for their reasoning; as a result, the point of divergence is very carefully set out and grounded in a sustained effort of understanding. More generally speaking, I talk only about authors that I can go along with far enough to say that, although my separation from them is costly to me, it also benefits me because I have passed through the school of their challenges. Those with whom I do not have this relationship of productive conflict, I never speak about. This explains a number of my silences, which are the result not of ignorance, nor of disdain, nor of hostility; they come solely from the fact that I do not *encounter* these authors. To employ Greimas's categories, they play the role neither of helpers nor opponents; they are in a neutral position. They are located in places where I simply do not go.

• *You give some unforgettable examples of this relation of productive conflict in the three volumes of* Time and Narrative,[9] *with your discussion toe-to-toe with Saint Augustine, Aristotle, Husserl, and Heidegger.*

• I had – but I would be incapable of saying when – a sort of flash of insight, namely the intuition of a relation of inverted parallelism between the Augustinian theory of time and the notion of *muthos* in Aristotle's *Poetics*. It was this sort of sudden collusion between *distentio animi* in Book XI of the *Confessions* and Aristotelian *muthos* that was not only crucial for what followed, but seminal; the idea, to paraphrase the one we were speaking of earlier, that time is structured like a narrative. This is the card I played in that book: how far can one go in the presupposition that time becomes human only when it is recounted, that the passage by way of the narrative is the elevation of the time of the world to the time of man?

• *Looking back upon your course from* The Voluntary and the Involuntary *to* Oneself as Another,[10] *with lengthy detours through Freudian theory, linguistics, structuralism, and so on, do you see a series of broken lines or a trajectory whose thread is apparent to you?*

• You are placing me here on the terrain of self-interpretation, and my own is of no more value than anyone else's.

● *Perhaps, but of no less value either. What is the interpretation of the reader of yourself that you are?*

● I am not entering into the choice between the alternatives, continuous/discontinuous. What I believe, or at any rate what I can tell about myself, is that each book is determined by a fragmentary problem. I very strongly hold to the idea, moreover, that philosophy is addressed to specific problems, to well-circumscribed difficulties of thought. So metaphor – it is first of all a figure of style; narrative – it is to begin with a literary genre. My books have always been limited in scope. I have never posed massive questions of the type: what is philosophy? I deal with particular problems. The question of metaphor is not that of the narrative, even if I do observe that there is the continuity of semantic innovation from one to the other.

I see the tie between my different books in another way. After having completed a work, I find myself confronting something that has escaped it, something that flies outside its orbit, becoming an obsession for me, and forming the next subject to examine. I cannot account for this subterranean tie. Why did the question of narrative impose itself on me after metaphor? Of course, I could draw a line between the two: in both books, it is a matter, as I have just said, of semantic innovation, in other words of the question: how do we create meaning in speaking? We create it by placing together incongruous semantic fields – this is metaphor – or by constructing a plot – this is narrative. So there is a certain homogeneity of the two subjects, under the sign of semantic innovation. But to what extent is this simply a retrospective discovery? I believe that anyone who writes has this experience of a theme that at first prowls on the edges of consciousness, then comes to put itself at the center and, finally, becomes an obsession.

The last time this happened to me was when I had been invited to give the Gifford Lectures in 1986. So this was only a short time after *Time and Narrative*. My first reaction was to ask myself what I was going to talk about. I told myself that after all I had to come to grips with the question of the subject. This forced me to take a recapitulative path in which I consider, in succession, the field of language, that of action, and that of narrative identity, before arriving at ethics and ontology.

The connection between one book and another is never the same from one instance to the next. *Freud and Philosophy* in a certain sense got away from me, since it was supposed to be a response to *The Symbolism of Evil* but instead became a book on Freud. *The Rule of Metaphor*[11] is, finally, in a critical relation to *The Symbolism of Evil* and to Eliade in the sense that in it I was asking myself if there was not a structure of language that had been studied more thoroughly, that was better known than the symbol – itself a vague notion used in so many different ways, from the symbols in chemistry to the symbol of the monarchy. By contrast, thanks to the long rhetorical tradition, we understand better how metaphor operates. I asked myself then whether I could not pour back into a kind of rhetorical receptacle all of the diffuse problematic of the symbol, providing it with a strong semantic framework. In fact, what I produced there was a semantic theory of symbols. One could say, then, that what I did in *The Rule of Metaphor* was to take a step back since I returned to the theme of *The Symbolism of Evil* after having passed through Freud, but also after having encountered the linguistic tools I did not possess at the time and which I did not even know then: propositional semantics, pragmatics of language, the theory of utterance. It is here that my stay in the United States was entirely decisive; encountering Max Black, in particular, was very important since it allowed me to become acquainted with theories of metaphor that rested not on deviant naming but on deviant predication.[12]

You wanted to know if there was continuity or rupture between my books: here is a particular type of continuity, which proceeds by returning, taking a step backwards. The same is true for the narrative, which I had encountered long before *Time and Narrative*, when I was publishing *History and Truth* (1955),[13] and even – myths already being narratives – as early as *The Symbolism of Evil*.

In this way, one can say that the theme of the new book is off-center in relation to the preceding one, but with a return to subjects that had already been encountered, touched upon, or anticipated in earlier discussions. What had been a fragment becomes the new envelope, the totality.

But I am particularly aware of the fact that each book has a limited scope. And it is from the reflection on its limits that the obsession with a new subject arises. Just as the theme of memory now torments me as not being treated in either *Time and Narrative* or in *Oneself as Another*.

• *In speaking of theories of metaphor, you alluded to the grafting of Anglo-Saxon philosophies onto your own. Your teaching in the United States must have opened up for you vast domains that were completely unknown, at that time, to most French university professors.*

• I could almost say that the American university was above all for me a great library and a great bibliography! An open bibliography that then became unavoidable. I discovered authors, works, and doctrines whose very existence was unknown to me. It is enough to go through the bibliography of the works consulted for *The Rule of Metaphor* and *Time and Narrative*. This enabled me to balance off my Germanic background without in any way erasing it: I continue to owe just as great a debt to Kant, and I would be willing to say that I have never ceased to be, ultimately, a sort of post-Kantian, if only through Husserl and Nabert – even a post-Hegelian Kantian, as I jokingly call myself.

• *You mentioned, but only in passing, the composition of* Time and Narrative. *We obviously cannot go into these three volumes in detail, there being no replacement for a careful reading of them. Could you at least say something about the general architecture of this work?*

• I would like to begin with two guiding concepts: those of "configuration" and of "refiguration." They gave me a better way to approach a question I had examined in *The Rule of Metaphor* under the title of "metaphorical reference," but then it had been hastily. In that work, I was concerned with the problem posed by the capacity displayed by language to reorder the experience of the reader. At the end of the book, I had only postulated that, when language is reorganized in a creative way by metaphor, a breakthrough is made in experience, that is to say, we are invited to read our own experience in accordance with the new modalities of language. But there was a link missing in this last chapter: the role of the reader.

This problem seemed to me to be mastered better in *Time and Narrative*, since I devoted two entirely distinct sections to it: one concerned with configuration, namely the narrative operations at work within language, in the form of emplotment of actions and characters (these are the first two volumes); the other concerned with refiguration, namely the transformation of one's own experience under the effect of the narrative, and this is the object of the third volume in its entirety. The problem of configuration is treated in three language practices: first, placing myself in the field of ordinary language of conversation, I open a lengthy discussion on the mimetic character of language, and I try to show that the notion of *mimesis* itself functions in a dialectical manner, as being first imitation, next reconstruction, and, finally, the transformative capacity of experience; then comes the second discursive field, history; and, lastly, the third discursive field, fiction.

But whether it be in everyday language, in history or in fiction, I remain *within* the milieu of language. This is why I deal only with configuration, reserving entirely for the third volume the ultrasensitive, and ultracontroversial, problem of the movement of language outside of itself and its capacity to redirect, restructure an experience, to produce a new manner of inhabiting the world.

So far as history is concerned, I have to specify that in *Time and Narrative* I am interested in only one problem: to what extent is history a narrative? This is why in my current investigations on the relations between memory and history – which I shall discuss later – I am trying to fill an obvious gap in this approach, a gap that was determined by the selective and exclusive nature of the question posed. At that time, this question was of great urgency for me; we were still in the era marked by Fernand Braudel and the *Annales* school, a period that had witnessed the retreat of events and narratives, the demise of political history, diplomatic history, the history of battles, and so on, to the benefit of a history that could be termed more structural, taking into account forces of gradual evolution and, consequently, of long duration. In *Time and Narrative* I make the necessary concessions to this discipline to assure myself that, if history is narrative, it is so in a completley different way than ordinary language, which rests on the direct, immediate storytelling of speech: with history, one is dealing with a highly constructed narrative. I take as an example favorable to my thesis what at first appears to be a counterexample: Braudel's great book, *The Mediterranean and the Mediterranean World in the Age of Philip II*; I try to show that, ultimately, this is a grand narrative in which the hero is the Mediterranean. The end is not marked by the death of Philip II but by the disappearance of the Mediterranean as a historical hero and its effacement as the center of the world.

Today, it seems to me that this quarrel generates less heat.


- *What was the reaction of the historians?*

- I was invited by them on several occasions; I had good relations with the historians, unlike what had happened with the psychoanalysts. With François Furet, whom I saw often at Chicago, where he became the head of the Committee on Social Thought; with Roger Chartier and, more recently, with François Bédarida concerning the problems of the history of the present day. In general, historians have extended a warm welcome to my works, after an initial phase of distrust, which was not directed against me but against the philosophy of history, under the pretext that, if a philosopher is concerned with history, it is necessarily to do the same mischief as . . .


- *Hegel?*

- No, worse! As Toynbee or Spengler. But in *Time and Narrative 1*, I am interested only in the history of historians, and I refrain entirely from delving into the so-called philosophy of history, whether it be

Kantian, Hegelian or post-Hegelian. I remain within the field of the historians.

It was my understanding that the historians were pleased to see a philosopher attacking history from the side of epistemology, for they themselves do methodology rather than epistemology. The question whether history is scientific has not really been discussed since Raymond Aron, Henri Marrou, and more recently Paul Veyne, the latter being closer to Foucault than to me on these matters.

My work with the historians never assumed a confrontational style but contributed instead to a common investigation around certain critical points: the concept of event, for instance, with Pierre Nora and Krzystof Pomian, who is the most philosophical of the historians. At the time I was not familiar with his book on *The Order of Time*. It is a very important work and I would no longer write *Time and Narrative* in the same way today, after having read it.

To remain a moment on the problem of the epistemology of history, I would like to say that, since *Time and Narrative*, I have published a better informed study of the current discussion, in which I have clearly shifted away from the problem of the narrative.[14] I have tried to distinguish various manners in which history can be considered a science: first, documentary history, where one can answer *true* or *false* to the presentation of facts; this is the level where we solve questions such as, "How many prisoners were in the Bastille on July 14, 1789?" Next, explanatory history, which includes a discussion on the respective roles of social and economic forces, an evaluation of the place of politics in relation to these, and the narrative element tied to domain of events. Then, a final level, which I had not encountered at the time I was writing *Time and Narrative*: the level on which are forged the grand categories such as the Renaissance, the French Revolution, which depend more on interpretation and writing, the notion of historio*graphy*, of the writing of history, understood in its strongest sense. Three levels, then, from documentary history which possesses criteria of verification, explanatory history open to controversy, to the history that can be called poetic, since it is one of the great plot constructions (*affabulations*) forming the self-understanding of a nation through its founding narratives.

Returning to the thread of *Time and Narrative*, in the second volume I tackle the problem of the question of fictional narrative, running up against the problem of the permanence of great narrative structures; once again, and in what I think is a fruitful manner, I go to battle with structuralism in the arena where it has always operated best – the narrative. The structuralist forms of narrative theory occupied me for some time, and at the end of the book, I venture analyses of three "novels on time": one in English, *Mrs Dalloway*; a second in German, *The Magic Mountain*; the third in French, *Time Regained*. I try to put these examples to the test of my conception of the simultaneous emplotment of the story recounted and of the characters.

The third volume of *Time and Narrative* is devoted to the problem of refiguration. How does a language restructured by emplotment lead to a rereading of our own experience in accordance with the main lines of the narrative? I return here, in a more plausible and better argued fashion, to a thesis present in *The Rule of Metaphor* as a sort of grand postulate of language, namely that the relation between language and reality, experience or the world, whatever term you like, is a dialectical one: given that the sign is not the thing, that the sign is in retreat in relation to it, language is constituted marginally, in a sense, in relation to experience and becomes for itself a spoken universe. Whence the legitimacy of the discourse of linguists who exclude the extralinguistic from their field and resolutely confine themselves to language; this is the strength of the Saussurean school – considering that it is from sign to sign, then from book to book, in a vast relation of intertextuality, that the universe of language is constituted. This is perfectly legitimate, as a first stage – the moment of exile – of the operation of language, which, at the limit, "celebrates itself," to borrow an expression from Roland Barthes.

The counterpart to this exile is the moment when, following Benveniste's expression, language is "poured back into the universe." He was able to formulate this moment as a linguist to the extent that he – unlike Saussure, who constructed his entire theory on the sign and on the differential relations between signs – began with the sentence, which he called "the instance of discourse." However, it is the sentence – and not the lexical sign – that possesses not only a *signified* but also an *intended*, that is to say, it aims at reality. The thesis that I maintain is that language's power of refiguration is proportional to its power of distanciation in the moment of its self-constitution in the universe of the signifier. This is the general thesis, the front on which I have always fought: language, in my opinion, means (*veut dire*) the world because it has first left the world; in this way it initiates a movement of reconquest of the reality lost by the prior conquest of meaning in itself and for itself.

Against the backdrop of this general thesis, I maintain a second one: if it is indeed in this manner that scientific language operates more or less directly, literary and poetic language, on the other hand, operates in a more subtle, more indirect manner, inasmuch as the chasm between language and reality has reached much greater depths. Precisely by reason of the dimension of *muthos* proper to language. It is not by chance that Aristotle chose the term *muthos* to designate both the fact that what we are dealing with is a fable and the fact that this story is ordered; it is the idea of a fable that is ordered and the ordered as fable. This is the moment of configuration, or the moment of the exile of language. And the moment of the return to reality, this is the moment of refiguration, which I believe I dealt with better for having set in place a mediator between these two moments, the border-crosser: in other words, the reader. For, if the reader lives in the unreal world of the fable, she is at the same time a flesh-and-blood being who is changed by the act of reading. As Proust said at the end of *Time Regained*, thanks to the book which serves as a magnifying glass, the reader can read his or her own life.[15]

Recognizing in this way the role of the reader as border-crosser is something I owe to Hans-Robert Jauss[16] and to what has been termed the school of "reception," which is moreover – it can be said in passing – a derivative, more or less heretical, branch of the hermeneutics of Dilthey and of Gadamer. I am astonished looking back on it not to have been attentive earlier to this role of the reader as mediator between language and the world, given that all Biblical exegesis, but also all of classical philology, rests on a history of readings, let us call them "acts of reading," to borrow the title of Wolfgang Iser's book.[17]

After setting this operative factor into place, ensuring the transition from configuration to refiguration, I return to my initial problem: time. In what way is time, as the fundamental structure of human experience, refigured by means of the narrative? This is where I establish the great, final confrontation of the book between the narrative and the temporal, on the basis of the three grand theories of time: those of Saint Augustine, Husserl, and Heidegger. The central argument is that each of these emerges reinforced by its passage through the grid of narrative. Reinforced in what sense? In that my rereading of Augustine, Husserl, and Heidegger from the perspective of narration seemed to me to be not a rejection of their philosophies but a reinforcement of their respective positions in relation, precisely, to cosmic time, which itself is not a recounted time. It is, as Aristotle said, only an addendum to movement. Indeed, if there is no one to recount the history of the universe since the Big Bang, if there is no narration of great cosmological events, there is no time. In this way I make narration the distinctive criterion separating psychical time from cosmological time. It is by this feature that time is snatched from physics.

• *These three volumes of* Time and Narrative *form a text of almost one thousand pages. How did the writing of an ensemble like this take place?*

• I wrote the essential part of it in an American research center, the National Humanities Center in Chapel Hill, North Carolina, where I spent an entire year and another long semester, having a vast library at my disposal and the tranquility for writing.

Only the conclusion was written somewhere else; it was requested by my editor, François Wahl, to whom I want to pay tribute here, for he has always been a very demanding reader to whom I owe a great deal. This conclusion is in part a self-critique. I read over my work asking myself the question: Where is the limit of this enterprise located? In what way does time, finally, escape the narrative? I had begun with a sort of mutual resemblance between a structured time and a temporal narrative; I had at the end, then, to draw up the balance sheet and see in what way time folds back upon itself, escaping the grasp of narrative. If I had succeeded in my design to hold time captive in the nets of narrative, I would have fallen back on the idealist positions against which I never ceased to struggle: namely, that the subject would be the master of meaning, that it would hold within the narrative all the meanings that time is capable of assuming. But world time, cosmic time, is structured after the manner of the very production of the world and not after that of the production of the narrative. To make this confession was perhaps a sort of final homage to Heidegger.

I firmly hold that there will always be two readings of time: a cosmological reading and a psychological reading, a time of the world and a time of the soul. And that time escapes the claim of unification. This leads me directly to the Kantian theme of the inscrutability of time: time advances, flows, and the very fact that we speak about it only through metaphors shows that we have no domination over it, not simply practically or instrumentally, of course, but also conceptually.

• *You say: a final homage to Heidegger. But this could be a homage to Bergson ... You never speak of him. How is this silence to be interpreted?*

• Here you touch upon something for which I feel great remorse. But when I try to make amends for this silence in my head, for want of making amends in my writings, I say to myself that I could not have done justice to him as I believe I did do justice, perhaps to Heidegger, but in any event to Augustine and to Husserl. I am placed in an irremediably critical position with respect to him for two reasons. First, because of the idea that if time is structured, it is as a result of its contamination by space. Second, that if time is fragmented, it is from the effect of the necessities of action. I had already been distanced from this conception of an indistinct temporal flow, free of any structuring, by Bachelard's book on the instant.[18] There he pleads for a sort of muscular time, with beginnings, breaks, and completions; and he supports the idea that it is by no means a failing for time to be structured. I felt myself from the outset to be far removed from the problematic of duration. But nevertheless I still have a doubt and a regret, because my criteria are valid only against *The Immediate Givens of Consciousness* and not against *Matter and Memory*, to which I would now like to return in considering the problem of memory. *Matter and Memory* is really Bergson's great book; with that enigmatic beginning: "We are going to pretend for an instant that we know nothing of the theories of matter, nothing of the theories of the mind, nothing of discussions about the reality or ideality of the external world. Here I am, then, in the presence of images . . ." It is like an inaugural myth. It is at any rate what is most Berkeleyan in Bergson.

• *From* Time and Narrative *to* Oneself as Another, *it is, you say, the theme of narrative identity that forms the link. Where does it appear?*

• I conceptualized the notion only at the time of my rereading, when I wrote the conclusion of *Time and Narrative* for François Wahl; this is where the expression formally appears, representing to me the principal achievement of this work. It is most curious that the expression came to me only in a sort of reflection on the work already completed, whereas in reality it was already at the heart of the book, with the notion of the "emplotment of the character." But let us leave *Time and Narrative* there.

Allow me to take *Oneself as Another* a bit farther, starting with the theme of the "capable person" which I value highly today. The six chapters of the book that come before the section on ethics respond to the question of "I can": I can speak, I can act, I can recount about myself, and so on. This question gives rise to a series of figures of *who?* For the question of the capable person is, successively, the question of determining *who* can speak, *who* can act, *who* can recount, *who* can impute actions to himself or herself? The question of the narrative appears here again, but only as a third question, that which posits the relation to time; the relation both of the speaking subject and of the acting subject, but whose temporality is thematized by the narrative. It is here that I take full possession of the notion of "narrative identity" which had only been sketched out in the conclusion of *Time and Narrative*. I delve into the heart of the problem of personal identity, in an extremely rich field of investigation in the area of Anglo-Saxon literature. I ventured a distinction between two figures of identity, which appeared to me to be more than a linguistic distinction, but one that included a profound structural difference between what I call *idem* identity, sameness or *mêmeté*, and *ipse* identity, selfhood or ipseity. I then gave a concrete example: sameness is the permanence of a person's fingerprints, or genetic code; on the psychological level, it is what is displayed as character – the word "character," moreover, is interesting, being the term used in printing to designate an invariable form. While the paradigm for *ipse* identity is, for me, making a promise. I shall hold firm, even if I change; it is an identity that is willed, sustained, one that proclaims itself despite change. In this sense, the notion of narrative identity is made explicit philosophically only through the grid of this distinction, of which I had no idea when I glimpsed it for the first time.

I was very interested by the limit-experiences that are held to be those in which *ipse* identity is thrust back to confront its own interrogative form: *Who am I?*, without the response that could be provided by identity understood as sameness. For me the model of this situation is Musil's *The Man Without Qualities, ohne Eigenschaften*, which is better translated as: *without properties*. That is to say, without sameness.

• *On the level of critique, that is of philosophy, you hold strongly to the question* Who am I? *in the face of all reductive and objectifying philosophies. But on the level of conviction, or of spirituality, must one not renounce identity?*

• Perhaps there is indeed a level of meditation where one has to renounce the very concern expressed in the question: Who am I? If I remain within the framework of a reflexive philosophy, the force of this question implies the force to resist objectification, naturalism. I have to fight to the end, then, as a philosopher on behalf of identity, prepared to renounce it – in the strict sense of the word – at another level; we shall return to this no doubt when we talk about religion. This is probably, anyway, the background of the criticisms that Derek Parfit levels at identity, when he says that "Identity is not what matters";[19] this is almost no longer a statement of a philosopher.

• *Initially, the last three chapters of* Oneself as Another, *devoted to ethics, were not part of the book.*

• This book was, in fact, completely reworked after the Gifford Lectures, where it had been constructed in an entirely different manner. The area I have just mentioned covers the first chapters of the book, which ended with a discussion of what I called the "exalted cogito" in Descartes, and the "humiliated cogito" in Hume and Nietzsche, and by an appendix, required by the founder of the Gifford Lectures, under the title of "natural theology." In order to satisfy this rule – which had become quite strange – following my predecessors as best I could, I had written two chapters, one on the narrative of vocation in the prophets, in which I discussed problems of identity in the construction of prophetic identity, and the other on the appropriation of Biblical writings by an ecclesiastical subject. What is a subject that situates itself in line with the reception of the "Great Code," to borrow Northrop Frye's expression?[20] I did not retain these two studies in the definitive French version and have published them elsewhere,[21] in order to keep the promise I have made to myself not to mix the philosophical and the theological. In addition, I freed myself from the weight of the discussion opposing the "exalted cogito" in Descartes and the "humiliated cogito" in Hume and Nietzsche, ending in the self's attestation of the "wounded cogito." I noted in this regard that the cogito is like the father: sometimes there is too much, sometimes not enough. I did not know at that time that this judgment was soon to rebound on me. At any rate, I put this discussion in the introduction to the work, so that I could keep the way open for a discussion of the figures of the capable person (*Who* speaks? *Who* . . .), an investigation that was well suited to be placed under the aegis of the "wounded cogito."

But I cannot leave unmentioned the tragic circumstances in which the most important reworking of the original text of the Gifford Lectures, as they were delivered in February of 1986, took place.

A few weeks after our return from Edinburgh, our third son, Olivier, the child of the return from captivity, the child of peace, killed himself, the very day I was in Prague with our friends of the Patočka group. This catastrophe was to leave an open wound which the interminable work of mourning has not yet healed. Even today, I am in the grip of two alternating reproaches: one is not to have been able to say no at the right time to certain tendencies, the other not to have perceived, or heard the call for help uttered from the depths of distress. In this way, I shared the terrible lot of so many fathers and discovered this silent fraternity that is born out of equality in suffering. A few weeks after this disaster, in Chicago, where I had taken refuge, I accompanied my old friend Mircea Eliade to the threshold of death; and I found myself overwhelmed, in a certain sense, by the – apparent yet insistent – contrast between two destinies, only one of which will have left the trace of a work, and the other, nothing of the sort, at least not to human eyes. What I shall perhaps have to say later, here, about the memory of God – a confession of common faith or of personal myth – has something to do with this too human contrast, which stands out against the merciful equalization of death and suffering.

It was upon returning from my spring classes in Chicago that I harnessed myself to the task of extending the field covered by the Gifford Lectures and of drawing out the ethical implications of my considerations on the capable person and on personal identity. This was the subject of a seminar given in Rome in the setting of the University of Rome, La Sapienza, and thanks to the generous hospitality of Professor Franco Bianco.

This part of what, then, became *Oneself as Another*, and which I call, with modesty and irony – whether feigned or not, I don't know – my "little ethics," is structured in three chapters which some have reduced too summarily to a debate between a teleological, neo-Aristotelian ethics, involving the idea of a good life, and a deontological, more Kantian approach centered around duty and obligation. But I value almost more highly the third chapter which is devoted to practical wisdom, to taking new decisions in the face of difficult cases: the hard cases of law, medicine or everyday life.[22] I prize this advance, starting from an initial level, where one answers the Aristotelian question, What is signified by the pursuit of the good life?; moving toward a second level where one replies to the Kantian question, What is it to obey duty?; to reach a third level, where one asks, What is it to resolve an entirely novel ethico-practical problem? – this is the problem of practical wisdom, which I connect to the hermeneutics of "application" under the aegis of Aristotelian *phronesis*.

These three chapters have a twofold structure: vertical and horizontal. I have just spoken of the three-leveled, vertical structure. But each of these levels is constituted by three terms: the same, the other who possesses a face, and the other who is a third party, the subject of justice. My problem is to transport this triad from one level to the next. And to begin with, to constitute it on the first level, by saying that ethical life is the wish for personal accomplishment with and for others, through the virtue of friendship and, in relation to a third party, through the virtue of justice. This leads me to say that justice is already a structuring component on the lowest level. It seems to me important to stress this initial characterization of the just as a figure of the good; it is the good with and for another, for another who does not have a face but who is the *socius* that I encounter in institutions; it is the other of institutions and not the other of interpersonal relations. On the second level, I pursue the fate of this triad, reformulated in terms of self-respect, respect for the other and of all the normative forms of justice through procedural structures. The third level arises out of the encounter with tragic situations. This is where I confront all the perplexities: the self without the support of sameness is confronted with the question: How can one decipher one's own life in situations of uncertainty, of conflict or of risk? The strongest aspect, in my opinion, is that relating to what becomes of justice when the language of law has to be spoken in a singular situation. I am pursuing today an investigation into the just and justice that takes into account this twofold grid of the problematic of ownness, of the proximate and the distant, horizontal and vertical axes.

• *You have mentioned several times your intention to work now on the problem of memory. From what perspective are you thinking of approaching it?*

• Through the relation between memory and history. This pair seems to me to escape the framework, the short-circuit, of time/narrative which caused me to miss it.

As concerns history, I was interested only in the question of knowing up to what point explanatory history remains narrative, but there are lots of other aspects of the problematic of history. I would like to escape the exclusive nature of the question of narrative.

With regard to time, at the end of my conclusion I sketched out the idea that there are other ways of speaking of it besides the narrative, in particular the lyrical. Today I believe that the profound conflict between the time of the world and the time of the soul can only be stated poetically, in the most popular form of poetry – in which it is repeated that life is short and death is certain – as in the most finely wrought, let us say, from Baudelaire to Yves Bonnefoy. Having wagered everything on the narrative, finally, gave short shrift to other manners of speaking of time, singing it, deploring it, or praising it, as we see, in the example of the Psalms and of Ecclesiastes.

I should like to take these questions up once more in terms of the self-constitution of memory in passive syntheses, after the manner of Husserl, and in placing these reflections under the sign of the *Zusammenhang des Lebens*, the cohesion of a life. How does a life follow after itself? I stress the fact that this is indeed a life and not a consciousness. I am right now reflecting on the theme of life, which I had always fled; following the early Husserl, I am very suspicious of *Lebensphilosophie*, of the idea of a philosophy of life.

• *And yet you took it up in* The Voluntary and the Involuntary.

• Yes, but as a matter of fact under the heading of the absolute involuntary. At that time I had not wanted to be crushed by the problem of death; I wanted in this way to give its rightful place to the theme of birth.

The level of life, as human life, is also that of desire; and hence it is the first level of ethics. In *Oneself as Another*, I defend the idea that, before the morality of norms, there is an ethics of the wish to live well. So, I encounter the word "life" at the most basic level of ethics; now this is also the level on which memory is constituted, beneath discourses, before the stage of predication. With the narrative, one has already entered into predicative discourse. Between time and narrative, the primary fastening, which is memory, was missing.

Memory interests me also as collective memory, from the perspective of contemporary events: the commemorations of fiftieth anniversaries that we experienced in 1994 and 1995 take us back to the time that I would call the time of the friction of memory and of history; the last survivors of that epoch, including myself, are about to cede their place to the historians. If there is a final moment when history intersects with memory, it is the commemoration of fiftieth anniversaries. These anniversaries are the times of the final confrontation between the memory of the survivors and the work of the historians.

Philosophically, the problem that I, along with many others, am struggling with is that of collective memory; it was treated by Halbwachs[23] by preterition or by evidence too facilely gathered. *Who* remembers, when one speaks of collective memory? Is it an abuse of language? Or a metaphor? Or could the notion of collective memory be retrieved philosophically by employing Husserlian categories from the Fifth of his *Cartesian Meditations*, namely, the constitution of what he calls "higher-order personalities,"[24] like the nation, the state. Then, collective memory would be to these higher-order personalities what individual memory is to persons. For it seems to me that memory in the strict sense, in the primary sense, is incommunicable. How can it be collective if it is first of all *mine*? "Mineness" of memory; *my* memories cannot be *your* memories; there is no transfer from one memory to another. If one holds onto both threads at once, namely the possessive character of memory and the contribution of memory to personal continuity, then the question of the *Zusammenhang* of collective memory arises with the full force of its enigma. This is the problem I am wrestling with now.

# Chapter 4

# *Politics and Totalitarianism*

- *You have mentioned several times here what you call "the political labyrinth." Long before you yourself were involved in the episode at Nanterre, you had written a seminal article called "The Political Paradox." Since then, things have changed a great deal, even at the level of politics as such, with the implosion of the Communist block.*

- It is true that my subsequent reflections in political philosophy have stemmed from this initial text. Its context is not unimportant: I had written it just after the Soviet invasion of Budapest, and it appeared in an issue of *Esprit* called "The Flames of Budapest."[1] At the time of this terrible event, I was asking myself how it was possible that the Communists – and we had many of them among our friends, especially at that time – could so easily condone political violence.

    In a certain manner, the interpretation that I was sketching out was rather benevolent with respect to Marx, since it consisted in saying that there is no thought of the political as such in the written work of Marx, that in him politics is a blank page. In the Marxism of Marx, I perceived the gap which it seemed to me was responsible for the Machiavellian development of Leninist and then Stalinist politics: the failure to have recognized the specificity of the political dimension. By underscoring to excess the role of the economico-social dimension, Marx had behaved as though there were but a single source of evil: the oppression of the workers by money – money which had been reified by capitalism and had thereby lost its proper link with living labor. From this perspective, the sole evil to be eradicated was exploitation; and it became a matter of relative indifference to determine which political instruments were appropriate to the task. And it is no accident that Lenin, in *What is to be Done?* and in *The State and Revolution*, practices a sort of synchretism in his political philosophy, combining several heterogeneous doctrines: for this is not what is essential for him. This is why he can draw from the libertarian tradition of nineteenth-century communists as well as from the democratic tradition of the Commune or from different communes – Flemish, Hanseatic, Lombardian, and so on. It is noteworthy, however, that he never mentions British democracy, despite its very ancient parliamentary practice, and even when he recalls it in trying to pin down the example of Manchester . . . One could always say that if Marx had developed all the aspects of his work, he would have examined the political as one of the alleged "superstructures"; but the mere fact of placing it among the "superstructures" would only have served to stifle any autonomous political reflection.

In reaction to the events of Budapest, what I was concerned with, then, was the problem of the specificity of the political with respect to the economic and social.

Today, what preoccupies me is instead the problem of its relation to the juridical and to the plane of morality.

I have returned to the specificity of the political as a result of my interest in the juridical domain. And in particular as a result of a series of works to which I alluded earlier: those of Michael Walzer, with the question of the plurality of spheres of law; those of Thévenot–Boltanski, with the question of the means of justification; and those of Jean-Marc Ferry, with the idea of the orders of recognition. These works question the institutional unity of the political, and make it difficult to situate it in the great constellation of institutions. Is the political really one of the "spheres," to speak like Walzer, one of the "cities," even one of the "worlds," to speak like Thévenot–Boltanski, or has it an irreducible, all-inclusive character, defined by a feature no other institution possesses, namely sovereignty? With all the requirements it includes, but also all the difficulties and paradoxes. It is exactly this question of juridical pluralism that sent me back to the problem of the political paradox, which I was raising in the fifties.

Not that juridical pluralism leaves the political problem untouched; it is rather that it suffers a kind of equivocation in Walzer and in our compatriots, because the "civic city" is treated as one of the cities, as one sphere of belonging among others. It is true that, in a perspective that could be termed "distributionist," according to which society is represented as a grand operation of the allocation of shares – the distribution of market goods but also of nonmarket goods, such as security, health, education – power is one of the things that can be distributed; an election is a distribution of power. But, precisely, what is distributed in this last example is heterogeneous with respect to all the other goods to be distributed: for it is, ultimately, sovereignty, that is to say, what is supreme in the ultimate order of decision.

- *Why do you say that the element of authority is heterogeneous in relation to the other goods distributed?*

- I have always been struck – this is what I called the political paradox – by the two-sided nature of political power.

On the one hand, its rationality. This is the dimension amplified by Hegel, since he makes it the figure of the Spirit that thinks itself, the *objective* Spirit to the extent that it represents more than the interests that are present; Hegel recalls, in *The Philosophy of Right*, that the political is grafted on the economico-social order (which today we call "civil society"), which he designates by the name of "external state." The political is thus at a different level and has a different structure. This is why, among other reasons, he says that the political cannot be the result of a contract, because this would be to employ the categories of civil society, in which a contract is a relation of confrontation and of negotiation, whereas one does not negotiate belonging to the political; one belongs to it in a manner other than by choice. Hegel gave the political an organic character, despite the dangers inherent in organicism; but he preferred these dangers to those of the individualism of the contractualist tradition.

The rationality of the political is expressed essentially by the fact that a state is governed by a constitution. It is striking in this regard to note that the failure of the French Revolution is never to have succeeded in stabilizing violence in a constitution; the numerous abortive constitutions that it produced are at the same time the graveyard of the rational; and the Terror has something to do with this. This rationality has numerous implications: first of all, the fact of ensuring territorial unity, in other words the geographical unity of jurisdiction of the apparatus of laws; next, ensuring a time-span greater than that of the ephemeral existence of a human being or, as Hannah Arendt said, accomplishing the deferral of mortality; finally, of permitting, as Dilthey has admirably shown, intergenerational integration, that is to say, meshing a received tradition with projects engaging the future of the historical community considered as a whole. The rationality of the State is tied to this relay function, linking heritages and projects, projects that are always threatened by the absence of memory characteristic of purely instrumental rationality; for technique lacks a past, it erases its traces as it advances and has in view only the tool yet to come, performing better than the preceding one. The state is precisely what resists the domination of the technological that has no memory, in joining the heritage of generations with the projects of modernity fashioned by the markets, hence by production, consumption, and leisure.

But the state has another face, rationality has its other side: the residue of founding violence. This too belongs in part to a heritage, but to a singular heritage, the nature of which is increasingly puzzling to me. The political is almost without origin: I mean that there has always been politics before politics; before Caesar, there is another Caesar; before Alexander, there are potentates. . . As though, somehow, it was the tradition of authority, much more than the authority of tradition, that constituted the blind spot of sovereignty. No one knows where this comes from. Hannah Arendt liked to quote the Latin formula: *Potestas in populo, auctoritas in senatu* – "Power comes from the people, authority comes from the Senate." And, by the term "Senate" is to be understood not only the Ancients who met in session and who, regardless of the age in which they lived, are still the contemporaries of the rest of the people; it is, if you like, the antiquity of the Ancients.

To my mind, this implies something of a different nature, which is the trace left by the violence of the founders; for, basically, there is probably no state that was not born out of violence, whether by conquest, usurpation, forced marriage, or the wartime exploits of some great assembler of territories. One might believe that this is a heritage that will be gradually eliminated, reduced to a minimum by constitutional rationality; but the constitution itself restores this irrational in the form, precisely, of the capacity of decision of the prince. In Hegel, one might believe that this element is related to the fact that he has a monarchy in mind; but I think that he is speaking for all regimes, including our own. There is, finally, someone at the top who decides; whether it is a threat of war, a response to some extreme situation, or simply imposing a judicial decision by force. We discover here the residual violence that Max Weber had in mind when he said that the state is the recourse to legitimate force as a final resort. This is at any rate how one decides whether or not there is a state. Recall Kennedy at the time of the missile crisis; there had to be *someone* who absolutely had at his disposal the secret code to trigger nuclear power. There is in every state a power of decision, a capacity for willing, an arbitrariness, which is of an entirely different nature than the rational wish to live together of civil society. I have turned this problem over and over, because I believe that we cannot avoid it if we want to think the political philosophically, that is to say, as an advanced form of rationality but one which also includes an archaic form of irrationality. We are obliged to come to terms with this, and it imposes on the citizen a duty of vigilance – vigilance with respect to the outbreaks of violence that are inscribed in the very structure of the political.

• *Isn't this idea of the paradox of the political also found in Hannah Arendt?*

• It is true that I have also tried to present this paradox on the basis of Hannah Arendt's analyses, in order not to continue to revolve around the categories of rational/irrational, sense/nonsense. I had been struck by one of her ideas in particular, which I reformulate in saying that the political is presented as an orthogonal structure, with a horizontal plane and a vertical plane. On the one hand, then, there is the horizontal tie of wishing to live together: this is what she calls *power*, which occurs only to the extent that people want to coexist. This wishing to live together is silent, generally unnoticed, buried; one does not remark its existence until it falls apart, or when it is threatened – this is the experience of the country in danger, that of the great defeats (*dé-faites*), which are also periods in which the political tie comes undone (*dé-fait*). In addition, there is the vertical, hierarchical side, which was what Max Weber was thinking of when he introduced the political into the social, at the beginning of *Wirtschaft und Gesellschaft*,[2] through the vertical differentiation of the governing and the governed; it is to this vertical dimension, obviously, that he attached the legitimate, and ultimate, use of violence.

Perhaps the enigmatic character of the political comes from this imbalance in structure; we undoubtedly feel it to be desirable that all power should emanate from the wish to live together, that the vertical relation be entirely absorbed within the horizontal relation – this is in a sense the desire for self-management – but perhaps this would also be the end of politics, including the end of its benefits in the sphere of linking the generations together and of reconciling traditions and projects. It is possible, in the final analysis, that this corrective function of politics can be exerted only if a compromise is found and worked out between the hierarchical relation and the consensual relation. Following this line, the democratic project would then be defined as the set of measures that are taken so that the rational prevails over the irrational, but at the same time so that the horizontal tie of wishing to live together in general prevails over the irreducible, hierarchical relation of command and authority.

I have returned to this problem by another path, within moral reflection, starting with the notion of "authority." Authority is a very troubling thing, to the extent that it refers by contrast to autonomy. Basically, is not political contractualism a transposition to the political body of the autonomy of the individual in the moral sense? How is autonomy to be defined? By saying that freedom is the source of its own law and that the moral law is here that of freedom; in Kantian terms, what we have here is a "fact of reason," a synthetic *a priori* relation. But even with this notion of autonomy, already on the moral plane – and so prior to the political fact – we run up against something that resists complete absorption in the definition of freedom as giving itself its own law. This resistance is displayed first in the figure of exteriority: this is the dimension that Levinas has explored so well, the exteriority of the other who summons me to responsibility, who constitutes me as a responsible subject. Next, in the fact of superiority, which could be illustrated by the relation master/disciple, whether this be the Socratic tradition or the Jewish tradition of the master of justice – both traditions appearing to me to be united in Saint Augustine's admirable *De Magistro*. Finally, after exteriority and superiority, one runs up against the enigma of anteriority: before the moral law, there is always a moral law, just as before Caesar, there is always another Caesar; before the Mosaic law, there are Mesopotamian laws, and before these are yet others, and so on. Here we find a sort of always-already-present, which causes any effort to discover a dated beginning to fail as it encounters the perspective of the origin. It is as though there were a dialectic of the origin and the beginning: the beginning should be able to be dated in a chronology, but the origin always slips away, at the same time as it surges up in the present under the enigma of the always-already-there.

- *This is a dialectic which has other examples.*

- Yes, we can find a curious manifestation of this on what could be called, in the broadest sense, the "literary" plane, under the enigmatic form of the incessant rewriting of laws and myths. Let us take the case of myths of origin. Here too, prior to any given myth of origin, there is always another. Before the Biblical flood, before Noah, you will find the Mesopotamian flood. It is as though the receding origin engendered an interminable process of rewriting. In the order of myths, as in the moral and political order, we find a dehiscence of this sort in the relation between the ideally dated beginning and the receding origin, which one attempts to overtake through the processes of rewriting.

But we observe the same phenomenon in the sphere of what could be called institutional rewritings: all those who thought they could start from zero have been forced to conceive of an earlier paradigm and to draw their authority from it. The most striking example is that of the French Revolution: the revolutionaries produced a new calendar, with a year zero, a day zero; but all of this referred to the Roman model, which itself was patterned after an earlier model for the founding of Rome; if you recall Titus Livius.

It is genuinely troubling, in my opinion, that the political repeats on its own level the enigma of the cosmic and the ethical. One can perfectly serve as a model for the other, and I readily allow that one might say: it is because there is first the enigma of the political that the origin is also a beginning, and that this beginning bears the figure of commandment – and, anyway, isn't the typical beginning the commandment of the king or the master? This reasoning was, essentially, that of the Scandinavian school of Biblical exegesis, termed "royal ideology," for which all the ethical, political, and cosmic dimensions of ancient Israel were reconstructed around the figure of the king. But I think that this is just one of the possible ways in because, conversely, one could say that the figure of the creator and that of the master of justice arise directly outside of the sphere of political power. So I believe that one has to admit the heterogeneity of the cosmic, moral, and political problematics and their reciprocal contamination.

● *But, finally, if the political always finds something that it presupposes, does this not mean that the question is not entirely within the competence of the philosopher?*

● The philosopher's service in this matter is to show, on the one hand, that *politics*, as the intrigues of power, does not exhaust the *political* as a structure of human reality; and on the other hand, that the political does not exhaust the entire anthropological field, since we find on other levels as well – moral and religious – the problematic of anteriority, of superiority, and of exteriority that we might have believed to be specific to the political. A problematic, moreover, which should not be allowed to exercise too great a fascination – let us recall what Gadamer has said: there is superiority only when it is *recognized*. The interest of the theme of recognition is to reintroduce reciprocity into an essentially asymmetric relationship. But one would also have to add, in that case, that recognition remains a recognition of superiority; recognizing superiority is the act of a disciple who accepts being taught by a master. And I think that this relation of mastery is interesting to the very extent to which this is not the master/slave relation, but something else that is entirely specific.

● *Although in the political type of recognition, between the citizen and those in power, criticism must remain possible.*

● But, in recognition, I absolutely include this dimension. For recognition is never something extorted, nor even something conceded through fear, intimidation or seduction, that is to say, finally, by means of sophism. It is because it is critically admitted that it is full recognition.

Perhaps this is the problem of democracy: how to educate citizens in critical adherence when as citizens they are never in the position of engendering the political sphere starting from themselves? It is on this doctrinal point that I part ways with Claude Lefort, who, faced with this enigma of the origin of power, insists on the absence of any foundation proper to democracy; for him, democracy is the first regime that is founded on nothing, only on itself, that is, on a void.[3] Whence its extreme fragility. I try to say, for my part, that it is always founded on the anteriority of itself in relation to itself. Can this be called a foundation? If so, it would be in the sense in which one speaks of founding events. But these presumed founding events do not escape the enigma of the receding origin, or, to put it better, of the dialectic of the immemorial origin and the dated beginning.

However, it is true that with the word "democracy" the vocabulary becomes a problem; I remember well what Aron used to say – this upset us, but he was absolutely right – "Democracy = definition of good government. It is the adjective attached to it that counts. Popular democracy, liberal democracy. . ."

• *In the current malaise of democracies to which you allude, is a large roll played by the fact that citizens are in the situation of never being able to engender the political sphere starting from themselves?*

• I do believe that this is one of its aspects. This malaise has much less to do in the present phase with the residual violence of the vertical relation, violence against which citizens would have to be on their guard, than with a certain difficulty the political has in finding its marks, or if you prefer, the difficulty the contemporary state has in situating itself in relation to civil society.

This is first of all because the nation-state finds itself today sandwiched on the plane of sovereignty between higher levels of sovereignty – Europe, international pacts, the United Nations – and lower levels of sovereignty – regional powers, municipal powers, and so on. Above and below, the sovereignty of the state is hemmed in. It is true that federal states, like the United States or Germany, have in this regard a hierarchy that is much less rigorously codified than our own.

But the malaise exists in those nations as well, and it is essentially tied to the fact that the sovereignty of the state has become indecipherable from within itself as the spheres of membership that govern civil society have become more complex. It is here that we come across the authors I mentioned at the beginning of this discussion, those who minimize the political dimension, reducing it to just one of the spheres to which citizens belong. The fact that this reading stems from a phenomenology of the social bond and of relations of interaction, and that this phenomenology, as a description of appearances, is acceptable – this is certain; in effect, we do not function at every moment as citizens; we conduct ourselves from time to time simply as citizens – for example, when we go to vote – but much more often as producers or as consumers. This is what explains that we might have the impression that the political is just one activity among others. But, in my opinion, this is to lose sight of the fact that even when we are not involved in politics, the state continues to encompass all the spheres of belonging with respect to which we pay allegiance. With regard to the state we do not have an allegiance *comparable* to the one we have for a university or a football team; the tie of citizenship is always presupposed by all the others. It is at one and the same time encompassing and encompassed, and I think that this is the new form, more insidious, less violent than in the 1950s or 1960s, that the political paradox has taken: during the period of Stalinism – to sum it up – it appeared clearly in the dramatic form of a split between the rational and the irrational in the arbitrary exercise of power; today, the risk is rather in the disappearance, or in the indecipherable character of political membership. If the state is lost . . .

• *Could you say more about this encompassing-encompassed character of the tie of citizenship?*

• I mean that membership in the political body is not of the same nature as membership in one of the other spheres that define our roles, our rights, our obligations, our advantages and our responsibilities. The "city" in the political sense is not reducible to the sum of the "cities" to which we belong, to the sum of the "spheres" of allegiances that make up civil society.

• *But then why do you say "encompassed?"*

• Because the search for or the exercise of power is one competitive activity that occupies us among others. If we are going to a political meeting, we go to a place that is different from the one where, for instance, we do our shopping. It is this that might have given the impression that we function only episodically as political beings, in the same sense as we function sporadically as consumers or as producers, or as professionals with a specific competence.

The rules by which one belongs to the political body are of an entirely different nature, and they are codified differently depending on the country. For example, the relation between nationality and citizenship can be a function of a law of blood or a law of the soil. In Germany, even if you are a longstanding resident you will never become German; on the other hand, you are able to vote in certain elections. In France, a foreigner can never vote. So the rule of membership in the political body is absolutely specific, even in relation to secondary political decisions. The right of asylum, the right of minorities, the loss or acquisition of nationality, the manner in which one is regarded as a member of a given political body: all of this obeys rules which are those of the city as encompassing and not as one of the cities situated in a topography of spheres of belonging.

Another example is provided by the limits of the jurisdiction of a state – for the territory does not simply constitute a geography but also a space of validity of laws, beyond which other laws are valid. The space of jurisdiction of a state is what shows that membership in the political body is truly primary.

There is, then, a relative indeterminacy in what is of the order of the political and what is not; we have difficulty situating the state, it being at the same time the encompassing institution and one of the institutions functioning in an intermittent manner, through discontinuous operations such as elections, demonstrations, and so on. I think that this is a new aspect, and perhaps the most noticeable current aspect, of what in the past I called the political paradox.

● *Doesn't the difficulty come from the fact that, if everything is not political, everything is capable of becoming so? Smoking, until recently, was part of the private sphere; but today it is the object of regulation by the state.*

● But what sign indicates that it is political? The fact that the prohibition of smoking in certain places is linked to sanctions. You can be punished if you smoke where it is forbidden. It is the sole mark of its political character, along with the fact that this measure has come from the state as legislator.

● *It is precisely for this reason that a parliament is required, so that the rule cannot be established arbitrarily.*

● This is an aspect of the political we haven't yet mentioned at all, the separation of powers, the relation between powers and power. This is obviously of great significance; in France, we have followed a direction other than that of Montesquieu, which was adopted by the United

States of America; we opted for a different division, between the executive, legislative, and judicial, which is not actually a power in the full sense, but a sphere of competence, an authority.

In returning to the initial framework, one could say that the legislative is the place of rationality, continually in the process of constitution and revision, while the executive is the place of the ultimate use of force. I very much like Éric Weil's definition of the state: it is the organization, he used to say, of a historical community that allows it to make decisions.[4] There is first of all in this definition the idea of a historical community: it is not the state that creates the latter, but the state frames it. Next, there is the idea of an organization of powers with a view to making decisions: this is the dimension of the will of the state, with a hint of what I called "residual violence."

Residual rather than constitutive; because violence is not the whole of the political, but its dark side. It implies a constant threat of resurgence, but it is not, in my opinion, constitutive of the state.

• *Would you not say, then, that this is where the novelty of democracy lies, in the measures it takes against the residual violence of power?*

• This is, in fact, how I see the specificity of democratic systems, rather than, as Claude Lefort does, in their capacity for self-foundation or for founding themselves on a void. For him, this is doubtless a means of ascribing value to the originality and the novelty of democracy. But I think that, with respect to their foundation, democracies are heirs. They are heirs to regimes possessing hierarchical structures, in other words, to theologico-political systems. It remains true that the classical theologico-political regime is outmoded; the claim to found the political realm on a theology, or, to return to our framework, on the vertical axis of authority alone, itself dependent on a divine authority, this claim is at an end, and I mourn it. But it does not follow that everything belonging to the theologico-political domain has lost its meaning: if something still remains, it is in the direction of wishing to live together that one must look, rather toward the vertical structure. I mean very precisely in the direction of wishing to live together as the practice of fraternity. I am convinced that there are in this regard, in the notion of the "people of God" and in its composition of perfect ecclesial reciprocity, genuine resources for conceptualizing a political model.

In this regard, one would have to look at the history of Biblical Israel, which is absolutely singular. Reread Second Isaiah:[5] " 'Console my people, console them,' says your God. 'Speak to the heart of Jerusalem and call to her that her time of service is ended . . .' " On what power do these hopes rest? On Cyrus! Cyrus is named twice in the Second

Isaiah:[6] "I am he who says of Cyrus, my shepherd – he will fulfil my whole purpose, saying of Jerusalem, 'Let her be rebuilt,' and of the Temple, 'Let your foundation be laid.'" And also: "Thus says Yahweh to his anointed, to Cyrus . . ." Here we are dealing with an *external* theologico-political realm. It is because Cyrus conducted a policy that could be called multicultural that he authorized the exiles, the people of the *gola*, to return to Jerusalem; he acted for the benefit of a politics that was not their own, and it was in this way that the Hebrews were able to devote themselves to the rebuilding of the Temple. Certainly, there were moments of autonomy in the history of Israel, especially with Esdras and Nehemiah, and the development of a sort of theocracy, but without political power. Political power was in the hands of the Persians, the Hellenist empires, and then the Romans. You have here a singular example of a religious sphere which did not produce an authoritarian type of theologico-political system. The entire history of the death and resurrection of a people through the experience of exile, the questions surrounding the founding of patriarchal traditions, in other words, the great work of what is now termed the school of the Second Isaiah, consists in rethinking and in reconciling two entirely different traditions: those of Abraham and of Jacob – the tradition of the fathers – and that of Moses, that is to say, of the first exile out of Egypt. In a sense, fusing together Abraham and Moses. Indeed, this reconciliation of diverse traditions was possible only because it constituted a reconciliation with the past through the remembrance of the destruction. It seems to me to be possible to revisit this Biblical schema today, after the death of the theologico-political in the theocratic style – and this is, moreover, probably the fundamental Christic schema, that of death and resurrection. Here, we find the possibility of an absolutely original theologico-political domain, capable of subsisting after the disappearance of the authoritarian theologico-political sphere, that in which the ecclesiastical anointed the political, while the political fortified the ecclesiastical with the strength of its secular arm; the exchange of the secular arm and the holy chrism, this is *our* theologico-political framework, and this is what has died.

Historically, it is this type of theological foundation which was succeeded by our democracy. In this sense, one cannot follow Claude Lefort in saying that it is henceforth without foundation, unless the authoritarian type of theological foundation is the only one possible. Now I think that it did, in fact, consist in an ideologized form, and that it is simply the theological ideology that has died. But democracy, to the extent that it continues to be viewed as a paradox, still benefits from the reality of the transmission of power and from the tradition of authority. The democratic originality would then be found in the measures taken

to administer the political other than by relating authority to anointment by the religious.

We should not restrict ourselves too narrowly to the *Roman* framework of the theologico-political, Roman in the twofold sense of
imperial Rome and of Vatican Rome. I spoke of the history of Israel. But
one can also think of the example of seventeenth century Puritanism,
where there is an entirely different manner of uniting the religious and
the political than what we have known here, through the divine
justification of political authority. This is something that Tocqueville
had perfectly recognized and which, according to him, constitutes the
specificity of the American model.

- *You say that democracy has succeeded the authoritarian form of the
theologico-political, in relation to which it represents a break. But
today, we are accustomed to think of it in relation to the totalitarian.*

- This twofold reference has to be preserved, for it is true that the
democratic break has been made along two lines. On the one hand, you
are right, this has occurred in relation to totalitarianism, which is in
many respects unprecedented, and, on the other hand, in relation to the
authoritarian tradition which is not to be confused with totalitarianism
for the former has demonstrated its credentials: the attempt to found
public authority on divine authority, on the presumed authority of a
supreme legislator, master of the cosmos, is something that has to be
regarded in its true greatness. Democracy was first constituted as it
broke with the authoritarian tradition, and it later asserted itself in
opposition to totalitarianism, an opposition that has forced us to
redefine democracy itself.

- *How do you interpret the advent of totalitarianism in the twentieth
century, if it is true, as you have just said, that it is unprecedented?*

- There is in totalitarianism something that constitutes, at least in large
part, a great innovation: the project of producing a new man, the claim
to start from zero. In this regard, I am haunted by the same disturbing
question that Hannah Arendt struggled with her entire life: how was
this possible?

One has to manage to think together and to coordinate two opposing
approaches, which are a little like two ends of the same chain: on the
one hand, what I would call a way in by absolute evil; on the other, a
way in by historical explanation. I do not know if anyone has ever tried
to combine these two approaches.

Remember Malraux's statement, which Jorge Semprun chose as the epigraph to his admirable book *L'Écriture ou la vie*: "I am searching for the crucial region of the soul where absolute Evil confronts fraternity." Even if one does not want to move too quickly in the direction of an inverted theology by speaking immediately of absolute evil, how can one entirely avoid ascribing the principle of totalitarianism to it? For by what is it recognized? What is its natural inclination? It is first of all totalizing human relations by dissolving all other social ties; it is producing a mass-humanity, such that it no longer obeys any organizing principle other than the state, incarnated in the person of the Leader. It is, therefore, not by accident that totalitarianism resulted in extermination, that is to say, the infliction of mass death: through the destruction of interhuman bonds, humanity becomes a *massa perdita*, in which the moribund and the dead are almost indistinguishable. This is the case, first and foremost, of the Jews, but one must also think of the others who were exterminated, of all the others; don't forget that Buchenwald was initially opened to imprison the German Communists and all those who were considered deviants in relation to the norms of the Nazi state; and some, like Margarete Buber-Neumann, even experienced two deportations – the Soviet and the Nazi.[7] It was as though these people were exterminated twice.

Is this not where the essence of totalitarianism is to be found, in the *institutional* extermination made possible by the elimination of everything that organically formed the social fabric? *Mass deaths* are the sign or the index of the exterminating character proper to the totalitarian regime; they testify to the fact that death is not an accident but the step-by-step contamination of those who are already dead in the direction of the moribund. There is, at the very source of totalitarianism, a proliferating experience of death. If one does not go as far as this idea of *massa perdita*, the real difference between an authoritarian regime and a totalitarian regime is not apparent. Not in the Crusades, for example, nor even in the Inquisition do you have the idea of institutional death; in them, one observes acts of extermination, to be sure, but not mass death. This is what is emblematic of totalitarianism and signals its advent.

● *At the opposite end from this way in through absolute evil, there is, you said, historical explanation.*

● Historical analysis proceeds step by step; it seeks to fill in all the gaps, and the gaps between the gaps, by explaining gradually the entrance into totalitarianism. Saül Friedländer has shown this in the case of Hitler's Germany.[8] The history of Nazism is the history of an authoritarian regime that made itself accepted as such by the Germans, by masking as long as possible its totalitarian nature. In voting massively for the National Socialist party in the July 1932 elections, the Germans displayed their adherence to a strictly authoritarian regime; the totalitarianism properly speaking was instituted only after Hitler was named Chancellor, and bit by bit, Hitler was able to hide the totalitarian toward which he leaned behind an authoritarian screen. It was, moreover, in this way that the "final solution" was imposed: progressively, bit by bit; at first the project of deporting Jews to the East, then to Madagascar, and it was only as these projects were shown to be unfeasible or as they were judged insufficient that Hitler came to the implementation of generalized extermination.

• *So you agree with the functionalists, against the intentionalists who feel that Hitler had always had the plan of the mass destruction of the Jews, as early as* Mein Kampf.

• I tend to think that both are right . . . One could say in a sense that Hitler recognized, at the moment when the decision of the "final solution" was formally taken, what he had always wanted, but without ever having expressed it by a strictly political will; I would be tempted to say that he had wanted it *pathologically* – and this, in fact, as early as *Mein Kampf* – but not *politically*.

• *You say that one must not move too quickly toward an explanation in terms of absolute evil; but doesn't the historical explanation move too slowly?*

• This is really why the two ends of the analysis should be taken up together. To explain the irruption of evil, is this not to absolve it? The German discussion of the *Historikerstreit* is very interesting from this point of view.[9] For, by showing that there are causes for the rise of Nazism, the responsibility of the actors would tend to be diluted and even to disappear: this was bound to occur, so no one is guilty. If this risk is to be avoided, nothing must be explained and evil must be given its absolute character of an irruption. But this point of view is very difficult to link together with a historical analysis, or with a reflection on political philosophy, which, for example, tries to think together the two forms of totalitarianism – Soviet and Nazi – and attempts to bring to light what the two regimes had in common. But, on the other hand, when one comes to mass extermination, one is indeed faced with the dissimilar in the pure state, with evil as essential dissimilarity. It is impossible to compare forms of evil, to totalize them, precisely because evil is by nature dissimilar, diabolical, that is to say, dispersion, division. There is no system of evil; evil is in each instance uniquely unique.

How to hold together the structural unity of totalitarianisms as political projects and the radical dissimilarity of the figures in which evil is embodied? Perhaps one would indeed have to look in the direction of the notion of "embodiment". . . or rather of anti-embodiment, of inverted embodiment, where the horrible, the abominable take the place of the admirable, the venerable. . . Here, thought stammers in the face of what I have called on occasion the *tremendum horrendum.*

• *On one side, then, absolute evil as irruption; on the other, the gradual mutation of the authoritarian into the totalitarian, through strictly political operations.*

• Up to the point where a line is crossed. The gradualism of historical or political explanation reconstructs the progressive development that envelops the irruption of the horrible, which, on the contrary, is not gradual. But in reality, this is always the way evil progresses: it irrupts in progressing, so to speak. Kierkegaard and Kafka, who would have to be read together, never ceased to go over and over this mystery of crossing over the boundary. In *The Trial* and in *The Castle*, evil is in a sense rampant; the phases of its progression are innumerable, and suddenly it is there. Its unclassifiable character is concealed in the gradualism of its progression. And this is undoubtedly what happened in Germany.

• *In the case of Germany, did democracy not contribute in large measure, by its weaknesses, by the ineptitude of the political calculations on all sides, to the advent of Nazism?*

• There would undoubtedly be much to say about this. That a democracy was the bed of totalitarianism is an irony of history; a ruse, not of reason, but of unreason.

For it is true as well that the progression of mass-humanity occurred through a poorly structured, or weakly structured, democratic regime, as was that of the Weimar Republic. Paradoxically, in destroying the hierarchical structures characteristic of the authoritarian tradition of the Germany of Wilhelm II, the democracy of the 1920s eliminated all the factors of resistance to the totalitarian; it struck down what I shall call the "structuring structures" of society.

I remember very well meeting in 1933, at a congress of Christian Socialists that was held on the island of Fanø, one of the representatives of this authoritarian tradition, heir of one of the great Prussian squires, the theologian Bonhöffer. Hitler had just come to power. But Bonhöffer already knew that he would be against him all the way. He was the incarnation of the authoritarian, the sense of clear hierarchies; in his world, on one side were those who commanded and, on the other, those who obeyed. This had nothing to do with the massification of totalitarianism, or even with the rough sketch of mass-humanity specific to the structureless democracy of the Weimar Republic. And do you know how far Bonhöffer's resistance led him? To tyrannicide. Bonhöffer, indeed, was one of the artisans of the failed plot against Hitler and he finished with his head on the execution block.

But democracy contains this risk: by striking down the structuring structures, the intermediary bodies and all the corporations, it isolates the citizen in the face of the general will. This is the Rousseauian universe, with all of the new possibilities it implies. Karl Popper saw in all the enemies of the open society, from Plato to Rousseau, the involuntary artisans of totalitarianism.[10]

• *Does this mean that you construe totalitarianism as a pathology of democracy?*

• I would not want to go that far. I am speaking only of the twentieth-century democracies, and of the weak resistance that they have put up against totalitarianisms. The German democracy capitulated, perhaps under the influence of antimilitarist socialism – to which I adhered! – perhaps also due to the fact, as I was saying, that in destroying all the hierarchical structure, it left a sort of empty place that totalitarianism was going to fill. Pacifism disarmed the state, but the German state, through its poor functioning, was itself the state of a "disarming" society. In this respect, the comparison with the French Third Republic is not inappropriate: it too was "disarming" in the face of the irruption of totalitarianism.

Perhaps it is finally in terms of facilitation that the advent of totalitarianism should be conceived: what facilitated the gradual arrival of Hitler into power, the step-by-step advance toward the authoritarian, then the camouflaged leap from the authoritarian to the totalitarian, crossing over a boundary?

But I still run up against the same difficulty: how to preserve intact the dimension of the *tremendum horrendum*, keeping intact as well the gradualism of explanation?

• *When you speak of totalitarianism, you refer exclusively to Nazism. Would you say the same thing about Communism?*

● Probably. But with two reservations concerning the comparison. First of all, as I told you, I think that one cannot compare forms of evil. But also for a more personal reason: the community to which I belong, the Western and Christian community has little to do with the history of the Gulag; however, it is absolutely implicated in the history of the Shoah. A certain theological antisemitism, in the form of the accusation of deicide, is incontestably one of the elements of what I called the factor of facilitation of the advent of totalitarianism. This implication – however indirect one believes it may be – remains for Christians a form of guilt, which they have to genuinely and unreservedly repent, much more, finally, than (certain) "silences" of the churches.

These "silences" of ecclesiastical bodies are not the only incriminating ones. Where and when did we hear the voice of the university as a social body, as a dimension of civil society? The fact is that the German universities did nothing to protect their Jewish colleagues. They contributed in this way to ending the extraordinary effort at assimilation of the Jews who came from Lithuania, Poland, and Russia after having been expelled from their ghettos by pogroms. This effort was in the process of succeeding; the synthesis of Jewishness and of Germanness – this synthesis that Hermann Cohen had himself conceived,[11] before developing his own conception of Judaism – was destroyed just when it was reaching its maturity. This forms an integral part of the Occident, of the complicated history of love and hate, of assimilation and rejection, that from early times has run through the relations between Jews and non-Jews.

● *Does the category of "crime against humanity" seem to you to be a good juridical construction of what you call* tremendum horrendum?

● It is probably an indispensable – yet debatable – effort to give a juridical form to the discontinuity between war crimes and mass extermination. When countries are at war with one another, they function as authoritarian regimes in relation to one another, following the Schmittian categories of friend-enemy;[12] they commit acts that correspond to this type of relation, and these are acts of death; what are called "war crimes" correspond to an excess tied to this functioning of authoritarian regimes.

But war crimes are not acts of mass extermination. In the latter case, what is at issue is the very fact of being born this or that, the fact that extermination is the reverse side of birth; it is being born that is the crime. The son of a resister is not a resister; but the son of a Jewish woman is a Jew.

In what case, then, is the term "crime against humanity" appropriate? It is perfectly appropriate in the case of the Shoah, if not exclusively, at least in an exemplary manner. For this is where, in a very specific fashion, the designation of the victim was made on the basis of birth. But then what about other genocides? It is true that the term "genocide" is sometimes abused; there is a certain inflation in the use of this term. But it is also true that those who suffer it have the right to see it as a genocide, since they are designated as victims by reason of who they are and not for what they have done. It is through them, individually, that the crime passes. Here we find a manifestation of what I earlier called the dispersion of evil, its discontinuous, and properly diabolical, irruption. The enigma of the noncumulative character of the figures of evil in specific events is not without an effect on the notion of genocide, which perhaps participates in a nontotalizable dispersion.

As you can see, I am quite hesitant about this notion, which incontestably has great power in the framework of what could be termed militant thinking, but possesses less clarity for a conceptually organized philosophical reflection.

Moreover, there is in the category of crimes against humanity, in the fact that it was applied retroactively, a certain violation of the tradition of penal law; it is after the fact that the acts committed previously are defined in this way. Of course, one can say that they were *already* crimes against humanity; but then one finds oneself on the plane of ontology, although this too is not without a certain justification, since these acts had themselves ontologized the victim, by designating that victim by reason of his or her birth. What occurs is something like an ontological transfer from the nature of the victim to the definition of the act. Nevertheless, the juridical tradition resists this approach.

• *One can also look in the direction of a moral categorization and invoke, as Jankelevitch did, the imprescriptible.*

• Strictly speaking, the imprescriptible is not a moral, but a juridical, category in the sense of that which is not susceptible to prescription. Now, with the idea of prescription we touch on a blind spot of the law, inasmuch as we invoke a sort of erosion over time of the right to punish. I am leaving aside the other uses of the term, outside of the impunity acquired over time, in particular the prescription concerning property rights, what jurists term "acquisitive prescription" in order to distinguish it from criminal, penal prescription. Prescription in this sense is an unwarranted privilege, which benefits the criminal under the pretext that society cannot indefinitely pursue delinquents. Invoking the imprescriptible is in a sense returning to the idea of a law on which time would have no hold. But then the law would begin to resemble its opposite: vengeance, which is insatiable and never ending. In this way the idea of prescription has acquired a sort of honor, despite its intellectually scandalous character. The *Oresteia* and *Iphigenia* by Goethe testify to this paradox of the erosion of vengeance and, by extension, to the paradox of the conversion of a vindictive justice into a benevolent justice.

The debate over the imprescriptible must be set against this backdrop. The imprescriptible would amount to denying that time can provide certain types of criminals with impunity, represented by the prohibition of pursuit, judgment, and condemnation beyond a period of time set by law. What complicates matters is the sort of contamination that is produced in the mind of the public between the deliberate suspension of prescription (which has the value of a double negation, prescription being already the negation of the obligation to pursue in view of avenging the violated right) and the entirely positive assertion that certain purported natural rights have an immutable value, and are for this reason inalienable and, consequently, declared imprescriptible. We have all read this in Rousseau. It seems that slipping from one meaning to the other is facilitated by the gesture common to both types of imprescriptibility, that of setting the force of the law outside of time.

If you will permit, I shall add to this already complicated picture another source of confusion. In the mind of the public, there is scarcely any difference between the imprescriptible and the unpardonable. To the extent that the notion of prescription belongs to the juridical domain, to the same extent pardon belongs to what I call *the economy of the gift*, hence to the religious, let us say to grace in the broadest sense of the term. Now, if one can legislate concerning the imprescriptible, one cannot concerning the unpardonable. For pardon is what the victims alone can give. It is also what they alone can refuse. No one can decree in their place that a given monstrous crime should one day be pardoned by the close relatives of the victims or those who escaped the horror. No one controls the time of suffering and the time of mourning. Is there, then, nothing to do but be silent and wait for time to do its work of erosion? I do not believe so. To ask for pardon remains an open *option*, which lies on the very plane of politics, as recent historical gestures have indicated: I am thinking of Chancellor Willy Brandt, of King Juan Carlos with the Inquisition, and of other heads of state. In inscribing the request for pardon in the political sphere, as Hannah Arendt asks, the authors of these courageous gestures have perhaps contributed to opening a breach in the imprescriptible and in the unpardonable. A breach that would not be the result of the simple wearing away by time, not only of suffering, but of justice itself. A breach that would truly be the combined action of the *work* of remembrance, the *work* of mourning, and of the *request* for pardon.

# Chapter 5

# *Duty of Memory, Duty of Justice*

• *You returned to the question of the "political paradox," you were saying, by reflecting on the law. This interest in juridical matters is something rather recent in your intellectual journey. How do you justify it?*

• I have the feeling of filling in an incredible gap in my own philosophical culture: whether in the teaching that I received or in the teaching I have done over the decades, the absence of any reflection on the juridical domain appears to me, retrospectively, a tremendous shortcoming. In philosophy, we gave it a very minor place; and although we speak a lot about the "state of law" (*État de droit*), the common practice in France is to pass directly from the moral to the political.

Think, *a contrario*, of the place held by law in the natural law school[1] – Grotius, Pufendorf, Burlamaqui – but also in Leibniz, in Kant, and in Hegel, who wrote an entire work called *The Philosophy of Right*. In this great philosophical tradition, law has a permanent place with, undoubtedly, the strong conviction that it constitutes a conceptual, normative, and speculative domain irreducible to either the moral or the political.

Irreducible to the moral, because law represents exteriority, in relation to the interiority of obligation: law indeed implies conformity to an external rule and, what is more, it assumes the legitimacy of coercion; here are two criteria of law compared to morality as defined by Kant. Lying is not punished, but defamation is.

Irreducible to the political to the extent that the question of legitimacy is never entirely exhausted by that of power. Power is itself in quest of legitimacy, and so it is in a position of petitioner with respect to the juridical, as is expressed in the idea of constitutional law.

• *If you were to imagine a pedagogy for the philosophical teaching of law, how would you conceive of it?*

• I think one would have to proceed by concentric circles. I would show that the first encounter that we have with the law, as citizens, the first circle if you like, is penal law. For justice encounters its contrary first in the thirst for vengeance, which is a powerful passion: justice consists in *not* seeking vengeance. Between the crime and the punishment, to return to well-known categories, lies justice and, consequently, the introduction of a third party. In the first instance, this is the state, obviously, since there is no law if there is no state, but it also implies the existence of a *corpus* of written laws; then an institution like the courts made up, in its turn, of those who are recruited for their competence and reputation for independence – the judges. State, written laws, courts, judges: this is what constitutes the exteriority of the first circle of the juridical. In addition, between the crime and the punishment, the operation of justice interposes a just distance by means of deliberation; it is in the trial that the distancing between the aggressor and the victim takes place, victim and aggressor who are not defined juridically until they stand as opposing sides in the same trial. They then become the plaintiff and the defendant; this change of status results from the very fact of the mediation by the juridical authority.

Philosophically, it is very interesting to see that the form of discourse employed in this arena is argumentation. I have recently become interested in the relation between argumentation and interpretation: how does one find the law under which it is appropriate to place a new case? The problem arises in particular in what Ronald Dworkin terms "hard cases":[2] we find a current example in France in the scandal of the HIV-contaminated blood. To begin with, the law invoked, a law relating to the sale of defective products, was too weak; but now it is clear that we have moved toward too harsh a designation – that of poisoning; adjustments will have to be made, and there is some discussion, for instance, of involuntary poisoning.

The designation of the infraction, in juridical matters, involves an enormous work of interpretation. What is one to call this offense? Homicide by negligence? Involuntary homicide? One has to find the legal pigeonhole that corresponds to the list of features defining the offense; and often one has to invent the rule under which the case is to be placed.

On close examination, we see that there are, in fact, three interpretive moments. In the first place, what we call a *case* is, in reality, the interpretation of a story: someone tells what happened. And we know that there are always several ways to recount the same things. Secondly, in order to know under what law to place the case, we must see in the panoply of laws the one that possesses a sort of presumed affinity with the case; consequently, there is a work of interpretation of the law as a function of the case; but also a work of presentation of the case as a function of its suitability to the law. Thirdly, the adjustment of one to the other – the mutual adjustment of the process of interpretation of the law and the process of interpretation of the fact – in short, the matching of these two interpretations with one another.

The case of the trial is equally interesting philosophically from another point of view, because it allows us to address the current Habermasian problem of "open discussion": how closely does the juridical approximate the model of open discussion, without limits or obstacles? We see right away that there is an unbridgeable distance between this model and the reality of the trial. For in a court no one is ever in a situation of infinite and open discussion. I see at least three constraints: first, the fact that the defendant is not present of his or her own free will; next, the fact that the parties do not speak whenever they feel like it, but each speaks in turn; finally, the fact that the decision takes place in a limited time and that the judges have an obligation to conclude the proceedings.

We are dealing with a very specific operation of rationality, which is, in a word, that of rhetoric. Provided, however, that the word "rhetoric" is taken in its strong sense, as that which is most clearly distinguished from sophistry, and as involving the use of probable reasonings concerning matters of controversy. This is the stuff of a trial, with the assault of words and the competition of arguments. In a scale model, marked off by the rules of procedure, we have here a paradigmatic example of categories discussed in philosophy: deliberation and decision. It is truly astonishing that we fail to draw upon this resource in the teaching of philosophy.

Between moral rationality and the rationality of the state, so bound up with violence, this first juridical circle constitutes a region of intermediary rationality, in which the presupposition is precisely the break between discourse and violence, to recall Éric Weil's famous opposition at the beginning of *Logique de la philosophie*; the trial is, in this regard, the privileged place for an ordered and ritualized discussion.

The second circle of the juridical is much wider. The trial – and in particular, the criminal trial – constitutes in reality only a segment of the law; it could be called the judiciary aspect of law. But the juridical is much broader; too often, because of excessive dramatization, it is as though everything hinged on imposing the sentence. But civil law is already in itself irreducible to criminal law; the obligation to repair damages is not equivalent to the obligation to submit to a punishment; from criminal to civil, there is already a significant broadening.

The notion of "damage" should be placed within this second circle, which is that of *contracts*. For life in society is not based only on its conflicts but also on the giving of our word, on exchanges of words. And conflicts arise precisely when someone's word is broken, when one party believes that the other has not kept the commitment made. Here we find ourselves in the vast domain of the mutual obligations which bind us to one another.

- *In what way is this philosophically instructive?*

- In that we have here a sort of staging and dramatization of an important ethical core which, in my view, allows us to correct a purely conflictual vision of human relations: that of promising. The bonds of promising touch something fundamental, even if only on the level of language: language is itself entirely a fiduciary institution. When someone speaks to me, I believe that he means what he says – to paraphrase the Anglo-Saxon theorists of ordinary language. I *believe* that there is an adequate fit between language and meaning. This is the option of "charity," and it is the primary fiduciary core in the enormous mass of contracts that we make with one another. Here, then, we see in operation one of the most basic convictions and probably the one most irreducible to any change of mores: one must keep one's word. *Pacta sunt servanda*, agreements must be kept.

This fiduciary relation, step by step, includes contracts and obligations within a space of jurisdiction, but also extends to relations between states, with the problem of treaties on the international level. And, of course, it is not by chance that the right of individuals has stemmed from reflections of this sort, on the alternative that the contract offers to conflict. Here again, the dialectic of conflict and contract could constitute an area of extremely strong philosophical teaching.

Through this, we can enter the third circle of the juridical, still broader than the second, in which we would understand the fact that society as a whole is a system of distribution of roles, of tasks, and of burdens. Not in the sense in which distribution is opposed to production, but in the sense in which shares are distributed, whether this be in the form of market goods, remunerations, patrimonies, financial resources, or whether this be in the form of nonmarket goods, such as security, health, or education. But this also includes citizenship: a society distributes citizenship by establishing rules for opening its doors, laws about immigrants, procedures of nationalization. This includes, finally – and this is the most difficult thing – the distribution of positions of authority and of command.

- *Why is this the most difficult?*

- Because we touch here on the problem of the definition of justice and on the impossibility of a uniquely arithmetic conception of distributive justice. A purely arithmetic conception does not work everywhere, does not cover the entire social field because, if one can say with Rawls that the first principle of justice is equality before the law, it remains that most social and political problems consist in the necessity for unequal distributions. Take an institution like the university: everyone cannot be part of the administration, everyone cannot exercise power. It is not only, not necessarily, a matter of power in the political sense of sovereignty, but of the exercise of authority in an institution: authority cannot be divided up in an egalitarian fashion. As a consequence, the problem is always to know if there are distributions that are more just, or less unjust, than others. I would note, moreover, in passing that in Plato and in Aristotle the word *adikos* (unjust) always comes before the word *dikaïosunè* (justice): perhaps this is indeed the way we initially enter into the problem of justice, through the feeling of *in*justice, through the feeling that there are unjust apportionments. Indignation is then, faced with what we feel is unjust – the cry "It is unjust!" – the first expression of our sense of justice. But indignation has its limits; in particular, it fixes itself on a demand for arithmetic equality.

We have all had the dream of equal shares for all; but very few social problems can be resolved by the equality of shares, because there is no doubt that a generalized egalitarianism would be associated with a violent society, in which an extremely strong power would be required to keep everyone at every instant in a position of equality. An egalitarian society cannot be a free society. We find a dialectic here, which is at first glance surprising, between liberty and equality.

When we enlarge the circle of justice to the dimensions of a dynamic of distribution, we encompass the first core – which is that of conflict, with its penal resolution – within a broader reflection on exchanges, in order to arrive, finally, at an even wider vision of apportionments. Conflicts, exchanges, distributions; conflict representing the tightest core, the most visible one, and distribution – in the sense of apportioning shares – being the broadest, the most encompassing.

- *In your first circle, you mentioned the example of the contaminated blood and the specific problems it poses of adjusting the case to the rule and the rule to the case. But it also poses the no less difficult problem of responsibility. How far does this extend?*

• Here we touch on a hazy term, under which at least two different things are placed. First, the fact of being the direct cause of acts whose consequences could have been foreseen and which lead either to compensation for damages in civil law or to a penalty under criminal law. This schema assumes that one can follow in a more or less linear fashion the thread that goes from intention to consequences, passing through the act. Things become more complicated as soon as there are several action processes, several protagonists, as is generally the case. They are further complicated in the case of an institution, with the phenomenon of hierarchy that it presupposes: you are no longer dealing simply with intertwined chains of responsibility, but also with interlocking hierarchical relations.

In this way we reach another sense of the word "responsibility." We are led to it starting with the sense we just mentioned. From the idea of a genuine cause of an action, we pass to the fact of being able to be held accountable for one's actions, of being able to give an accounting. I have investigated the metaphors implied by imputation, *account, counting*. In Latin, *putare*, in German, *Rechnung*, in English, *accountability*, in French, *rendre des comptes*. To be responsible is to be able to give an accounting to one who asks you. I believe that seeking to locate responsibility in the capacity to *answer for* is moving in the wrong direction; more precisely, to be responsible is to answer not in response to a question but to the request to give an accounting.

The whole question is then to determine what becomes of the capacity to give an accounting in the case of a hierarchical structure. Is the minister responsible, in this sense, for the least act of the least of his subordinates? It might be said that the gravity of a position of authority consists in being able to bear the consequences of the acts of one's subordinates. With this question, we touch upon the second meaning of the idea of responsibility. There is in this regard an expectation on the part of the public, the expectation of prudence, not in the sense of precaution, but in the sense of vigilance. In order to give sufficient gravity to an administrative post, perhaps it is necessary to go that far, perhaps this is the price to be paid for being able to be at the head of a command structure: being able to be held accountable for the acts of one's subordinates. This relates, moreover, to what I was saying about the difficulties of distributive justice, for a society also distributes, along with positions of authority, positions of responsibility.

• *But then it becomes very difficult to define a penal responsibility, a criminal responsibility?*

• This is the problem discussed in the past by Jaspers concerning the question of German guilt.[3] Should there be a distinction between criminal responsibility – which always implies persons – and political responsibility, which involves a system of governors, even if they have not themselves been criminals in the sense of having directly committed acts contrary to the law? I think that we must remain faithful to this distinction and adhere to it firmly. Criminal responsibility is always individual; and if, for example, one day those who committed crimes in Bosnia are to be tried, these will have to be specific individuals. This responsibility differs from the political responsibility of a state, as the ensemble of institutions that made possible, and sometimes authorized, at any rate allowed, criminal actions to take place. This sort of state has a duty to make reparation. This is what the German state has understood with respect to those who escaped extermination: as much as it considers itself to be responsible in political, civil terms for the crimes of the Nazi state, in the name of the continuity of the nation, it nevertheless is not to be considered criminal, any more than are the citizens of present-day Germany, unless, specifically, they have committed crimes. The individualization of sentencing is a fundamental attribute. And anyway I believe I recall that the problem of determining whether, collectively, the Nazi Party could be declared criminal was argued forcefully at Nuremburg. Generally speaking, the idea of collective imputation was rejected; and it seems to me that the judges were obliged to proceed by enumeration, by defining the crime in each instance for each offender.

• *What do you think in this regard about the argument advanced by François Mitterrand to establish that the French state did not have to seek forgiveness for the crimes committed by the Vichy government?*

• I was very skeptical about the coherency of the argument on behalf of a break with respect to institutions. Less because of the regular election of Pétain than because of the fact of the continuity of the same historical community. The fact that there was an institutional break does not mean that there was not a continuity of the nation precisely as a historical community, incarnated in the vast network of the institutions of civil society that are framed by the state. This is why I had the feeling that there was an obligation for the state to take in hand the totality of our history. What Clemenceau said about the Revolution is true here as well: you have to take it as a whole. You have to take our history as a whole, and within it is the slice formed by Vichy. We would not only be more honest but we would be freer if we were to pass judgment on ourselves. No one would relate to their own personal history in the manner we have been asked to relate to our national history; no one would say, "I was not the same, I was someone else." Contrary to what is claimed, the continuity is beyond debate, in particular in the public sector: if you open the register of high officials in 1948, you will see that two-thirds of them were already in their positions in 1942 . . . Have you seen the plaque that was placed at the Vel' d'Hiv'? To name the Vichy government, the following circumlocution was found: "the de facto authority termed French state." We were told that the French State of Vichy has no relation to the republic that we form. But the republic is not an entity; it is only the form of the state.

• *If you reject the idea of a collective offense, then the accusation that has weighed on Germany becomes very questionable.*

• The problem anyway is not crystal clear, if only because of what we were saying earlier regarding responsibility: through a duty of vigilance and by virtue of the chain of command, a superior is responsible for the acts of subordinates. Perhaps the Husserlian notion of "moral person," of a collective subject, would have to be reintroduced here; that is to say, a "personality of a higher rank," stemming from intersubjective relations through a sort of objectification. It seems to me that, without going as far as a veritable nominalism hostile to any reification of collective entities, and with the help of Max Weber's analyses at the beginning of *Wirtschaft und Gesellschaft*, one can defend, as a well-founded analogy, the idea of a "moral person." In this case, because the moral person is a subject of law, could one not try to give a penal definition of the offense with which it could be charged? Can a moral person commit an offense? If so, one could speak of a collective offense, but not of a collective crime, crime requiring an ascription in each case to a particular individual.

This question borders on another one, which troubles me a great deal – we touched on it earlier: it is that of collective memory. I encountered it in connection with two different orders of motivation.

I have encountered it first, as I told you, because I am a member of that generation which is disappearing and which is the last to have witnessed the horrors committed between 1933 and 1945. Now these are not memories that are personal ones. It is really the collective memory that is the place of humiliation, of demands, of guilt, of celebrations, hence of veneration as well as loathing. Here, we need the concept of collective memory which the historian critically reworks; we need the concept of collective memory in order to have a point of application for the critical operation of history. In a reciprocal manner, collective memory can counterbalance the tendency of history to render official a *certain* state of memory, an ideological memory. For example, a large part of nineteenth-century history was the history of political power; history was then conceived of as being in the service of national grandeur, in the service of a certain collective memory which it supported without exercising its function of critical vigilance. Official history is, if you like, a collective memory that is officialized rather than criticized. It seems to me that this dialectic of history and collective memory is very interesting, each taking the lead in turn.

Memory exercises two functions: it ensures temporal continuity, by allowing us to move along the axis of time; it allows us to recognize ourselves and to say *I*, *my*. History in its turn contributes something other than the feeling of belonging to the same field of temporal consciousness, through its recourse to documents that have been preserved in a material form; this is what enables it to tell in other terms, to tell from the point of view of others.

• *But when the history has been written, when collective memory has submitted to the critical work you mention, then it still has to be reintegrated into the collective memory, be reappropriated by it.*

• This is perhaps the other meaning of the word *history*, no longer the history of things that have been done, but history in process, that of the actors – in other words, the history that has a future. It is very important to place history in the sense of historiography – which knows only the past slice of time – back within the history that is lived, that is being made, and that has a future. I am thinking of what Raymond Aron said in his 1938 thesis on the limits of historical objectivity,[4] when he proposed that the task of the historian was to "defatalize" the past; in other words, to place oneself in the situation of the protagonists, who, themselves, had a future; to place oneself back in the situation of uncertainty in which they found themselves when they were waiting for, fearing, hoping for, and in any case lacking knowledge of, what would come after.

It may well be that memory in this way outstrips the history of historians. For memory is always the memory of someone who has projects. Or in other terms, those of Koselleck,[5] it is in the relation between a horizon of expectation and a space of experience that both history *and* memory have to be placed. It remains that it is memory that has a future while history interprets a slice of the past, forgetting that it once had a future.

This is why, to the idea of defatalizing the past, I would add the idea of rescuing an unkept promise. For people of the past had hopes and projects, many of which were unfulfilled; a good number of our utopias would be empty if we could not fill them with promises of people of the past that were undelivered, thwarted, or destroyed. Basically, every period is surrounded by an aura of hopes that were not fulfilled; it is this aura that permits renewals in the future, and perhaps this is how utopia could be cured of its congenital illness – believing that one can start over from zero: utopia is instead a rebirth.

- *You mentioned two orders of motivation that led you to reflect on the problem of collective memory. What is the second one?*

- Recent events in Europe, after the fall of communism; we find people as they were seventy-five years ago; it is almost as though they had been taken out of the deep-freeze. They seem to display at times an excess, at times a lack of memory. I find this case troubling, and I wonder if it is really one and the same memory that is at once excessive and lacking. I think, for example, of those peoples who dream only of the epoch when they were in full glory: greater Serbia, greater Hungary . . . Their memory is afflicted with the memory of humiliations suffered in the loss of their great ambitions; in sum, it is a memory that obeys what Freud called the "repetition compulsion" and which he defines, quite aptly, as an instance of acting-out that occurs when the work of memory is lacking. There is a form of forgetting that results from this lack to which he opposes an active forgetting that implies, on the contrary, a work of construction. The latter form of forgetting is selective, and this is what enables us to construct an intelligible narrative. This is also what permits forgiveness, which is not the contrary of forgetting – as is too often believed – but presupposes it. For what forgetting does it presuppose? The forgetting of the debt and not of the facts. Quite the opposite, one must keep track of the facts in order to enter into a therapy of memory; what has to be cured is the destructive capacity of these memories.

Let us, however, be very prudent in the use of the category of forgiveness, which must not be transformed into an exigency or into a claim: "But what? You don't want to forgive me?" The first notion, here, is that of request, and every request for forgiveness must be able to admit of refusal, that is to say, the unforgivable. Without this, it is meaningless. But it is certain that, when forgiveness is given, it has immense curative value, not only for the guilty party, but also for the victims. For it permits the reconstruction of a memory, in the same manner as, in the analytical cure, the patient reconstructs an intelligible and acceptable memory. Forgiveness shatters the debt but forgetting does not.

The caricature of this, in our legislation, is amnesty, since it purports to erase the debt *and* the fact. Amnesty, it has been remarked, is an institutionalized form of amnesia. Today, for example, you do not have the right to say that a particular general stationed in Algeria was a criminal: you can be sued for defamation because amnesty was declared. It is true that here we are no longer in the religious realm of regeneration but in the political realm, and that, in this realm, amnesty contributes to the public tranquility that forms one of the responsibilities of the state. In this way, in certain cases, public tranquility can imply amnesty; the slate is wiped clean. But with all the dangers that forgetting presents, permanent forgetting, amnesia. Amnesty is a constitutional power which should be used as infrequently as possible.

# Chapter 6

# *Education and Secularism*

● *Your university experience on both sides of the Atlantic has given you the opportunity to see to what extent the separation between the religious and the political is drawn differently in different national traditions. What we call secularism (*laïcité*), in fact, covers quite diverse things.*

● It is very difficult to sort out within the question of secularism what is specifically French and what may have a claim to universality. Let us not forget that our conception of secularism is directly tied to the history of the relation between the Catholic Church and the state. The political order, in France, acquired its autonomy in opposition to what we have called the theologico-political order of authoritarian regimes, in which the Church assured the legitimacy of the state. In this manner, the public sphere became equivalent to the autonomy that Kant reserved for the moral dimension.

But it must immediately be added that France is, in this area, only partially specific; for one cannot help but relate the French situation to a wider European question, which we also have to admit is not always uppermost in the minds of the French. The starting point would have to be the resolution of the wars of religion in central Europe, with the Peace of Westphalia in 1648, for it was here that for the first time a federal state was defined – still weak, and still extremely loose – the Germanic Holy Roman Empire, but nonetheless accepting several religions within its space of sovereignty. For Europe, this was a fact of great importance, but as it happens this fact was not really integrated into French history, just as the foundation of the United States by the dissidents of established churches was not integrated into our historical consciousness; the consequence of this in the United States was to open up an entirely different space from our own, in which the political and the religious are in a nonconflictual relation. We must never lose sight of this, so as not to be tempted to consider our solutions to be the better ones – solutions which have to be placed back into a cosmopolitan setting in which others exist as well. We must always remember that our universalizing intention is in part a claim, and that it calls for the recognition of others in order to be confirmed in its aim.

Having said this, it seems to me that in the public discussion there is a misunderstanding concerning the differences between the two uses of the term *secularism*; the same word designating two very different practices – the secularism proper to the state, on the one hand, and that proper to civil society, on the other.

The first is defined in terms of abstention. It is one of the articles of the French Constitution: the state neither recognizes nor supports any religion. This is religious freedom in negative, the price being that the state itself has no religion. This goes even further; this means that the state does not "think" in these terms, that it is neither religious nor atheist. We are in the presence of an institutional agnosticism.

This secularism by abstention implies, logically, that there be a national administration of religious creeds, just as there is a minister of the Post Office and Telecommunications. The state has, in particular, an obligation for the maintenance of religous buildings, which, since the separation of church and state, are the property of the latter. This duty incumbent on the state shows that the separation of the two authorities does not take place in an atmosphere of mutual lack of awareness, but requires a strict delineation of their respective roles: a religious community must take the form of an association of worshipers, endowed with a public status, which obeys certain laws relating to security, public order, respect for others, and so on.

On the other side, there exists an active, dynamic, polemical secularism, tied to the spirit of public discussion. In a pluralistic society such as our own, opinions, convictions, professions of faith are freely expressed and published. Here, secularism seems to me to be defined by the quality of public discussion, that is to say, by the mutual recognition of the right of expression, but even more so, by the acceptibility of the arguments of others. I would willingly connect this to a notion developed recently by John Rawls: that of "reasonable disagreement." I think that a pluralistic society rests not only on "overlapping consensus," which is necessary for social cohesion, but on accepting the fact that there are unresolvable differences. There is an art of dealing with these, by recognizing the reasonableness of the parties present, giving dignity and respect to opposing viewpoints, and acknowledging the plausibility of arguments invoked on all sides. In this perspective, the most I can ask of others is not to subscribe to what I believe to be true but to present their best arguments. It is here that Habermas's communicational ethics is most fully applicable.

If I have not yet spoken of schools, it is because this question is always taken up too hastily, without the prior precaution of distinguishing the two forms of secularism: the negative form, that of absention, which is that of the state; the positive form, of confrontation, which is that of civil society. Now what makes the problem of the schools difficult is that they occupy a middle position, between the state, its expression as a public service – in this regard, the schools have to include the element of abstention which characterizes the state – and civil society, which charges the schools with one of its most important functions: education. Education is one of the primary social goods – to borrow once again one of John Rawls's categories – which has to be distributed. This task does not belong to the state as such: education is one of the things a society distributes in its function of dividing up roles, rights, obligations, advantages, and burdens: distributing education is the province of civil society. This is so true that alongside the secularism of the state it was necessary to inscribe the freedom of education. What, in fact, does the expression "freedom of education" signify? That it is one of the functions of civil society to provide education, but under certain conditions, also to be found in other areas, such as in law or medicine; in particular, that of satisfying the requirements for examinations. In other words, the very fact that the Constitution recognizes the freedom of education shows that this is not defined entirely by the public authorities.

As a result, within public education, it seems to me that there is an obligation for civil society – and here it is a problem of wisdom – to come to terms with the plurality of opinions characteristic of modern society. I distinguish two aspects of this necessary compromise. An aspect involving information, first. I find it absolutely incredible that in public education, under the pretext of the secularism of abstention characteristic of the state, there is no real presentation in any depth of the great figures of Judaism or of Christianity. We end up with the paradox that children are much better acquainted with the Greek, Roman or Egyptian pantheon than with the prophets of Israel or the parables of Jesus; they know everything about the loves of Zeus, the adventures of Ulysses, but they have never heard of the Epistle to the Romans or the Psalms. Now these texts are the foundation of our culture, much more so than Greek mythology. It is true that this presents us with a problem that is difficult to resolve. Who would teach these subjects? Historians? Religious people? Undoubtedly, it is a real problem; but the fact that it is never raised is not normal. Just as it is not normal, once again, that students do not have access to their own past, to their own cultural heritage, which contains, besides the Greek heritage, Jewish and Christian sources. In history, they hear about the wars of religion, but has anyone ever clearly shown them the issues around which these wars unfolded, the meaning, for example, of predestination in Luther, the eucharist for Catholics, what the debate over the ordination of priests implies?

Alongside the aspect of information, which the schools should ensure, there is the aspect of training in discussion. If the secularism of civil society is a secularism of confrontation between carefully weighed convictions, then we must prepare children to be good participants in discussions; they have to be initiated into the pluralistic problematic of contemporary societies, perhaps by listening to opposing arguments presented by competent people. Of course, one would have to determine the age at which this ought to begin and the proper dosage of this type of instruction. But it is, at any rate, certain that this problem cannot be avoided indefinitely. One example among others of this cultural deficiency: we now have children who go to the museum who are perfectly incapable of understanding what the entombment is, what the Virgin and Child represent, or even the Crucifixion. Now this religious thematics travels through all of Western painting, from Byzantine mosaics and Roman frescoes to Gauguin's yellow Christ and Dali's crucifixion. This is an incredible amputation of culture.

In other words, the unstable and difficult position of the schools has to be recognized as such and so justify the beginning of negotiation. Just as we have committees for consultation on ethics to discuss the borderline cases presented by biology, we should have an agency for the discussion of problems concerning religious education in the schools, an agency staffed by representatives of the state as well as those of civil society.

Moreover, it would be wrong to believe that the secularism of abstention suffices unto itself; there is a kind of circularity between the two forms of secularism, absention and confrontation, or more precisely, the former exists only by reason of the latter. For it is to the secularism of confrontation that is entrusted the task of producing at a given moment of history the desire to live together, that is to say, a certain convergence of convictions. The secular state never completely practices the secularism of abstention; it rests on what Rawls calls "overlapping consensus." According to him, democratic States function well only in historically determined conditions, when three components are present: a liberal conception of religion – that is to say, religions that accept the idea that the truth of which they are the repository does not exhaust the entire range of truth; that are not liberal by condescension, or by constraint, but by the conviction that there is truth to be found elsewhere; an Enlightenment tradition that admits that the religious order has an admissible, plausible significance, that it is not reducible to the Voltarean category of "infamy"; finally, a Romantic component with its original values of love of nature, of life, of creation, values that are by no means exhausted by ecologist movements, but that form a vitalist component, an element of enthusiasm alongside the element of religious conviction and the element of rationality coming from the Enlightenment.

• *Do you have the feeling that today we are going in the direction you would like to see, toward a redefinition of secularism and toward the reintroduction of the religious within the confines of the schools?*

• Not yet in any clear way. But we have nonetheless, almost silently, given up for the most part extreme positions. The ecclesiastical authorities, in any case the Catholic leaders, have abandoned the claim of being the only ones to teach what, according to them, is the truth of Christianity; for a long time, the fear that people other than priests would talk about religion was certainly one of the causes of the retreat that I mentioned. On this plane, I think that there have been profound changes in attitude. In addition, on the secular side, we also see an opening: the idea is dawning that there might be something to be done in teaching, even if no one is sure exactly what. It will certainly be necessary for the French to make some comparisons, in this and in other areas, and to ask themselves how these problems are being resolved elsewhere.

For, when we look around at the various solutions adopted in Western countries, what is striking is the great diversity, which contrasts with the equalizing of these same societies when it comes to work and production on the one hand and to leisure on the other. Perhaps this is a reaction to this broad leveling that we see a kind of retraction, not only on the plane of ethnic ideologies but also on the cultural plane of the defense of educational systems. It is astonishing to observe to what extent, in Europe, we are slow in establishing something like a circulation between the different systems of education. I think that it is through a detour of this sort that changes will emerge, when more teachers and students in France have personal experience of the Anglo-Saxon and German systems. There are all sorts of possible and imaginable solutions: catechism at school or not, taught by specialized teachers or not; the proportion of public and private instruction, depending on the country, varies widely. To the extent that the educational systems are the product of history, and of very different histories depending on the country, and to the extent that they were tied to the slow production of the modern state, with or against ecclesiastical authorities, with or without the support of heretics or dissidents in the churches, it is understandable that their diversity is great. This is a history of great complexity which we have heavily schematized in this country, thinking that this schematism was universal.

It is in this way that the Republic, in this case the Third, was constituted in and through its confrontation with the church. It is probably true that, historically, the war of 1914–18 was an important turning point. And then one must not forget the recognition of democracy by the Vatican, tardy though it was, after the condemnations uttered against it throughout the nineteenth century. All of this explains that the Catholic, or formerly Catholic, countries encounter particular difficulties that are not found in Protestant countries, even if one cannot jump to the conclusion that they are always better off. Certain countries have considerable institutional lags: for example, in Sweden, Lutheranism continues to be a state religion. It is here that we see to how great an extent the religious as well as the political are tied to a history. Each of these histories is already complex, but their intersections make them even more so. I think that in order to examine problems tied to secularism, one must have a greater historical sense and a less ideological one.

For example, one of the difficulties of the French problem – and perhaps of Latin countries in general – has to do with the fact that the Catholic Church has been, and remains, a form of monarchy and that it therefore constitutes a model of authoritarian politics. Moreover, it would be an illusion to believe that the political order has definitively broken with any reference to the theological: at the roots of the political, at its foundation, there is the enigma of the origin of authority. Where does it come from? It is something that has never been settled and that causes the shadow or the ghost of the theological to continue to haunt the political. Consequently, to produce the secularism that exists in France, it was necessary to combine together, in a constructive dialogue, a model that ceased to be monarchical in the political order and a model that continued to be so in the ecclesiastical order. The debate over public and private schools would become clearer if the historical points of reference were restored.

Moreover, the term *private* is itself a source of confusion. It has two meanings: *private* can mean not public; it is in this sense that a school may be said to be private. But *private* can also mean that which is on the level of individual convictions. I well understand that no church accepts being pushed back into the private in the sense of the interiority of the soul: every church thinks that it has a public side, in accordance with the other reception of the term, as nonindividual. And *private* itself has two senses: that which is not the province of the state, and that which is not the province of the community. All these words have a complex usage; and, as always, one of the tasks of philosophical reflection is to clarify concepts. Clarify your language first, the Anglo-Saxons are constantly telling us, distinguish the uses of the terms . . .

• *The problems of secularism and the schools has returned to the forefront in France with the matter of the Islamic veil. What is your position on this?*

• It first has to be said that the Muslim religion has become the second largest in France, after Catholicism, and that we have, in line with the duty of hospitality, a duty of comprehension. We have too great a tendency to view Muslims only from the perspective of the threat of fundamentalism, and we forget the opposing threat that weighs on them, namely disintegration – at least that is what my closest Muslim friends tell me: they do not view us as former colonialists, that is to say, in terms of a relation of submission and subjugation, but as a threat of disintegration. They judge our societies as taking the path of disaggregation and they refuse to become victims of this as well. The question of Islamism is this *as well*: a sort of protection, in some respects a panic, in the face of a threat of decomposition. I would go so far as to say that in our suburbs, the capacity for resistance characteristic of Muslim families, whose communities remain vibrant, thanks to religion, can be the opportunity for the disintegrated fringe of our own culture. It may well be that in the proximity of what we call moderate Islam, this massive presence may effectively represent a fortunate opportunity for our society, countering the elements of decomposition that are undermining it. What in them remains intact could be a promising element for us.

The difficulty of the problem you raise, and of all those that are related to it, has to do with the novelty of the situation in which we find ourselves. We are dealing with Islam as it irrupts within the French political arena, with a new religion that has not participated in our history, which was not one of the religious sources at the origin of the constitution of our nation, not during Antiquity, not during the Middle Ages, not even during the Renaissance. What is striking here is the novelty of the partner, and what is more, of a partner that has not produced what Christianity, willingly or forcibly, produced: the integration of a critical dimension within its own convictions. It is very characteristic of Judaism and of Christianity that they ultimately performed the difficult marriage of conviction and critique; but, by the same token, Islam cannot espouse our manner of distinguishing between the theological and the political, since it rests on the idea of their organic unity. Will it one day be able to make this critical distinction between the political and the religious? Is it obliged to pass through the same process of secularization as we did, a process despite which the Christian ecclesiastical communities try to survive? I would hesitate to take our own grid of secularism as the sole model and to apply it directly to Islam. A friend who studies Islam said to me that a follower of Islam in line with average orthodoxy – in other words, not an extremist – will always see the West as Christian, even if it is dechristianized, that is to say as a territory in which a *false* religion is practiced. For the essential basis of Islamic religious teaching consists in saying that there was, of course, some truth in Judaism and in Christianity, but that it was falsified by their writings and that it could therefore not be integrated into Islam without bringing these falsifications along with it. Our secularism can be perceived by Muslims only as a crazy idea stemming from a false religion; when an Iman hears it said that the laws of the Republic are higher than those of religion, he hears something that is quite simply inconceivable for him.

Let us not forget either, when we reflect about the future of the relations between communities, that from now on the market economy permeates Islam just as it has permeated our own society; as a result, Islam is also confronted with the universalism of the market economy, which is a product of modernity proper to Christianity. In the course of its process of decomposition, Christianity has produced the ideology of the market economy, which captures Islamic societies from behind, or from beneath – if only because of the oil. In this way, they are in the world economy and also in the international political community, through wars, through international law and, so, through the ideological minimum contained by the coexistence of states.

Nevertheless, we are confronting a problem that is very difficult to pose, because it is entirely new for us. To be sure, the West has had relations with Islam in the past; but when they were not hostile relations, they were located on a very high intellectual plane, between doctors, lawyers, theologians or philosophers; there was a Judeo-Islamic-Christian golden age, but that was in the Middle Ages.

Now that the Muslims are here with us, with the twofold status of resident aliens possessing rights and a resident permit, or, in the name of the law of the soil, as French citizens of the Muslim religion, must we follow our own criteria in admitting them to school, without making any concessions, or must there be negotiations on the basis of the idea, precisely, that the school is the place of a secularism intermediate between that of abstention and that of confrontation, the site of what

I would call a third secularism? I think that it is because we did not develop this concept of "third secularism" that we find ourselves defenseless, and that the only solutions we have come up with have been repressive ones. This seems most regrettable to me. And I confess I am shocked by the fact that, as concerns the veil, we have offered no other solution to young Muslim girls. With regard to Judaism and Christianity, it is thought that one can speak of discreet signs and ostentatious signs: a choice is offered. Where is the alternative to the veil? And anyway, what would be the ostentatious form of a Catholic sign? Someone coming to school carrying a cross on their back?

I cannot help but think that there is something ridiculous in the fact that at school a Christian girl can show her buttocks while a Muslim girl is forbidden to cover her head. Here too, let us begin by looking at what others have done. How have the English gone about this? They accept, recommending discreet veils. Take the question of school holidays. In France, these holidays usually correspond to the religious feasts of Christendom. But in the United States, classes are closed on Yom Kippur and on Rosh Hashana.

- *Because of the size of the Jewish community?*

- Yes, but also because the Americans are used to being flexible in coming to agreements. In France we have not yet learned to resolve these problems in a manner agreeable to all the parties.

Spontaneously, I would have been in favor of accepting the veil. If it had been accepted, perhaps the number of cases would have not multiplied as they did. The refusal will favor its proliferation at the doors of the schools. And we will end up with the paradox that we will deprive of an education precisely those girls for whom school would have been a means of social advancement and even of liberation with regard to the family. This is the twisted effect of the decision to outlaw the veil. Or these students will be sent to private instruction, but a kind which will not offer the same guarantees or the same structures as the private parochial schools, also the product of a long history of negotiation. For example, will we be able to give to the Muslim schools the equivalent of accreditation that the other private schools have? For, even in religious schools, there are very precise rules on religious pluralism. Will these be respected in Islamic schools?

Another point complicates the situation of the French state even further with respect to its Muslim residents: the grip of foreign countries on the fundamentalists among them. At the present time, the Western countries are in a conflictual relationship with the fundamentalism of Islam. Can one imagine in this context a French Islam that would not be in any way the spearhead of powers that are simultaneously religious and political? One must not forget, for example, that King Hassan II is also the Commander of the Faith, and that King Hussein of Jordan is a descendant of the prophet. Then, of course, when their emissaries are imams, and when these imams tell the young girls "Carry on – do not give in!" one does not know what to think. Only that there are extreme biases in this matter: on one side, we are dealing with a secular state that is somewhat rigid in its criteria, and on the other, with an Islamic thrust that is testing the capacities of resistance of that state, pushing it to make a mistake.

Since Napoleon, the Republic has managed to deal with diverse religions, not in their ecclesiastical structures of doctrines and authority but in the particular juridical forms that religious societies constitute; it is in this way, for example, that the consistory was created for Jews. We will have to be able to create for Islam in France the equivalent of what the Protestants and the Jews obtained from Napoleon.

● *The Catholics, nevertheless, strongly resisted this up until the beginning of the twentieth century. When Combe's law was enacted, the Republic had to use gendarmes to go get children on the farms. . .*[1]

● The very fact that you cite these events shows the regressive character of the situation we find ourselves in at this time. We have come a long way since the period you mention.

Once again, the difficulty lies in the unprecedented nature of the situation. All the great immigrations that France has known in the nineteenth and twentieth centuries came from Christian or Jewish Europe: the great masses of immigrants were made up of Poles, Italians or Spaniards, who posed no major problem. Muslim immigration comes as an intervention into a history which had followed its own course and which had attained a certain balance, a sort of conflictual consensus that is the very model of good consensus in pluralistic societies.

● *Ultimately, don't you think that in the secularism of our Western countries, there was the illusion of a total evacuation of the religious?*

● All the European peoples are, we have said, Latinized and Christianized barbarians. This means that religion had not only the function of educating individuals but also the function of institutionalization.

I am in complete agreement with Marcel Gauchet on this point in saying that the religious produced the institutional even outside of the ecclesiastical.[2] The history of the Middle Ages shows perfectly that most of the great institutions were generated after the ecclesiastical model, whether it be the university, municipal government, markets or intellectual societies. As a consequence, it is not possible to imagine an extreme situation in which the religious would have been totally eliminated from the self-understanding of cultures and from the modern nation-state. It is an integral part of their formation, of their *Bildung*. In this sense, one can say that secularism is a secularization, that it is tied to the process of secularization.

But it may also be, as I suggested earlier, that there is something in the political itself that prevents it from going to the end of its own project. There is in it a sort of backdrop or residue, which is not simply the result of its historical origin, that is to say of its derivation from the religious, but which is due to its constitution, its archeology in the twofold sense of the term: chronological and foundational.

This is why it is not incomprehensible that an intersection of the political and the religious could occur again, in certain specific historical circumstances, in particular in periods when the social bond is unraveling. This is the case of Serbia, but it could also be, in the near future, the case of Russia where we see the churches beginning to function again as agencies of legitimation, as the authorizers – in the literal sense of *giving authority* – with regard to the political. We are in the presence of a return to anointment of the political by the religious. Is this not, after all, what Stalin had in mind when he called upon the Orthodox Church to carry out what he called "the great patriotic war?" This is obviously terrifying because in religions one also learns to die; here, fundamental motivations are extorted for reappropriation by the political, whereas the history of the political has consisted in eliminating these motivations to win its own autonomy.

It is true that, in the present case, this drift is also explained by the inabilty of the political to find a stable solution to another problem: the relation between the frontiers of the state and the division into separate ethnic groups. It is in this context that the religious enters as a third party, in order to give weight to ethnic differences in redrawing the contours of the political.

• *The situation in the former Yugoslavia and in Russia is not unique; in the Middle East, between Israel and the neighboring Arab countries, we find the situation as well, where the political is overlaid with the religious and the ethnic.*

• This case is infinitely more complicated to the extent that *Israeli* now refers first to a type of citizenship. But to what extent is this citizenship defined in reference to a Biblical religious heritage, on the one hand,

and, on the other, to the history of the Jews of Europe, victims of persecutions in Christian countries? This is what is difficult to say. In addition, one must not simply identify the Palestinians with Islam: a good proportion of them are Christians. Likewise, one must not identify *Israeli* and *religious Jew*, the latter being Orthodox or Liberal: let us not forget that Israel finds itself today, all things being equal, in the situation of France at the beginning of the twentieth century, with a war between the religious and the secular.

The religious or the political, which is the more important in the Middle East? There is no doubt that there has been a religious basis to the war that has afflicted them, in the sense that the relation to the land is considered sacred on both sides. For the Jews the land of Israel is not just any place; and our spirit bristles at the idea that they could have been sent to Madagascar or somewhere else; in a certain manner, there is a historical relation, if not of belonging at least of mutual correspondence between this people and that land. But it is also true that the Jewish people are defined not by their land but by a founding word. Just as it is also true that the al-Aska mosque of Jerusalem is considered by the entire Muslim world as one of the holy places of Islam.

Sometimes, in moments of despair, I think that here is really a sort of theological, or antitheological, irony in the idea of a Land that is twice promised, twice given . . .

# Chapter 7

# *Biblical Readings and Meditations*

● *You are one of those rare philosophers who engages in a philosophical work and in a work of reflection of a religious nature. How do you reconcile the two undertakings?*

● It seems to me that however far back I go in the past, I have always walked on two legs. It is not only for methodological reasons that I do not mix genres, it is because I insist on affirming a twofold reference, which is absolutely primary for me.

In the course of my reflections, I have given this a number of formulations, perhaps the most precise of these, the one I prefer today, is expressed by the relation between conviction and critique – to which I ascribe, moreover, a very strong political sense, from the perspective of democratic life: we form a culture which has always had strong convictions, intertwined with certain moments of critique.

But this is only one manner of expressing the polarity of conviction and critique, for philosophy is not simply critical, it too belonging to the order of conviction. And religious conviction itself possesses an internal, critical dimension.

● *Does religious conviction appear to you to belong to the order of experience?*

● I have vigorously resisted the word "experience" throughout my career, out of a distrust of immediacy, effusiveness, intuitionism: I always favored, on the contrary, the mediation of language and scripture; this is even where my two affiliations confront one another.

I would say almost bluntly that it is not on the basis of the same texts that I do philosophy and that I feel my membership in a community, in a Christian tradition. It would almost be from one textuality to another that I would establish the balance. As concerns philosophical textuality, if we differ over the long list, we all have the same short list: Plato, Aristotle, Kant, probably Hegel; and among the moderns, one might hesitate between Nietzsche, Bergson, Husserl, Heidegger, Nabert, Jaspers, and so on. The list of fundamental texts in philosophy is not the list of texts forming the religious corpus. I place great importance on the mediation of writings, which are different from one sphere to the other, even if the activity of reading draws them closer. As for the Biblical writings, by these I mean the Hebraic Bible, the New Testament of the early Church and what is most directly theological and exegetical in the Fathers. Augustine has always enjoyed, in my eyes, a sort of preference. This does not prevent the exchange between these two bodies of texts – even in the topological sense – nor does it exclude placing Augustine on the side of philosophy, which is what I did when I made use of his analyses on time in Book XI of the *Confessions*. Conversely, Homer, Hesiod, and the tragic poets have always seemed to me to be situated in an intermediary zone between the prophets of Israel, on the one hand, and the pre-Socratic philosophers and Socrates, on the other.

It is indispensable, when one enters into this universe of Biblical interpretation, to distinguish clearly between the different types of reading and of approach, otherwise one has the impression of a perpetual dialogue of the deaf. Each type of reading, and hence of interpretation, serves different objectives and begins from presuppositions which are not only separate but often even opposite. A historical reading must not be encumbered with dogmatic prejudices any more than the official reading of the church should be content to remain blissfully ignorant of what is brought to light by archeological work, such as the deciphering of the Dead Sea Scrolls. The philosophical reading of Biblical texts must not, in its turn, ignore the confessional side or the historical and philological investigations.

Between the Greek texts and the Biblical sources, the difference should nevertheless be modulated. This I have discovered recently, on the occasion of the exegetical revolution of the last few years in the domain of Old Testament studies. For over a century, these rested on the hypothesis of four sources – Yahvist, Elohist, Deuteronomic, Sacerdotal – thought to have extended over seven or eight centuries of writing. Now this theory which was long the feather in the cap of the historical-critical method and of theologians and exegetes, had allowed the construction of a coherent vision of the theology of the Old Testament, based on the accumulation of a series of proclamations, of kerygma, unified in the final kerygma of Judaism. In light of this presumed coherence, a global opposition between Judaism and Hellenism appeared justified. Today this edifice is being demolished. The crisis of the Babylonian exile becomes the primary reference point for reassembling the multiple traditions preceding the exile. It seems today that their writings and rewritings occurred in a much shorter time and their unification seems to have been more or less imposed by the Persian authorities on the return of the captives. For the slowly progressive, convergent, and unified vision of the Jewish writings would be substituted a more contrasted, even more polemical, vision of the Hebraic Bible, inviting a reading that would itself be plural. The most interesting reading would seem to move backwards; one would start with Deuteronomy (whose peculiar character Spinoza was one of the first to underscore) as well as with the histories of Judah and of Israel between the monarchy of David and the Exile – guilt-ridden histories, marked with the Deuteronomic seal – then one would move from these to the Mosaic block concerning the bestowal of the Law and then, even further back, toward the legends of the patriarchs, placed under the sign of benediction and promise rather than of commandment and accusation. The reading would conclude with the sacerdotal vision of a good creation, spoiled by man, such as we read it in the first chapter of Genesis.

This is, of course, a hypothesis regarding the composition of the different books.

• *Why is this "shift" imposed on the reading of great significance to you?*

• It is so for several reasons. First, because this indicates that one is dealing with concurrent theologies, broadly tied to the problem posed by the catastrophe of exile and by the problem of reconstruction upon the return from Babylon. To enter into this Jewish polemic is to initiate an intelligent reading, spurred by alternative complicities, for example, between the Deuteronomic heritage and the sacerdotal heritage, or between the theology of the Law under the sign of Moses and the theology of benediction and of the promise under the sign of Abraham. Next, because it is the mark of the tensions and polemics in which Israel is confronted by its other: a more or less external other (baalism), a frankly external other (Persian culture) and an entirely other (Hellenistic culture).

This final point of friction is, for us philosophers, of the greatest importance. Indeed, the writings that are at issue are those that the scribes of Judaism classified in a different category than that of the Torah and the prophets – *nebiim*: Proverbs, Psalms, Ecclesiastes, Job. I am interested by the idea that these writings should be read in competition with the founding writings of Hellenistic culture, Homer, Hesiod, the tragic poets, the pre-Socratics. To the very extent to which orthodox Yahvism stems from a polemic within Judaism confronted with the challenge of exile, to the same extent these writings are to be placed in a relation with respect to the Greek texts we have just cited. Certain exegetes would even like to go farther back and make a parallel between the Deuteronomist "historians" and Herodotus. It seems that I am moving away here from the vision of two separate worlds, Jerusalem facing Athens!

- *Would you say, then, that we are dealing with two different, but perhaps compatible, manners of thinking?*

- Yes, undoubtedly, as long as it is a question of comprehensive reading, or as some say, of *descriptive* theology. I insist on the fact that one has the right to speak of a Biblical *thought*, at the origin of the immense theological labor that unfolds through the writings of ancient Israel, and that this is so despite the lack of a speculative language, as Biblical thought had available to it only the narrative, legislative, prophetic, hymnic, and sapiential genres. Nevertheless, a varied "saying God" opens through its polemical turn to internal and external critique.

But I would not want to stop here, for philosophical thought, as it was articulated in Greece, is not directly opposed to the comprehensive reading I have just mentioned but only to the kerygmatic readings that were given of it by the *confessional* theology, at work within the Biblical writings and especially through the great historical traditions of the Synagogue and the Church. The recognition of a word that would be that of another is not self-evident, once the historical-critical method has led the comprehensive reading to admit that it is multiple. The history of Jewish and Christian communities clearly shows that it has not always been the same center of organization, and the same guideline, that have been taken as normative. In this way, the Christian Church of the early times read the Jewish writings in a different way than the Rabbinical school, which shaped Judaism properly speaking, at the expense of other rival schools. In particular, those that were tied to the apocalyptic movement which the multiple theologies of the primitive Church continued to a great extent to embrace. Discerning a word of God for today requires an applied hermeneutics centered on predication in the broadest sense of the term. In this regard, Karl Barth[1] continues to convince me that what theologians call "dogmatic" consists in a conceptual and discursive ordering of predication, which relates a word held to be founding with a circumstantial judgment on the present and the future of the communities of faith.

Must one then resign oneself to a gaping abyss between a descriptive reading and the listening of faith? I do not think so. I have not yet said anything about the in-between represented by canonical reading, that is to say, reading applied to the sort of intelligibility produced by the final version, the final composition of the text as it has been transmitted, once codified and sanctioned by the authorities of the communities at the origin of the histories peculiar to the Synagogue and to the Church. The canonical reading is there to warn us that the historical-critical method is itself only one type of reading, placing Biblical texts alongside the texts of all other religions and all other cultures. The canonical reading has its own rules by which it takes into account the message that the final writers of the ultimate compositions of the Bible wanted to transmit. After all, it is this final text that, historically, has been efficacious. This is, in part, the case of the ensemble that is called the Pentateuch, which became the Hexateuch, if we add Joshua to the first five books of the Hebraic Bible. And if the correspondences, analogies, and cumulative reinterpretations predominate there, the canonical understanding must not be reduced to these modalities of interpretation alone.

I would like to cite here, still in the context of the canonical reading, the considerable work of Father Beauchamp,[2] who, without neglecting the historical-critical method, adopts the structure of three "writings" proposed by the rabbis, while incorporating this reading into the Christian hermeneutics of the Fathers and the medieval scholars, for whom the "other" Testament was the reinterpretation of the first. He justifies his approach by the fact that, in a canonical reading limited to the Old Testament, the interpretations, reinterpretations, and cumulative reformulations of the same promises and the same alliances abound, thus making the Christian hermeneutics the actual extension of a hermeneutics already at work in the Hebraic canon.

To my mind, it is at the level of this canonical exegesis that the theological and the philosophical begin to split apart. The closure of the canon becomes the major phenomenon that separates from the other texts those that stand as *authoritative* for communities, which, in turn, understand themselves in light of these founding texts, distinguished from all other texts, as well as from the most faithful commentaries. The nonphilosophical moment is here, in this recognition of the authority of canonical texts worthy of guiding the kerygmatic interpretations of the theologies of this profession of faith. I agree with those exegete theologians who say that these texts are said to be inspired because they stand as authoritative, and not the reverse. Anyway, the idea of "inspiration" is itself a psychologizing interpretation of canonical authority; in any event, the term is apt only perhaps for prophetic texts, where indeed a human voice declares that it speaks in the name of another voice, that of Yahveh. It is only to the extent that the title of prophet was extended to narrators, legislators, sages, and scribes that the Bible was held to have been inspired, with all the aporias related to this idea of a word divided. To be sure, the idea of authority has its own difficulties, but these are precisely those that have to be confronted in a discussion that places the Biblical world face to face with the Hellenic world. And it is in the framework of a canonical reading that kerygmatic theologies will differentiate themselves, and that they will then stand in opposition to the free reading of philosophical texts. Following this, two attitudes of reading are distinguished and stand confronting one another.

But one must still go a bit farther in this confrontation. It is with the kerygmatic readings – or if you wish, with the theologies of professions of faith – that the opposition between Jerusalem and Athens is the sharpest. Now it must be understood that the kerygmatic interpretations are also multiple, always partial (in both senses of the word), varying according to the expectations of the public, itself shaped by a cultural environment bearing the imprint of the epoch. Within Judaism, as I mentioned earlier to you, it does seem that it was a dominant rabbinical school that imposed its vision of history and its conception of the Law, without managing to erase entirely from its reading the Deuteronomic side, or the sacerdotal side. As for the Christian Church, there is hardly any need to stress the differences in the theologies implied in the four Evangelists, which the early Church had the wisdom to leave side by side, or the differences in the theologies of Paul and of John. Later, we shall see Luther making the Letter to the Romans the canon within the canon, at the expense of other possible interpretations. And who cannot recall even now the efforts by Martin Luther King to make the passage out of Egypt and the Exodus the supreme paradigm? The work within the reinterpretations, by turn divergent and cumulative, continues over the centuries and up to our own time.

I would like, finally, to bring the difference in texts down to a difference in the attitude of reading: the critical attitude will be more on the philosophical side, the religious moment as such not being a critical moment; it is the moment of adhering to a word reputed to have come from farther and from higher than myself, and this occurs in a kerygmatic reading within a profession of faith. At this level, one finds, then, the idea of a dependence or a submission to an earlier word, whereas in the philosophical domain, even in a Platonic perspective, even if the world of ideas precedes us, it is nevertheless by a critical act that we appropriate the reminiscence that takes on the sense of a preexistence. What seems to me to be constitutive of the religious is, therefore, the fact of crediting a word, in accordance with a certain code and within the limits of a certain canon. I would willingly propose, in order to develop this point, the idea of a series of hermeneutical "circles": I know this word because it is written, this writing because it is received and read; and this reading is accepted by a community, which, as a result, accepts to be deciphered by its founding texts; and it is this community that reads them. So, in a certain manner, to be a religious subject is to agree to enter or to have already entered into this vast circuit involving a founding word, mediating texts, and traditions of interpretation; I say traditions, because I have always been convinced that there was a multitude of interpretations within the Judeo-Christian domain, and so a certain pluralism, a certain competition between traditions of reception and of interpretation.

As for entering into this circle, I have on occasion said that it is chance transformed into destiny by a continuous choice. Chance, because one could always say to me that if I had been born somewhere else, things obviously would not have followed the same course. But this argument has never made much of an impression on me because imagining myself being born somewhere else is imagining myself not being me. If pushed, I would agree to say that a religion is like a language into which one is either born or has been transferred by exile or hospitality; in any event, one feels at home there, which implies a recognition that there are other languages spoken by other people.

• *Do you think that there are particular circumstances in which it would be possible to perceive something of what lies beyond the language within which you say you live?*

• Lately, in reflecting on the experience of death, and on what has been said to me by doctors who specialize in these end-of-life experiences in patients suffering from AIDS or cancer, I have had the impression that one can observe, at that moment, that the appeal to resources of courage and trust comes from farther than this or that language; it is here that today I would reintroduce the idea of experience. No one is moribund when he is going to die, he is living, and there is perhaps a moment – I hope so for myself – when, confronting death, the veils of this language, its limitations and codifications, are erased in order to let something *fundamental* express itself, which perhaps then, effectively, belongs to the order of experience. Life in the face of death takes on a capital L, and this is the courage of being alive up until death. I think, however, that these experiences are rare, perhaps similar to those lived by the mystics. I have no experience in this sense. I have instead been attentive to the interpretation of texts, to the ethical invitation, even if, beyond the duty and even the desire to "live well," I readily confess that there is a call to love that comes from farther and from higher.

- *We shall return later to what indeed appears to be a limit-experience that you associate with the act of dying. But before that we would like to know more about what you have just called the "fundamental" in terms of its relation to historical religions and, more precisely, to Christianity, which we have not yet talked about. Because, finally, this language you inherited, you still had to accept it as you began to speak it. Many people who live the same duality or the same bipolarity as your own often make use of one of the poles to neutralize the other or to leave it behind.*

- This is true. But I have no reason to censure this manner of thinking. I said earlier that it was a matter of "chance transformed into destiny by a continuous choice." This is where I encounter critical agencies, from Lucretius to Nietzsche, by way of Spinoza, Hume, and Voltaire. But I always trusted a ground of questioning that was ultimately more resistant, more profound, and that comes from farther back than critique itself. Critique is still always linked to powers that I master, whereas this giving of meaning seems to me, precisely, to constitute me both as a receptive subject and as a critical subject. The polarity of adherence and of critique is itself placed under the sign of this prior giving. I am, then, prepared to recognize the historically limited character of my situation and – to return to my comparison with languages – I would say that there is no manner of speaking that would lie outside of natural language. The sole resource that we have with respect to this plurality of languages is translation. Perhaps our problem today would be to determine if we are still in this relation of translation between a Jewish and Christian heritage and the other religions said to be monotheistic, although I have the gravest doubts about the nature, even the identity, that could be posited outside of Scripture of that God who would be Allah here and Yahveh elsewhere; for I believe that the naming of God is itself implied in the constitution of each of the "languages" mentioned, so that the word "God" is a sort of suspended word and one that designates perhaps something that others would not call God. Maybe in Buddhism this would be some-thing of the order of illumination; there are perhaps languages in which the word "God" does not function at all. But I recognize them as religious if I find three criteria in them: the anteriority of a founding word, the mediation of writing, and the history of an interpretation.

• *Does not the very fact of Revelation in the Mosaic heritage form a sort of duality? On the one hand, the anterior word is uttered, but on the other, it cannot be transmitted directly. There is the need for an intermediary, not only a man, who is Moses, but also the writing on the tablets, which themselves are not understood at first: they have to be shattered.*

• Yes, I strongly emphasize the fact that this relation of interpretation is consubstantial with the Jewish origin. The tablets were written and shattered; no one ever tried to *show* these tablets. And we speak of them in a writing that is also a writing on tablets. We return here to the mediation of writing. It is all the more necessary if, as I mentioned earlier, a plural reading of the Biblical corpus is inevitable, in which Mount Sinai is not the whole of the Hebraic Bible. For example, the tradition of the Patriarchs, with its theology of the blessing and the promise, perhaps says something other than the injunction and the commandment.

But I would not want to linger on the idea of "origin" attached to what is currently called revelation. The notion of the origin must itself be freed from the idea of a haunting by the past, unraveled well by psychoanalysts; it must be entirely dissociated from a beginning that one would try to date. It seems to me that going back in time toward some first thing is presenting it as chronologically prior, as a first that one could grasp. One finds oneself inevitably caught in Kantian antinomies. The origin, to my mind, does not function as an ordinal, as the first in a series, as a beginning that could be dated, but as what is always already there within a present word. This concerns an anterior of the order of the fundamental rather than the chronological. Obviously, it has its chronological trace: Moses precedes us in time. But Moses himself is preceded not only by traditions (which we can relate to the Mesopotamians), by all the millenary codes – at the time of Moses there were already at least two thousand years of speculations and of mediations – but especially by an anteriority that does not belong to the chronological order of temporal precedence. And Moses is preceded, in the final version of the Pentateuch, by the patriarchal traditions to which a long preface was added, Genesis 1–11, which concerns a humanity prior to the selection of Abraham. This backward flight in a reading that follows a regressive course is completely striking. It resembles a retreat of the origin in the search for an assigned beginning: we thus arrive at the magnificent sacerdotal narrative of creation, which begins both the writing and the reading for canonical exegesis. What the philosopher can retain is the idea of an anteriority that is not chronological.

One way of showing that the idea of origin does not coincide with that of a beginning in time is underscoring the place of the sapiential in Biblical writings. I am one of those who think that the sapiential genre extends beyond the writings placed under this heading. In particular, the sapiential is easily concealed under the narrative. I consider to be narrativized sapiential writings those accounts of the fall that are meditations of the sage, mediated by the only vehicle available, the narrative. Someone tells a story: there was a man who was good, then who became bad on the occasion of a certain event – which is a way of presenting in narrative form what appears in superimposed layers, as Kant well understood; in other words, the fact that the original goodness of man is more profound than the radicality of evil, a radicality that affects and infects a *penchant*, again to speak like Kant, without being able to equal the fundamental *disposition* toward the good. This superimpression, which is found in the depths of existence, is presented by the narrative chronologically. The sapiential texts function narratively, so to speak. But there are also prophetic texts, in which we encounter historical characters, such as Ezekiel, Isaiah, Jeremiah, who stand up to events threatening destruction by means of a word that is at once a word of mourning and a word of hope of reconstruction. This rhythm of destruction and reconstruction, of death and resurrection, is a grand model that we find again in the schema of the Passion – the cross, death, resurrection – but which one can say is already found in the Old Testament, in the rhythm of the great prophetic tradition: announcement of destruction, the actual exile, and the promise of restoration. This type of rhythm can be put in the category of "revelation" in the sense that, when I read this, I myself am constituted in accordance with this assertion-destruction-restitution rhythm; I do not draw it out of myself, I find it already inscribed prior to me. I return again to Kant – he is always my preferred author for the philosophy of religion – who, speaking of the figure of Christ as being the man pleasing to God, giving his life for his friends, declares that he could not have drawn that figure out of himself, and that he found it inscribed in a sort of imaginary or a schematism constitutive of the religious. In place of revelation, I would rather speak of a situation in which one refers to a constituting imaginary through the resources of religious language, by turn narrative, legislative, hymnic, and perhaps above all, sapiential.

- *In fact,* revelation *is a term you do not use readily. Why?*

- First, because it is too often reduced to inspiration, which I showed earlier is appropriate only for a certain category of text, and because, extended to the entire Biblical corpus, it introduces a psychologizing interpretation of canonical authority, which is the real guiding concept with which the philosopher and, before him, the kerygmatic theologian have to come to terms. In addition, the term "revelation" is suited only to a kerygmatic and not to a historical-critical reading, not even to canonical reading, which does not necessarily involve the reader in "putting into practice." And even the kerygmatic reading, apart from the choices and decisions it involves over the priority among the texts that "speak to us," is multiple: I mean that it is not reduced to a call to obedience – even if by this is meant "obedience to the faith" – but that it is also a call to reflection, meditation, to what the Germans call *Andenken* ("speculative form of meditation and reflection"), even to study, as the rabbis like to say, reading, discussing, interpreting the Torah, then held to be a lesson. This is clearly the case for sapiential writings, as well as for many narratives.

- *There is a text of the Pentateuch – Exodus 3: 14 – which is almost a required passage when one reflects on the relations between philosophy and religion.*

- I, in my own turn, have been interested in the "episode" of Exodus 3: 14, on which philosophers have written extensively because of the particular use that is made of the verb *to be* – "I am who am," "I am who I am," or "I shall become who I shall become," to translate as Buber and Rosenzweig do in German. This is a sort of speculative irruption in the narrative sphere, since after all Exodus 3 consists in a vocation narrative which strongly resembles many other vocation narratives, beginning with that of Gideon, and the most sumptuous being that of Ezekial, introduced by the grandiose vision of the temple, with the six-winged angels and the burning coal placed on the lips. In Exodus 3: 14, then, the narrative context of the vocation story is torn by a kind of speculative irruption, a sort of cipher, in which the use of the Hebrew verb *to be* was later assimilated to the Greek verb *to be*, the Septant having no other available. One must, therefore, make room in the Bible for a speculative order. This leads me to say – in recalling the dualism of the two systems of language formed by religion and philosophy – that Biblical thought does indeed exist. In this regard, I remain Kantian in saying that *Denken* (thinking) is not coextensive with *Erkennen* (knowing) and that this is a nonphilosophical manner of thinking and of being. It is indeed another manner of thinking (and of being), a nonphilosophical manner, that is transmitted by the prophets, the collectors of Mosaic and other traditions, and that shines forth in what is said by the sages of this Orient of which the Hebrews are a part.

At one period of my life, thirty years ago, under the influence of Karl Barth, I pushed this dualism quite far, to the point of excluding any encounter of God in philosophy. For I have always been mistrustful with respect to speculation termed ontotheological, and I had a critical reaction to any attempt to fuse the Greek verb *to be* and God, in spite of Exodus 3: 14. My mistrust of the proofs of the existence of God had led me always to treat philosophy as an anthropology – this is still the word I adopted in *Oneself as Another*, in which I border on the religious only in the final pages of the chapter on the voice of conscience, when I say that moral conscience speaks to me from farther away than myself; I cannot say then if it is the voice of my ancestors, the testament of a dead god, or that of a living god. In this case, I am agnostic on the plane of philosophy.

I perhaps had other reasons to protect myself from the intrusions, from the overly direct, too immediate infiltrations of the religious in the philosophical; these were cultural reasons, I would even say institutional reasons. It was very important to me to be recognized as a professor of philosophy, teaching philosophy in a public institution and speaking the common language, hence assuming the mental reservations that this entailed, even if it meant that I would periodically be accused of being a theologian in disguise who philosophizes, or a philosopher who makes the religious sphere think or be thought. I take on all the difficulties of this situation, including the suspicion that, in actual fact, I would never be able to maintain this duality in watertight compartments. At the beginning of *Oneself as Another*, I even proposed a language of transition, or rather a sort of armistice, when I distinguished between philosophical argumentation, in the public space of discussion and the profound motivation of my philosophical engagement and of my personal and communitary existence. By motivation, I do not mean the psychological sense that signifies having motives, which after all serve as reasons, but what Charles Taylor in *Sources of the Self* [3] calls "sources," understanding by this something that I do not master. The word "source" also has its neo-Platonic connotations and belongs to the philosophical religious language that may sometimes seem to be close to the specific, confessional religious, connoting the idea of a living source. It is not surprising to find analogies in both orders that can become affinities, and I assume this, for I do not believe that I am the master of this game, or the master of meaning. My two allegiances always escape me, even if at times they nod to one another.

- *In the exegesis of Biblical hermeneutics, is it not the case that the methods you describe above – from the historical-critical method to the kerygmatic readings – unavoidably incorporate philosophical concepts or arguments?*

• Yes, that is unavoidable, especially at the level of confessional theology which necessarily has recourse to the cultural language available to a given period. In this way, Biblical kerygma was transmitted in "languages," by turn Hellenistic, neo-Platonic, Kantian, Schellingian, and so on. On this mediation of philosophical language in the use of confessional theologies, I have presented my views in the texts that are found in volume 3 of *Lectures*,[4] where – and this is an interesting example of a form of mixed functioning – a general hermeneutics in Schleiermacher's sense (that is to say, a reflection on the nature of understanding, the place of the reader, the historicality of meaning, and so on) serves as *organon* for Biblical hermeneutics. But, inversely, the specificity of the religious serves as a cover for its own philosophical *organon*. By turns, one envelops the other. The condition of mutual enveloping is not uncommon. I have come across it, as I mentioned to you, in an entirely different sphere, within philosophical discourse itself: the philosopher may say that he includes a semiotic segment within his theory of language, and the semioticist may reply that he, in turn, does the semiotics of the philosopher's discourse. Something very similar occurs between theological discourse and its philosophical *organon*, including that of hermeneutical philosophy.

• *Let us now come to your relation to Christianity, which we have said little about so far, focusing as we were on the Hebraic Bible. Does not the philosopher have some difficulty in accepting the mystery of the Resurrection?*

• I do not regret this long sojourn with Moses, Abraham, the Psalms, and Job. It is the contact with these texts that creates divisions between historical-critical reading, canonical reading, and kerygmatic reading, which, in the final analysis, is the reading of faith.

We now come, then, to the New Testament and to its core, the preaching of the resurrection. Before speaking of the resurrection, I want to refer to an episode in the Gospel where the significance of the Passion and so of the death of Jesus is at issue; it is, in fact, first the Passion that is offered to our understanding. The text I am thinking of is the passage from the Gospel of Mark 8: 33, and Matthew 16: 23, the only time that Jesus calls someone Satan. This speech is addressed to Peter, whom the Catholic tradition of reading and interpretation of the Gospels makes the primary reference. Why this "outburst" by Jesus against Peter? Because he suggested to Jesus a kind of contract which is to attain glory without passing through Gethsemane. But the price to pay is, precisely, Gethsemane. It is here that an initial decision has to be taken, a weighty one with respect to philosophy. It concerns the sense to give to the Passion and the death of Jesus. A majority tradition, which is based in the New Testament, in particular in Paul, has understood this death in terms of sacrifice, the vicarious satisfaction given to divine anger. Jesus is punished in place of us. Another tradition, a minority one but in other ways more profound, and genuinely revolutionary in relation to sacrificial religions, as René Girard has eloquently shown, puts the main emphasis on the gracious gift that Jesus gives of his life: "No one takes my life, I give it." This nonsacrificial interpretation accords with one of the teachings of Jesus: "There is no greater love than this, that a man should lay down his life for his friends" (John 15: 13). I strongly support the liberation of the theology of the cross from the sacrificial interpretation. On this point, I find there is agreement, too, from such fine exegetes as Father Xavier-Léon Dufour, the author of *Lecture de l'Évangile de Jean* and *Face à la mort. Jésus et Paul.*[5]

In what way does this first decision open the way for a reinterpretation of the narratives relating to the resurrection? Here, I confess I move away not only from the dominant interpretation but from what is still the tacit consensus, at least, of dogmatic theologians. But this is perhaps where the philosopher that I am acts upon the apprentice theologian that moves within me. It has always seemed to me that the enormous narrative power of the accounts relating to the discovery of the empty tomb and the apparitions of the risen Christ blotted out the theological significance of the resurrection as a victory over death. The proclamation: "It is true; the Lord has risen" (Luke 24: 34) seems to me in its affirmative vigor to go beyond its investment in the imaginary of faith. Is it not in the quality of this death that the beginning of the sense of the resurrection resides? I find support for this in John, for whom the "elevation" of Christ begins on the Cross. It appears to me that this idea of elevation – beyond death – can be found after-the-event scattered narratively among the accounts of crucifixion, resurrection, ascension, Pentecost, which occasioned, retrospectively, four distinct Christian feasts. It is here that, perhaps once again pressured by the philosopher in me, I am tempted, following Hegel, to understand the resurrection as resurrection in the Christian community, which becomes the body of the living Christ. The resurrection would consist in having a body other than the physical body, that is to say, acquiring a historical body. Am I entirely unorthodox in thinking this? This seems to me an extension of certain words of the living Jesus, "He who wants to save his life, must first lose it" – an admirable statement that does not proclaim any sacrificial perspective – and also, "I have come to serve and not to be served." The comparison between these two texts suggests to me that the victory over death in the act of dying is not different from the service of others, which – guided by the spirit of Christ – extends into the diaconate of the community. This interpretation, I confess, is an expression of what Léon Brunschvicg would doubtless have called a "Christianity of the philosopher," to distinguish it from a Christian philosophy like that of Malebranche.[6]

● *Is not the idea that Christ could actually become king of the world, if he did not accept the cross, of the same order as the perversion to which Peter succumbs?*

● Yes, and moreover, the only other place in the Gospels where it is a matter of Satan himself is the narrative of the three temptations. Basically, the three temptations – which have nothing to do with sexuality, as the needless discussions occasioned by the recent papal encyclicals would lead us to believe – would have to be compared to problems of power: the power of money, of political authorities or of ecclesiastical authorities. This is much more serious than sexual questions: sexuality is probably pernicious and dangerous only to the extent that it may exercise a power over another whom it transforms into an object – in other words, when it no longer expresses mutual recognition, the mutual consent of one flesh to the other.

But I come back to the idea that the cross and the resurrection are the same thing: is it not astonishing that it is the Roman centurion who says, pointing at Jesus after he has just died: "Truly, this man was a son of God" (Mark 15: 39)? It thus comes to complete Jesus's cry: "My God, my God, why have you forsaken me?" which is also the beginning of Psalm 22. There is a sort of collusion, of commingling of the two moments of the same Psalm, the moment of lamentation, at the limit of accusation, and the moment of praise (we have, moreover, no way of going beyond this relation between lamentation and praise, which together form the two pillars of prayer). In the narrative of the crucifixion, Jesus says the beginning of the Psalm – "My God, why have you forsaken me?" – and the centurion pronounces the other half, the praise – "Truly, this man was a son of God." The twofold word, at the moment of the death of Jesus, anticipates the complete fulfillment of the resurrection in the other of the crucified, that is, in the community. Joining together lamentation and praise provides the sketch of an inchoate community which will enter into history beginning with Pentecost. It is noteworthy that Mark sees Jesus stopping with the lamentation, while Luke also ascribes to him the second half: "Father, into your hands I commend my soul" (Luke 23: 46). With Luke, the same person utters both the lamentation and the praise. The strength of Mark is to dare, or to obey a different law than Luke. It may even be that Jesus himself does not know that he was the Christ. And it is the community that recognizes this and states it, established as it is on this nonknowledge. This brings me to say that I do not finally know what happened between the Cross and Pentecost. In this regard, I am entirely prepared to admit that a theological sense is conveyed by the narration of the empty tomb and by that of the apparitions. But this theological sense is as if buried within the images of the narrative. Does not the empty tomb signify the gap between the death of Jesus as elevation and his effective resurrection as the Christ in the community? And does not the theological sense of the apparitions consist in the fact that it is the same spirit of Jesus, who offered his life for his friends, that now animates the handful of disciples, transformed, from the deserters they were, into an *ecclesia*? I know nothing of the resurrection as an event, as peripeteia, as turning point. Here, the entire empirical narrative appears to me to conceal rather than to give form to its theological sense, which, moreover, is multiple, as witnessed by the plurality of the Gospels and the discordant accounts of Paul and John.

• *The whole problem would then amount to knowing how to go about entering into the memory of a community still to come without assuming the apologetic or hagiographic mode, while remaining all the same absolutely exemplary.*

• The resurrection is stated by a community that is unavoidably historical, and so limited by its institutional apparatus – however minimal it may be. This is an essential debate, which was of great importance for the German Romantics: can the invisible Church be separated from the visible Church? I would compare this question to the following: could one find a primitive language that is not one of the natural languages? The reply is negative. Language exists only in languages. And the invisible Church exists only in visible churches. The problem is to take on this historical constraint without violence. When I say without violence, I am looking in the direction of Buddhism, because historical Christianity was not good at managing this relationship; it has often tipped over into extreme violence – the Crusades, the Inquisition, the wars of Religion, the English Protestants forbidding the Irish Catholics to ordain their priests, and so on. No historical community has been left untouched by this. In the past, when I reflected on violence, I observed that it grows and culminates when one approaches summits that are at one and the same time summits of hope and summits of power. The height of violence coincides with the height of hope, when the latter claims to totalize meaning, whether political or religious. Now even if the religious community is constituted outside the sphere of the political and even if it aspires to gather human beings around a project of regeneration other than a political project, it passes in its turn through the "parade" of power and violence. The church presents itself as an institution of regeneration. The eminent position of the religious, and its very transcendence in relation to the political, are not without certain perverse effects.

• *Transcendence in relation to the political, when this is not a form of collusion with it* . . .

• It is true that, historically, this has been the most frequent occurrence, the political demanding anointment by ecclesiastical power, and the latter soliciting from the political the backing of the secular arm. In this regard, I am reminded of what Hannah Arendt used to say about hell, namely that it is a political category, a notion forged to govern men. I believe this. It is a matter of making people afraid. Jean Delumeau demonstrated this mechanism magnificently throughout his work, in particular in his history of fear in the West.[7] I am happy that the preaching about hell has almost disappeared, perhaps because we have created hell here among us. The narratives about hell that one can read now seem silly, compared with the horrors of Auschwitz. One can say, unparadoxically, that hell has been overcome historically. At one time I was attracted, perhaps convinced, by what Karl Barth used to say, namely that hell exists for no one: not for the unbeliever who is indifferent toward it, nor for the believer since he has been delivered from it. This is a paradox, perhaps, that merits some thought . . .

• *What you say about "bracketing" the problem of the resurrection of the flesh, in a glorious body, should have as its primary ethical consequence a lack of concern about one's own salvation, but also, more deeply, a lack of concern with salvation as such in the sense of an afterlife. Would you go as far as that?*

• Yes, of course. I believe more and more that one has to divest oneself of that concern in order to pose the problem of life until death. Everything that I have tried to say about the self and otherness in the self, I would continue to defend on the philosophical plane; but, in the religious order, perhaps I would ask to give up the self. I have already quoted the word attributed to Jesus and which is undoubtedly one of the *ipsissima verba*: "He who would save his life must lose it." It may very well be that, philosophically, I must persevere in the defense of the self in opposition to the reductive claims addressed to it. I remain a reflexive philosopher, hence a philosopher of the self, of the *ipse*. But the shift to the religious question, which in Kantian terms has for its sole theme, unlike morality, regeneration – I translate: the restoration or the establishment of a capable human being, one capable of speaking, of acting, of being morally, juridically and politically responsible – this shift from the moral to the religious presumes a letting go of all the answers to the question "Who am I?" and implies, perhaps, renouncing the urgency of the question itself, in any event, renouncing its insistence as well as its obsession.

It seems more and more obvious to me that this culture of "detachment" – to borrow the magnificent title from Master Eckhart's writings and to enlist myself along with him in the tradition of Flemish mysticism – implies bracketing the concern with personal resurrection. In any event, the "imaginary" form of concern seems to me to have been abandoned, that is to say, the projection of the self beyond death in terms of afterlife. Afterlife is a representation that remains prisoner to empirical time, as an "after" belonging to the same time as life. This intratemporal "after" can concern only the survivors. They cannot help but ask themselves the question: What has become of our dead? Where are they now? What gives the desire for an afterlife a strength that is so difficult to overcome is the anticipation and interiorization, during my own life, of the question that my survivors will ask; yet I must not consider myself as tomorrow's corpse, as long as I am alive. Here I come back to an earlier point of our conversation where I referred to the hope, at the moment of death, of tearing away the veils that conceal the essential buried under historical revelations. I, therefore, project not an after-death but a death that would be an ultimate affirmation of life. My own experience of the end of life is nourished by this deepest wish to make the act of dying an act of life. This wish I extend to mortality itself as a dying that remains immanent to life. In this way mortality itself has to be thought *sub specie vitae* and not *sub specie mortis*. This explains that I by no means like nor do I use the Heideggerian vocabulary of being-toward-death; instead I would say being until death. What is important is to be living until the moment of death, pushing detachment as far as the mourning for the concern for an afterlife. Here I see the fusion of Master Eckhart's vocabulary and that of Freud: "detachment" and "work of mourning." After all, life advances only blow by blow, through abandonments and renunciations. At birth, the security of intrauterine life had to be abandoned; at twenty-five years of age, I knew I could never be a long-distance runner. In a more personal vein, and more difficult to confess, I had to abandon, in terms of my career and social position, the dream of being a Normalien, then that of being elected to the Collège de France.

Having said this, I do not feel especially affected by the ritual accusation, addressed to Christianity by Nietzsche and his successors, of possessing only a culture of suffering and of being inspired by the disdain, the calumny of life. More precisely, in order not to be subject to this reproach, I have to include within this work of mourning the assurance that joy is still possible when everything has been given up – and it is in this that suffering is the price to pay; not that it is to be sought out for itself, but it must be accepted that there is a price to be paid. To put this another way, when I reread Nabert, who always uses alongside each other the expressions "desire to be" and "effort to exist," I notice that the word "effort" is not absorbed by the word "desire"; for in effort there is always a price to pay. But this is to the benefit of life and its multiple beginnings and rebeginnings. This reminds me of what I wrote fifty years ago in *The Voluntary and the Involuntary,* when I asked that we reflect on birth rather than on death. After that, I came across, with a certain amazement, the exclamation of Hannah Arendt, as someone who was Jewish, quoting the Gospels which themselves quote Isaiah 9: 6: "A child has been born unto us."[8] For her, too, birth signifies more than death. This is what wishing to remain living until death means.

● *Do you reject, then, other possible meanings of the beyond that would not be reducible to the imaginary of an afterlife?*

● I am very hesitant here and this is so for a reason that goes beyond the fate of our desires, our wishes, our hopes. Detachment and the work of mourning are still located in the same time as the object of renunciation, namely an afterlife that would unfold in a sort of second temporality, parallel to that of the survivors. The reason is that we have no discourse available to think of the relation of time to eternity. We can only imagine it, and in a variety of ways, as I suggest with too much haste in *Time and Narrative,*[9] where I relate a variety of experiences of eternity that cannot be included within the Augustinian schema of the eternal present. These extreme experiences, which can also be very simple experiences (the birth of a child, accepting a gift, the happiness of shared friendship), give rise to what I am resigned to calling an analogical schematism of outside-of-time, of more-than-time. A schematism that is very difficult to distinguish from the simple imaginary, as we see in Kant when he resorts to this level of discourse.[10] Now, among the possible schematisms, I readily turn toward one that is suggested to me, precisely, by a Biblical expression speaking of the memory of God (I quote from the Jerusalem Bible for which I have a weakness): "what is man that you should spare a thought for him, or the son of man, that you care for him?" (Psalm 8: 4). You will notice the interrogative turn, which I retain in my speculation. Indeed, I am not unaware that in Biblical language memory is not reduced to a remembrance, under pain of slipping back into the time of history, but signifies something like concern, solicitude, compassion. This memory-concern has to do, in my opinion, with the dimension of the fundamental of which I was speaking earlier, of the fundamental turned toward us. Then, in line with this verse, I find myself meditating – *andenken*! – on a God who remembers me, beyond the categories of time (past, present, future). In order to give due weight to this digression, I venture to add to it a speculative extension in the wake of the process theology stemming from Whitehead,[11] where it is a matter of a God who becomes – and not who is, in the static and immutable sense of Greek philosophy, from which Augustine descended. Supporting this speculation on the schematism of the memory of God, I "figure" to myself that human existence that is no longer but which *has been* is in some way gathered into the memory of a God who is affected by it. As Hartshorne, the major disciple of Whitehead, said, existence gathered up in this way "makes a difference" in God.[12] I found a similar idea suggested by Hans Jonas in his admirable essay on the concept of God after Auschwitz.[13] He imagines a suffering God whom the good actions of men (in a Jewish perspective) would come to rescue, as it were. In the final analysis, my position with respect to personal survival is in complete accord with my interpretation of the resurrection of Christ. It is under the sign of this resurrection, which unites the gift of his own life and the service of others, that I place the present speculation. And it is in this sense that I hold it to be Christian, however peripheral it may be with respect to the dominant theologies. Regardless of this speculation, recognized as such, in which a certain nontemporal content is given to the temporal idea of a beyond, I would not want this to serve as a pretext for lessening the rigor required by the renunciation of the idea of afterlife, under the twofold sign of Eckhartian "detachment" and of Freudian "work of mourning." To use a language that remains quite mythical, I would say this: Let God, at my death, do with me as he wills. I demand nothing, I demand no "after." I cast upon others, my survivors, the task of taking up again my desire to be, my effort to exist, in the time of the living.

● *Is it a consequence of the bracketing of the concern for personal resurrection to devote oneself entirely to the duty of remembering with respect to those one has lost as well as with respect to those with whom one lives and risks losing?*

• Yes, it is. Because what alone survives, on the empirical and historical plane, is the life of the survivors. With this theme of the survival of the other and in the other, we are still within the horizon of life. What do I do with my own deaths in my memory? This is a problem of the living with regard to those who are no longer. And it affects me very directly after what I confided to you about the death of my son Olivier. But I do not have the right to interiorize, so to speak, this anticipation that I will have survivors in order to convert it into a representation of my own afterlife, in continuity with my actual life. In projecting myself into the other who will live after me, descendants and friends, I participate in advance in the duty of memory, as if I were, future perfect, the survivor of my death. But this should not lead us to an imaginary of one's own afterlife.


• *Does one not run into a problem raised by Hermann Cohen, who sees the necessity of the religious dimension in the limit attained by morality, which takes into account only the self, the "one," that which is common to all without being concerned with the irreducible suffering of the singular other? This would imply two orders: one, philosophical, ethical; the other, religious.*

• In any case, we find ourselves at this intersection without having chosen it. For us it is a given task to make these distinct orders communicate: that of philosophical morality and that of the religious, which also has its own moral dimension, in line with what I called the economy of the gift. This is what I would say today, after having spent decades protecting, sometimes cantankerously, the distinction between the two orders. I believe I am sufficiently advanced in life and in the interpretation of these two traditions to venture out into the places of their intersection. One of these is probably the fact of compassion. I can go rather far, from a philosophical point of view, in the idea of the priority of the other, and I have sufficiently repeated that the ethical is defined for me by the desire for the good life, with and for others, and by the desire for just institutions. Solicitude assumes that, counter to all cultural pessimism, I pay credit to the resources of goodwill – what the Anglo-Saxon philosophers of the eighteenth century always tried to affirm in opposition to Hobbes, that is, that man is not simply a wolf for man, and that pity exists. It is true that these are very fragile feelings and that it is one of the functions of the religious to take charge of them, to recodify them in a way, either along the lines of Second Isaiah, or along the lines of the Gospels of the death of Christ; but provided that this death be stripped of the ideology according to which an angry God would have to be satisfied under the pretext that, a man not sufficing, a being who was a god had to do it. In any case, it is the gift that has to win out over the vindictive idea that blood was the necessary price to pay. It is Girard who has accurately seen the singular nature of the Gospels, present already in the Hebraic Bible starting with Second Isaiah.

• *The voluntary gift of one's own life is not necessarily implied by morality. Is not something more than morality required?*

• Here again is one of the boundaries of the philosophical side explored by Jean Nabert, both in his *Éléments pour une éthique* and in his book on evil.[14] In one this is called "The sources of veneration," in the other "The approaches of justification." Nabert introduced the category of testimony which seems to me to be a place of intersection; in fact, Nabert, with whom I agree entirely, presented the problem in the following terms: how could empirical consciousness, with its weaknesses, its limitations, ever unite with founding consciousness? To be sure, a critical work on the self is necessary, but this can be mediated by the evidence of simple people who are not philosophers at all but who have tranquilly made the choice of effacing themselves, who have decided to take this path of generosity, of compassion, in which speculation in a sense lags behind evidence, and where these simple beings are more advanced than I. This advance of testimony over reflection is, so to speak, the gift that the religious offers to the philosophical, lending freely to it without requiring something in exchange. This would be the debt the philosophical owes to the religious, which lends to it the category of testimony.

• *This is yet another way of returning to the theme of life, which you have so strongly emphasized today.*

• There would certainly be a great deal to say about life in a nonbiological sense, at any rate in more than a biological sense. In my current speculation, I consider life, almost eschatologically, as an unveiling in the face of dying. In the one who, for the onlooker, is no more than a dying person, there still subsists a living being in whom the final spark of life shines. This spark strips away the veils of the codes in which the *fundamental* is enveloped during the entire time of empirical existence. Perhaps it is a sort of fantasy, but this is what presently occupies me in place of the fantasy of an afterlife. An afterlife implies the question

"Where are my dead?" in a sort of chronology paralleling the temporal existence of the living. How do the dead continue to exist, along a parallel path, in an elsewhere that would reduplicate the chronology of the survivor? This is what I must not anticipate, internalize, in the effort to think my own relation with death (which is still, I repeat, the gaze of one who is living – of a survivor) through the anticipated memory that others among the living, my survivors, will retain of me. But this anticipation of the way my friends and family will look back on me should not screen or veil my gaze as a living being on my death to come. It is under this strict condition that I am still permitted to speak of resurrection. Resurrection is the fact that life is stronger than death in this twofold sense: that it is extended horizontally in the *other*, my survivor, and is transcended vertically in the "memory of God."

• *It is striking that the human species has buried its dead from a very early time, and that, from this early date, there have been sepulchres.*

• Yes, but this is not a question for me who am going to die. It is my problem with regard to my dead, a problem of survivor and not of an anticipated afterlife. So it is a problem for the memory of the survivors and not a question that interests the anticipation of afterlife. The sepulchre is – along with language, the institution, and the tool – one of the four specific differences characterizing humanity as such. But I should not consider myself as "tomorrow's dead" which will only be the dead of my survivors. Is there behind the idea of the sepulchre the idea that everything does not cease there? Lacking a sense for a beyond-time, there is the cult of the dead, concretized by the act of burial and the whole liturgy of the sepulchre, which reaps the understanding – or rather the pre-understanding – of eternity, which I expressed earlier in terms of "religious schematism." In this regard, one must reaffirm the great cost of dissociating the idea of the beyond from the imaginary representation of an afterlife. It is this separation that the ritual of the sepulchre does not succeed in making, mixing together the beyond (of time) and survival, afterlife (in time).

• *Might this not be one way of capturing in an image the horizon of a reconciled humanity, which is, after all, the cosmopolitan horizon?*

• Construing this as a cosmopolitan idea detached from that of a personal future? Can one go so far as to detach the idea of the future of humanity from that of the *post mortem* future of the person? This is a big question. I construe it instead as a personal asceticism, and I do not want to allow myself to become fascinated by this question which would prevent me from posing correctly the problem of being alive up to the moment of death. What in philosophy is called "finitude" consists in distinguishing the end from the boundary. With the boundary, we look both ways: ahead and behind. With the end, we are always on the nearside without having anything with which to furnish the beyond.

If we are to believe the exegetes, the Jewish and then the Christian consciences did complete a certain course that, starting from a national project of survival, led to a personal project of resurrection. Christianity set the resurrection of Christ back within a culturally available schema, which was that of an afterlife. Ezekiel's prophecy of the dried bones, which had probably been a national prophecy, was reinterpreted and was transformed into a prophecy of personal resurrection. There was in the text, no doubt, a calculated ambiguity. One cannot say that it was strictly national or cosmopolitan – to employ the Kantian vocabulary in an extrahistorical sense – or that it was simply personalist. But it is certain that later Judaism, read by Christians, had personalized the idea of resurrection, which was a theme characteristic of what lay beyond the catastrophe of exile. The rupture of exile and of destruction, then reconstruction. This provides the tertiary structure: I live, I die, I am reborn. It was already constitutive of a tradition of later Judaism, and in a way Christianity placed the person of Christ in this structure, with his corporeal resurrection anticipating our own resurrection. This is how the dominant neotestimentary thought was constructed.

Where would I now situate myself with respect to this, if I am prepared to accept my heritage as a whole? Do I have the right to filter it, to sift through it? What do I believe deeply? It is enough for the time being for me to know that I belong to a vast tradition, and that men and women also belong to it who have professed with assurance and good faith doctrines from which I feel myself far removed. With them all I can apply to myself is Bernanos's remark: "It is easier than one thinks to hate oneself. Grace is to forget oneself. But if all pride were dead in us, the supreme grace would be to love oneself humbly, as one of the suffering members of Jesus Christ."

Speculation aside, I try to join a certain gaiety to the work of mourning. Yes, I would like someone one day to say of me: he was a very lively fellow, and not just a stern professor.

● *Do you mean by this that there is a given moment when mourning, however terrible, has found its place in existence?*

● Yes, and then everything is there for the taking. Applying to myself the statement at the end of the sacerdotal narrative of creation: "And God saw that it was good. Yes, very good."

• *This is a blessing; when contingency is blessed, we enter into another dimension.*

• We can only hope to tend in this direction. We catch glimpses of it, in brief flashes.

• *How does one escape these alternatives: thinking of God in the form of a person or in the form of a regulative idea in Kant's sense?*

• The regulative idea belongs to a very advanced philosophical development. I try to consider the question from within the religious field and not the philosophical, if that is possible. For there are instances of osmosis between the religious domain and the philosophical domain. In the most personalized religious sphere, in Buber for example, one finds a Thou but also the neuter, in the form of the anonymity of that which is fateful, of the "It had to be that." On the other hand, it is quite astonishing to see that Buddhism, as we know it culturally, in its most speculative forms, has always been integrated into cultural fields in which there were personalized divinities, even to the point of superstition. I do not know how these diverse components are integrated and function together, but I think that what is completely depersonalized in the divine finds its compensation in an extreme personalization of idols. For us, the configuration is perhaps the opposite: in the linguistic fields of Judaism, prophecy and narrative are highly personalized, whereas the legislative would be closer to the impersonal. However, the legislative is personalized by reason of its proximity to the narrative in well-known texts: "I am Yahweh your God" (Deuteronomy 5: 6). This is a declaration of liberation, a prophetic word that encompasses the commandment, in which the "thou" of "Thou shall not kill" can be said without there being an "I." The "thou" functions as "being addressed" but without revealing an "I" who says "thou."

I was very interested, from an exegetical point of view, in the dispute that took place in the 1950s and that led us to ask ourselves whether the narrative of Sinai did not join together two very different domains, one of liberation – highly narrativized – the other legislative – set off against the background of Mesopotamian lawgiving. What is interesting is that we read canonical texts, stemming from an intersection of two traditions, in which the legislative is narrativized by the word of deliverance – I who led you out of Egypt, I give you this law – and, inversely, in which the narrative is converted into ethics by the law given to a free people, a law that is the charter of liberation and that perfectly integrates the narrative and the legislative. What is highly personalized in the prophetic and the narrative is found to be combined in this way with what could be virtually neutral in the Law, since one can state the Law without knowing the lawgiver.

● *You were saying earlier that the naming of God is constitutive with respect to religions themselves. How do you apply this to the question of the relations between Judaism and Christianity?*

● God is a term that oscillates curiously between the common name and the proper name: Yahveh, your God. The word God is the name of the gods and Yahveh is the name of God, but which ceases to be simply one particular case in order to become, in its singularity, unique. But is the tetragram a proper name? The critique of anthropomorphism makes us say that there are forms of naming that are unworthy of God. This begins with Xenophane and continues through the half-philosophical, half-theological speculation on the divine names – the critique of the names that are unsuitable for God is at once the philosophical injected into the religious, but also a sort of asceticism internal to the religious that seeks to rid itself of what is unworthy of God.

There is certainly a very specific relation between Judaism and Christianity. I strongly resist the tendency in Christianity that consists in saying that Judaism is a thing of the past because it has been replaced by Christianity. I believe in the perenniality of post-Christian Judaism because the hermeneutical relation between Christianity and Judaism presupposes the solidity of Judaism. It seems to me that the Greek and Latin Fathers persisted in a certain fundamentalism of the Old Testament because, in order to become figures or types, the events, institutions and characters of the Old Testament had to possess their own substance and preserve it historically. The second element that compels us to recognize that Judaism has its own consistency is that this hermeneutical relation was already operating within the Old Testament, since we find a whole series of covenants each of which is a reinterpretation of the preceding covenant, and even the idea of the New Covenant, with Ezekiel and Jeremiah: the law will no longer be inscribed on stone but in the hearts of men. I am particularly attentive to the chain of covenants, of Noah, Abraham, and David, in which this phenomenon of cumulative reinterpretation is present. I would place the hermeneutical relation of Christianity to Judaism in the continuation of the relation of reinterpretation of the alliances, a relation internal to the Hebraic Bible. A third element of continuity consists in the fact that Christianity is grafted onto a minor branch of Judaism, the eschatological branch; it leads back, therefore, to what was already a dialectical relation within Judaism between the Rabbinical movement of the second Temple, tied to restoration (and which presents certain intolerant aspects, forcing Jewish women to end their marriages with pagans, for instance), and another variant of Judaism. Christianity, in this way, is placed within the continuation of a certain pluralism internal to Judaism.

Unfortunately, all this has been obscured by the conflict at the end of the first century and, especially, during the second century, at the time when Christianity moved out of the synagogue and when a mutual exclusion occurred. This is when the writing of a Matthew, for example, becomes very anti-Judaic, although the trial of Jesus was a Roman trial. I believe that it is theologically important to maintain the preponderance of Roman responsibility in the trial of Jesus in order to signify clearly that it is in relation to power that Jesus was condemned, which sets aside the accusation of deicide leveled against the Jews. The suspicion of deicide was the millenary crime of Christianity with respect to the Jews. It is necessary, as I have already said, to bear the burden of this. This drama takes it toll of the relations between the ecclesial and the power structure. We have encountered this enigma of the propensity of religions to tyranny. In this regard, the responsibility of historical Christendom is heavy. Nevertheless, I am grateful to the great Church for having resisted Marcion, who wanted to eliminate the Old Testament and to cut Christianity off from its roots, under the pretext that the novelty of Christianity was such that it could dispense with any prior base.

There remains the magnificent filiation of the Psalms, which are sung in churches as well as in synagogues; in several of the most well-known religious orders there is even a weekly reading of the one hundred and fifty Psalms. . . The place of the Psalms in the Hebraic Bible does, it is true, pose a problem, since the rabbis who presided over the elaboration of the canon placed them in the third group, after the Torah and the Prophets, and alongside the books of Wisdom, Ecclesiastes, and Job. The Psalms, which are the source of the greatest affiliation between Judaism and Christianity, form the counterpart to all the relations of power tied to the ecclesial constitution, tied also to the problem central to Judaism: how to survive the destruction of the Temple? The restructuring of Judaism around the Synagogue turned out to be parallel to the constitution of the Christian Church as an institutionalized confession. There were two parallel and rival processes of institutionalization, which brought about the great split. We have to remember that there was a time, at the beginning of our era, when Christians, at least the Judeo-Christians, met in the synagogue. But it is true that the great debate in Jerusalem between the Judeo-Christians and the pagan-Christians did not prevent the domination of the pagan-Christians. I gave a great deal of attention to the contemporary interpretation of the relation between Judaism and Christianity by Rosenzweig,[15] who, having himself been close to converting to Christianity, had the vision of a new complementarity in which Judaism, rejecting in a single stroke both the ghetto and assimilation, would be brought to rethink itself not only in terms of its cohabitation but even more in terms of a complementarity with Christianity. Rosenzweig says that one is born Jewish and that one becomes Christian, that is to say, that Judaism enjoys a natural rootedness, whereas Christianity is inscribed in history. Judaism's capacity to develop its singularity into universality would then pass by way of Christian mediation, which would perhaps not be the only one, but which would nevertheless be necessary. I am thinking again of the blessing of Abraham: "In thou, all nations shall be blessed." How could all the nations be blessed in Abraham if not through the historical relay of Christianity? Rosenzweig pushed cohabitation quite far, and the most beautiful pages of *The Star of Redemption* are devoted to the correspondence between all the Jewish and Christian holidays, except for the Jewish New Year. After Auschwitz there is a duty to convey Jewish thought before Auschwitz, in opposition to those who say that after Auschwitz thought is no longer possible. This would be not an error, but a fault; this would be to make Hitler right, when he wanted to strip Judaism of any future. There is here a kind of fraternity between Judaism and Christianity.

• *Since you are speaking of Christianity in a global manner, one cannot help but ask you how you interpret the relations between Protestantism and Catholicism.*

• Here too contemporary history seems to me entirely different from that of the sixteenth century, since the motives for the rupture scarcely exist. If we take the history of Luther, which was examined so well by Lucien Febvre in the work he devoted to him,[16] we see that this is a phenomenon belonging to the end of the Middle Ages, and that the essential question was to know whether or not one was "damned" and to what extent one could be said to be "saved." Our problem today is instead that of "sense" and "nonsense." This is a post-Nietzschean question which can no longer be expressed solely in terms of guilt, of sin, or of Redemption.

What is more, the problem of monachism seems to me to have changed its sense entirely. Luther was opposed to monachism by stressing the fact that it was the profane vocation, the laity, that was the bearer of vocation, whereas nowadays I would say that monachism serves as a counterexample: it signifies that there do exist human beings capable of living outside of money, of sexuality, and of relations of power. But we could certainly find in Buddhist monasteries as well similar spaces for drawing breath, for silence – all the things denied us by modern society, a society of noise, of covetousness, and of possession. The Christian cleric is no longer in the position of an extension of the Greek cleric, holding contemplative life above practical life, but represents a kind of counterexample to the society of production, consumption, and leisure.

It seems to me that the problem of the split between Catholicism and Protestantism rests finally on the problem of authority, and it is true that here there is, for the moment, an unbridgeable gap. But I am not at all interested in institutional ecumenism because I believe in the originally plural destination of Christianity – it is, undoubtedly, for this reason that I am not Catholic. My knowledge of Catholicism is that of a neighbor. I experience this in two ways: on the one hand, in terms of local, parish life – that of communities in proximity – and, on the other, in terms of intellectual, exegetic, philosophical, and theological work. In this way, I feel entirely at home with the Jesuits on the rue de Sèvres and with my friends at the Institut Catholique in Paris: they have the same problems I have, problems of sense and nonsense, and they also have problems with their own authority, their own ecclesiastical hierarchy; they simply live from the inside what I, for my part, perceive from the nearby neighborhood where I reside.

• *One of the difficulties posed by Islam in relation to us, as you were saying in speaking of secularism, is the fact that the societies in which Judaism and Christianity exist are secular societies. How do you interpret the phenomenon of secularization?*

• Every church is a visible church. It, therefore, enters into the domain of institutions in having to resolve problems inherent in power. Ecclesiastical society finds itself to be within the general institutional domain. One could describe the primary characteristic of secularization as a restriction of the field of influence of the ecclesiastical institution in relation to other institutions, and as the fact that all the other institutions can be conceived in their function and in the exercise of their authority independently from any reference to ecclesiastical communities. The distinctive feature is, therefore, first of all the enfranchisement of the entire chain of institutions of civil society in relation to that very specific society that is ecclesiastical society. Secondly, there is the interiorization of this process in each of the members of these institutions as we see them functioning as "orders of recognition," to return to Jean-Marc Ferry's vocabulary, each person being an agent in relation to a system. This relation itself is also deployed outside of the religious. One sees oneself recognized in one's effectiveness as a social agent, capable of intervening in systems that are *auto*nomous, the religious then being *hetero*nomous. A third feature would be the transformation of the historical horizon of the entire set of institutions, of the network it forms, as it shifts toward a future stripped of the eschatological horizon that was provided by the religious. First, there was a transposition of this eschatological dimension – let us say, of the "great banquet," of the final reconciliation – into rational language, which became the problem of ends in the Kantian manner, in which what remains of the perpetual is the horizon of relations between states. The second stage of this mutation of the historical horizon, tied to the loss of the link constituted by secularized forms of eschatology, consists in the appearance of a manner of living in a history without an ultimate end, hence a history moving from one brief deadline to the next, on the scale of feasible short-term projects shaped by different communities. The final sign of secularization would be the absence of any comprehensive recapitulative function, and so the dispersion of the circles of belonging of the communities. It is no accident that there are so many works today on the pluralism of the idea of justice, attesting to the absence, not only of a comprehensive historical project, but, in the present, of the impossibility of a recapitulation.

- *Is it conceivable to you that societies can exist without any eschatological perspective?*

- The question is to determine whether what intellectuals describe as secularization is the profound truth of our societies. It is a problem I pose to myself when I read works such as *L'Ère du vide* by Gilles Lipovetsky:[17] one never knows whether the descriptions that are given do not themselves contribute to the phenomenon, by accelerating it, and even creating it out of nothing, as if we were confronted by a sort of self-fulfilling prophecy in reverse; in reality, might not this antiprophecy of the absence of eschatology bring itself about by the mere fact of being uttered? As for knowing whether a society can live without eschatology . . . Perhaps not, but we are also in a crisis of replacement eschatologies – Communism, for example – which have played this role in the post-Enlightenment period. Perhaps we are fooling ourselves by believing that the end of *these* grand narratives was the end of *all* grand narratives. Maybe it is only the end of substitution narratives, which certainly leave behind them a very large void.

I deeply believe that critique is beneficial for the eschatological projection of what remains of the ecclesiastical core in our societies, stripped of the temptation of power. It remains a poor, disarmed word, which has no force other than its capacity to be said and heard. It rests on a sort of wager: are there still enough people who will hear this word?

For there is another phenomenon – I do not know whether it enters into the process of secularization, or whether secularization is an effect of it – which is the indefinite multiplication of signs in circulation in our societies, in comparison with the very small number of texts available in the Middle Ages. The small voice of Biblical writings is lost in the incredible clamor of all the signals exchanged. But the fate of the Biblical word is that of all poetic voices. Will they be heard at the level of public discourse? My hope is that there will always be poets and ears to listen to them. The minority fate of a strong word is not only that of the Biblical word.

• *In recalling your attachment to the duality of conviction and critique, you finally respond to the question of secularization by saying that it is impossible.*

• I do not know if it is impossible for society on a grand scale. I consider it impossible for me and for the communities in which I feel myself rooted and to which I am connected by ties of affinity, of neighborhood. This raises again the problem of my relation to other religions. I am quite distant from the notion of comparativism, which would claim to be based on some alleged confessional neutrality. One encounters language only from within some particular language. For most of us, we are rooted in a "mother tongue"; at best, we have learned another "tongue" but as one learns a language, that is to say, starting from a mother tongue and through translations. There are all the degrees from monolinguism to polyglottism. The same thing is true for the comprehension of a religion which always begins from a "religion from within" – which is not necessarily the relation of a believer to a confession. I have often used the expression "in imagination and in sympathy" to designate the capacity to hold as plausible – that is to say worthy of being pleaded for – a confession, a confessional structure of the religious. And it is only little by little, by approximations, that one can understand a neighboring confession and, through it, another that is close to it. Within the Christian space, starting from a confession that is Reformed Protestantism, I can understand what Orthodox thought or Catholicism is, or even, toward somewhat more hazy margins, the nature of certain sects. Starting from the same situation I can also understand the triangle of so-called monotheistic religions – Judaism, Christianity, Islam, as well as the religions without God, such as Buddhism, which I term religious because one finds there the reference to an anteriority, an exteriority, and a superiority – these three notions being constitutive of the manner in which I am preceded in the world of meaning.

● *And Islam?*

● I perceive it in a purely cultural, historical manner, but I do not know it well enough, and I do not see what it actually adds to what I find in the extreme variety of Judaism and Christianity. But this is perhaps due to my ignorance, and one has to believe that in it there is a spiritual force, for it is not simply by violence, or by conquest, that millions of people have been won over by it. This ignorance has to be remedied because it is here for the long run, alongside us and among us.

We would have to go back to the moment in the conversation when, in reference to the work of translation from one language to another (which I took as the model for the step-by-step understanding of one religion translated into the language of another religion), I alluded to the possible emergence of a fundamental, basic, essential dimension which prompts me to say that there is in them the same essential dimension as in ourselves. But I recognize this same essential dimension only in extreme situations, like that of death, or in situations of distress: the fraternity of the battlefield, "the fraternity of those who have been shaken," of which Patočka spoke.

● *Why not in the simplest acts of existence performed by everyone: love, relations with others, the loss of a loved one, the birth of a child, which are also limit-experiences?*

● You are right. And I would not want to conclude this reflection on tragic experiences alone. I changed the direction of the discussion with my reflection on the experience of the end of life. It is also a matter of linking up with other religions and great cultures on the basis of the way in which they deal, in a language different from my own, with these fundamental experiences. The thing I was trying to describe earlier, in speaking of exteriority, superiority, and anteriority, we could undoubtedly find in experiences of life and creation, which are also experiences of sharing.

# Chapter 8

# Aesthetic Experience

● *In your life, art has always held a prominent place; you regularly go to museums, you listen to a wide range of music. However, in your work, this dimension of human experience is singularly lacking, if we set aside your analyses of literature in* Time and Narrative. *What are your tastes, first of all?*

● I have great admiration for twentieth-century art: in music, my preference goes to Schönberg, Berg, Webern, the whole Vienna school; in painting, I would want to mention Soulages, Manessier, Bazaine. But these are examples that come immediately to mind, and I could think of so many others: Mondrian, Kandinsky, Klee, Miró . . . I returned, not long ago, to the Peggy Guggenheim museum in Venice: there I saw several admirable works of Pollock, a Bacon, and also a Chagall. I have a genuine passion for Chagall; looking at his canvases, I experience every time the feeling of reverence; reverence before this mixture, which belongs only to him, of the sacred and of irony – couples floating in air, a flying rabbi, somewhere in a corner a donkey, a violin player . . . But nothing must be excluded from one's admiration; one even has to learn in a sense to love everything. I long resisted classical painting; and then I went to see the great Poussin exhibition that was held in Paris in 1994. Obviously, it is something quite different from Pollock or Bazaine. What leaves me with reservations about it is the narrative assumption of most of the canvases. One has to be able to identify the stories being staged. But the eye educated by nonfigurative painting only manages to see the extraordinary play of color and of line and the perfect balance of the two. I was reading, moreover, in the catalogue of the exhibition that Picasso always returned to Poussin, as to his principal tutor in the art of painting.

I also love statuary: Lipchitz, Arp, Pevsner and the admirable Brancusi. It is true that it is often difficult for this art to move away from the figurative; but, when it manages to do so, the result is absolutely extraordinary. I am thinking, for example, of Henry Moore's great sculptures, in which the treatment of the human body – of the feminine body, in particular – is constantly allusive. And in the same stroke, things about the body are said that correspond to no anatomical description, and yet they induce unexplored relational possibilities and make possible the unfolding of new and original feelings: of plenitude and fecundity, of course, but this is still saying too little; of vacuity, more strangely, in the case of those hollowed figures that one can pass through, the effect is absolutely astonishing. We are here in a universe where polysemy reigns: I am thinking, in particular, of one of these sculptures, *Atom Piece*, located in Chicago near the university library, at the spot where the first controlled chain reaction took place. The sculpture consists of a shattered sphere that can equally represent the skull of a scientist, an atom that is exploding, or the Earth itself. In this case, the polysemy is obviously sought after in its own right. We are in the presence of an intention to signify that goes far beyond the event and seeks to gather together all the aspects that will be dispersed in descriptions: descriptions of the protagonists – the atom or the scientist – description of the events – the nuclear explosion or the still inert atom. There is in the work the capacity to make all these aspects ever denser, to intensify them in condensing them. And in speaking of this we can only distribute the polysemy along the different and diverging axes of language. The work alone gathers them together.

- *But are we not here, in this very case, on the edge of the figurative, from which you hoped sculpture would free itself?*

- If you like, but this would be something more like the polyfigurative, inasmuch as this art goes beyond the classical resources of the figurative. This would be comparable to the density of certain forms of language, such as metaphor, in which several levels of meaning are held together in a single expression. The work of art can have an effect comparable to that of metaphor: integrating levels of sense that are overlaid, preserved and contained together.

The work of art is in this way, for me, the occasion for discovering aspects of language that are ordinarily concealed by its usual practice, its instrumentalized function of communication. The work of art bares properties of language which otherwise would remain invisible and unexplored.

• *You are probably thinking of the analyses in* Time and Narrative, *which you mentioned during an earlier session.*

• It is, in fact, by way of the narrative that I have approached aesthetics up to now. As I told you, the narrative provided me with the opportunity to take a position on a problem that can be resolved neither with artificial languages nor even with ordinary language: the two-sidedness of the sign. On the one hand, the sign is not the thing; it is in retreat in relation to the latter and as a result of this it generates a new order that is organized according to an intertextuality. On the other hand, the sign designates something, and one must pay careful attention to this second function, which intervenes as a compensation with regard to the former, because it compensates for the exile of the sign in its own order. I recalled Benveniste's remarkable statement: the sentence pours language back into the universe. *Pour back into the universe*: the sign retreats in relation to things, and the sentence pours language back into the universe.

I told you that I set this twofold function of the sign in a vocabulary particularly appropriate to the narrative, in distinguishing *configuration*, which is the capacity of language to provide a configuration of itself in its own space, and *refiguration*, which expresses the capacity of the work to restructure the world of the reader in unsettling, challenging, remodeling the reader's expectations.

I define the function of refiguration as *mimetic*. But it is extremely important not to be mistaken as to its nature: it does not consist in reproducing reality but in restructuring the world of the reader in confronting him or her with the world of the work; and it is in this that the creativity of art consists, penetrating the world of everyday experience in order to rework it from inside.

Because the painting of the past few centuries, at least since the invention of perspective in the Quattrocento, has almost always been figurative, we should not be fooled about the nature of *mimesis* – and I shall maintain this paradox: it is in the twentieth century when painting ceased to be figurative that the full measure of this *mimesis* could be taken, namely, that its function is not to help us recognize objects but to discover dimensions of experience that did not exist prior to the work. It is because Soulages or Mondrian did not imitate reality, in the restrictive sense of the word, because they did not make a replica of it, that their work has the power to make us discover, in our own experience, aspects up to then unknown. On a philosophical plane, this leads us to question the classical conception of truth as adequation to the real; for, if one can speak of truth in relation to the work of art, it is to the extent that this designates the capacity of the work of art to break a path in the real by renewing the real *in accordance with the work itself,* so to speak.

But music permits us to go even further in this direction than painting, even nonfigurative painting. For the latter often contains figurative remnants. I am thinking, for example, of Manessier's four magnificent paintings: *The Passion according to Saint Matthew, The Passion according to Saint Luke, The Passion according to Saint John, The Passion according to Saint Mark.* In these works there is something like an allusion to reality: forms of the cross against red, orange or pink backgrounds; the figuration is allusive, even recessive, but not entirely absent. In music, by contrast, there is nothing of the sort. Each piece possesses a certain mood, and it is as such, without representing anything of the real, that it establishes in us the corresponding mood or tone.

● *In music, too, there are examples of the Passion according to Saint Matthew or of the Passion according to Saint John . . .*

● One could say of sacred music, to the extent that it alludes to a religious content, what I said about figurative painting: it is when music is not in the service of a text having its own verbal meanings, when it is no longer anything but *this* tone, *this* mood, this color of the soul, when all external intentionality has disappeared and when it no longer has a signified that it possesses its full power of regenerating or recomposing our personal experience. Music creates feelings for us that have no name; it extends our emotional space, it opens in us a region where absolutely new feelings can be shaped. When we listen to a particular piece of music, we enter into a region of the soul that can be explored only by listening to *this* piece. Each work is authentically a modality of the soul, a modulation of the soul.

It must be acknowledged, moreover, that contemporary philosophy has to a large degree been found wanting on this chapter of the sentiments: many things have been said about the passions but very little has been said about feelings, and then about very few of these. Now each piece of music gives rise to a feeling that exists nowhere else except in that particular work. Could we not say that one of the main functions of music is to construct a world of singular essences in the realm of feeling? I am not far from thinking that it is in music that the exploration occurs, in a pure state, of our being-affected, on the subject of which Michel Henry has written some very important analyses.[1]

● *You have used the term "world" concerning the work of art; and you*

*said earlier that the world of the work confronts the world of the
spectator or the listener. In Malraux, too, the notion of* world *was
central, and it led him to the well-known statement: "Great artists are
not the transcribers of the world, they are its* rivals.*"*[2]

• I have always used this term, not out of concession, nor facility, but
as a strong term whose development can be traced through Husserl,
Heidegger, and Gadamer. What is a world? It is something one can live
in; something that can be hospitable, strange, hostile . . . In this way
there are fundamental feelings that are unrelated to any specific object
or thing but which depend on the world in which the work appears;
these are, in sum, pure modalities of inhabiting. I think that it is not by
reason of complaisance or rhetoric that we speak, for example, of the
"Greek world," even if this is each time on the basis of a singular work:
the work, which is itself a singular world, brings to light an aspect or
a facet of the "Greek world"; that is to say that it is of greater value than
itself – it refers to a sort of surrounding environment, it attests to a
capacity to expand itself and to occupy an entire space of consideration
or of meditation in face of which a spectator can situate herself. There
is no doubt that the spectator is placed opposite the work, confronting
it. But at the same time, she is in the midst of the world created by this
"opposite." These are two perfectly complementary aspects, and the
fact of being immersed in a world compensates for what could be the
pretense of mastery in the simple face-to-face with the work: a world
is something that surrounds me, that can submerge me; in any case,
it is something I do not produce but in which I find myself.

Thus one cannot use the term "world," in a rigorous sense, unless the
work performs for the spectator or the reader the work of refiguration
that overturns expectations and changes horizons; it is only inasmuch
as it can refigure this world that the work reveals itself as capable of a
world.

This is a point I insist upon. For if one makes the work of art – be it
literary, plastic, or musical – simply the center of the constitution of an
unreal order, one removes its bite, its power over the real. Let us not
forget the twofold nature of the sign: retreat from and transfer back into
the world. If art did not have, despite its retreat, the capacity to come
bursting into our midst, into our world, it would be completely
innocuous; it would be struck with insignificance and reduced to sheer
entertainment, it would be confined to a parenthesis in our concerns.
I think we have to go as far as possible in this direction and maintain
that the capacity to make a return into the world is carried to its greatest
intensity by the work of art, precisely because the retreat made here is
infinitely more radical than in ordinary language, where this function

is blunted, attentuated. As the representational function is lessened – this is the case with nonfigurative painting and with music when it is nondescriptive – as the gap with reality grows wider, the biting power of the work on the world of our experience is reinforced. The greater the retreat, the more intense the return back upon the real, as coming from a greater distance, as if our experience were visited from infinitely further away than itself. We have a sort of counterexperience of this hypothesis in the example of photography as it is practiced by amateurs, when what we obtain is simply a double of the real, with a return to the origin by way of only a very small loop, and, as a result, its grasp on our world is infinitely less. As for art photography, it also claims, but at a much higher cost, to free itself from imitation, from mere representation, and also constructs its object on the border, so to speak, of the reduplication of reality. I have recently had the opportunity to admire a superb collection of "Fathers and Daughters" photographs by Marianne Cook of New York. Photography succeeds here in capturing the breaks in this subtle bond and the words unspoken in stretches of silence.

For a long time, the representative function in pictorial art was held to have prevented the expressive function from being fully deployed and the work from making itself into a world in competition with the real in a realm beyond all reality. And it is only in the twentieth century, when the break with representation has been completed that, as in the wish expressed by Malraux, an "imaginary museum" has been created, in which works of very different styles coexist, provided that each excels in its own realm. Everything can be brought together, just as in our big cities a Roman Catholic church and a skyscraper can exist side by side, or a Gothic cathedral next to the Georges Pompidou Center. For this to be possible, it was necessary that the signs had to be emptied of any external designation; only then could they enter into all sorts of imaginable relations with other signs; between them there is now a sort of infinite availability for incongruous associations. Everything can go together, from the moment that one admits along with Malraux that there is no progress from one style to another, but only within each style, moments of perfection.

• *The break with representation which characterizes twentieth-century painting and sculpture presents, among other problems, that of the limits of art: to what extent can we still speak of a work of art?*

• This is a domain in which I am ill at ease. Is it enough for a chair to be placed on a platform, in other words, to be diverted from its ordinary use, to authorize us to think of it as a work of art? The disappearance of the frame, in the case of painting, plays a very important role in this regard: the frame separated the work from the background, it constituted a sort of window through which the infinity of a world was hollowed out within these very limits. When this function is no longer exercised, we find ourselves confronting some very troubling cases; I am thinking, for example, of certain large panels by Reinhardt, entirely black, in which there are only modulations of black . . . I confess that I am somewhat at a loss in the face of examples of this sort.

- *You say that there is no progress in the history of art. But there is still a history of materials, where progress is not absent. The transformation of the Italian frescoes in the Renaissance was largely dependent on the transformation of the bases and the ability of the painters to prepare new mixtures of colors.*

- Certainly, but a painter can also, today, give up brushes for a knife or even for fingers; he may want in this way to add thickness to his material, roughness, erasing as it were the border between painting and sculpture. I am thinking of the works of Tanguy or Tapiès, which are almost bas-reliefs.

- *All the same, today one can no longer write novels like Balzac or Zola.*

- No, but why? The example is, actually, very interesting, because one of the functions performed in the past by the novel – taking the place of sociology – no longer has any reason to exist. However, the novel can make use of the extradescriptive properties characteristic of language; it can, ultimately, have cognitive significance, based upon the expressive capacity of language, a capacity that is independent of its descriptive function submitted to the test of verification.

Take the case of books on the experience of the concentration camps, and most recently that of Jorge Semprun, *L'Écriture ou la vie*. The entire book revolves around the possibility/impossibility of representing absolute evil. The difficulty is obviously extreme since it is a matter of imposing the canons of the narrative on a limit-experience; either the horrible does not pass into the narrative, or it does, but then the narrative breaks down and falls into silence. But in this book there is an element that is named several times, an obsessive element that is at the same time the extreme of the narrative and its impossibility: it is an odor, that of burning flesh.

Primo Levi, for his part, has chosen another path in *If This is a Man*: that of pure description, after the fashion of Solzhenitsyn in *One Day in the Life of Ivan Denisovich*; his book resembles a cold account, bordering on the documentary, as if the horrible could be said only in a sort of understatement, of *litote*; the understatement of the horrible. Through the bare bones of the language, in creating its own form of sensibility, the bareness of the situation is allowed to be signified, and it is not by *what* is said but by a certain bareness in tone that Levi obtains the desired effect.

• *This effect, produced on the reader, is doubtless the mood you spoke of earlier, the emotion that you assume by analogy with that of the creator.*

• Analogy in the sense of resonance, not of proportionality. I would say that the work, in what is singular in it, frees in the one who tastes it an emotion analogous to that which produced it, an emotion of which that individual was capable, but without knowing it, and which enlarges his affective field once he experiences it. In other words, so long as the work has not cut a path through to the analogous emotion, it remains uncomprehended and we know that this frequently happens.

The subject of aesthetic experience is placed in a relation comparable to the relation of adequation that exists between the emotion of the creator and the work that conveys it. What he experiences is the singular feeling of this singular suitability. On the question of the singularity of the work of art, I am indebted to Gilles-Gaston Granger's *Essai d'une philosophie du style.*[3] According to him, what constitutes the success of a work of art is the fact that an artist has grasped the singularity of a conjuncture, a problematic, knotted for her in a unique point, and that she responds to this by a unique gesture. How is *this* problem to be resolved? I am thinking, for example, of Cézanne's stubbornness confronting the Sainte-Victoire mountain: why always paint the same view over and over? Because it is never the same. It is as if it were necessary for Cézanne to do justice to something that was not the idea of the mountain – not the terms we use in general discourse – but that represented the singularity of *this* mountain, here and now; this is what has to be rendered, what insists on receiving the iconic augmentation that the painter alone can confer upon it. It is in terms of the singular that the question confines Cézanne to the Sainte-Victoire mountain or to the Black Castle, this morning at this hour in this light. And to this singular question a singular answer has to be given. Genius is found precisely here: in the capacity to respond in a singular manner to the singular nature of the question.

It is in this sense that I attempt, in *The Rule of Metaphor*, to take up once again the problem of reference in metaphor, what I have called the power of refiguration of the poem or the narrative. For the referential function is exercised in the singularity of the relation of a work to that to which it renders justice in the living experience of the artist. The work refers to *itself* in an emotion that has disappeared as emotion but which has been preserved in the work. How are we to name this something emotive to which the work does justice? There is a word in English that I find very appropriate – *mood*, which the French imperfectly renders as *humeur*. What the artist restores is the mood that corresponds to the singular, prereflexive, antepredicative relation to the situation of a given object in the world. The mood is like a relation outside of the self, a manner of inhabiting a world here and now; it is this mood that can be painted, put into music or into narrative in a work, which, if it is successful, will have the right kind of rapport with it.

But the fact that this mood can be, so to speak, problematized, in order to become a singular question calling for a singular response, that the experience of the artist, and what it contains that demands to be said, can be transposed in the form of a singular problem to be resolved by pictorial or other means, this is perhaps the enigma of artistic creation. The modesty or the pride of the artist – in this case, it amounts to the same thing – is probably to know at this very moment how to make the gesture that every person should make. In apprehending the singularity of the question there is the sentiment of an incredible obligation; in the case of Cézanne or Van Gogh we know that it was overwhelming. It is as if the artist experienced the urgency of an unpaid debt with respect to something singular that had to be said in a singular manner.

• *Nevertheless, it remains that this singular experience becomes communicable in and through the work.*

• This is indeed what is most astonishing, in other words, that there is something universal in this singularity. Because, in the last analysis, a painter paints to be seen, a musician writes to be heard. Something of her experience, precisely because it has been carried by a work, is going to be able to be communicated. Her naked experience as such was incommunicable; but, as soon as it can be problematized in the form of a singular question which is adequately answered in the form of a response that is singular as well, then it acquires communicability, it becomes universalizable. The work iconically augments the lived experience, inexpressible, incommunicable, closed upon itself. It is this iconic augmentation, as augmentation, that is communicable. So, to take one example, what is communicable in Van Gogh's *Church at Auvers-sur-Oise* is the perfect appropriateness of the means used to produce this unique thing which does not represent the village church that one can see by going today to Auvers-sur-Oise, but which materializes in a visible work what remains invisible, namely the unique and probably crazed experience that Van Gogh had of it when he painted it. The perfect resolution of the singular problem presented to the artist is grasped in the aesthetic experience in a prereflexive, immediate manner; in Kantian terms, one would say that it is the "play" between imagination and understanding, as it is incarnated in this work, which is communicable; in the absence of the objective universality proper to determinant judgment, reflecting judgment – to which aesthetic experience belongs – has, in terms of universality, only this play; this is what can be shared.

But there is no doubt that in this lies the great difficulty of reflections on art. For the aesthetic experience involves each time *a* spectator, *a* listener, *a* reader who is also in a relation of singularity with the singularity of the work; but at the same time, it is the first act of a communication of the work to others and, virtually, to all. The work is like a trail of fire issuing from itself, reaching me and reaching beyond me to the universality of humanity.

To follow the requirements of singularity to the end is to give the best chance of the greatest universality: such is the paradox that must probably be maintained.

• *But would it not be possible to seek the universality of the work in the direction of its formal rules of composition: the three unities for classical tragedy, the tempered scale for eighteenth- and nineteenth-century music, the canons of figuration and of perspective for painting?*

• Aesthetic rules constitute only a weak universality, close to common sense and its generalities; they are conventions, hence something agreed upon. But the universality to which the work aspires is something entirely different, since it is actually possible only through the intermediary of its extreme singularity. Take the example of nonfigurative painting: it is the nakedness of the singular experience that is communicated without the mediation of rules susceptible of being recognized within a tradition, without this element of normativity; the weak universality of generalities is broken, but the communicability is perfectly accomplished.

This is why I think that, already in figurative art, the beauty of a given work, the success of a given portrait belonged not to the quality of the representation, not to the fact that it resembled a model, not even to its conforming to allegedly universal rules, but to a *surplus* in relation to any representation and to any rule; the work could represent an object or a face with close resemblance, it could obey rules agreed upon in advance, but if it deserves to figure today in our imaginary museum, it is because *in surplus* it perfectly matched up to its genuine object, which was not the fruit bowl or the face of the young girl in the turban but the singular grasp by Cézanne or Vermeer of the singular question posed to them. From this point of view, one could then say that the split between figurative art and nonfigurative art is less than one thinks; for in classical painting, it was already this surplus in relation to representation that undoubtedly caused it to be said of a given portrait, among so many others that had an equally close resemblance to their model, that it forced us to admire it. One could say that nonfigurative painting freed what was in reality already the properly aesthetic dimension of the figurative, a dimension that remained veiled by the function of representation that fell to pictorial art. And it is when the concern with the internal composition alone was disconnected from the representative function that the function of *manifestation* of a world was rendered explicit; representation once abolished, it becomes obvious that the work expresses the world in a manner other than by representing it; it expresses it by iconizing the singular emotional relation of the artist to the world, which I have called the *mood*. Or, once again in Kantian terms, with the project of representation what remained of determinant judgment in the work disappears, and reflective judgment appears in all its bareness, containing the expression of a singularity which is seeking its normativity, and finding it only in its capacity to communicate itself indefinitely to others.

   One could say exactly the same thing about music: the elimination of tonality in Schönberg's *Pierrot lunaire*, then the invention of the twelve-tone system in his later works, achieves, in relation to the tempered scale used throughout the eighteenth and nineteenth centuries, the same break with familiarity as Picasso's nonfigurative style, where the human figure is cut, twisted, in comparison with the figurative style of Delacroix. The musical rules of the nineteenth century had nothing universal about them, they were merely nomic generalities that hid the genuine relation to the *mood* that each musical piece expresses. As in painting, the convention of the rules facilitated access to the works; communicability was not accomplished through singularity alone. And this is why very contemporary art is so difficult: it forbids any recourse to attached rules defining *a priori* what is to be beautiful.


• *If we follow the Kantian thread with you, are we not led to extend what you say about aesthetic experience to other areas? For, in Kant, aesthetics does not exhaust the entire field of reflective judgment, which also includes moral experience.*

• I believe that, between ethics and aesthetics, there can be a sort of reciprocal instruction around the theme of singularity. For, by contrast with things, but like works of art, persons are also singular conjunctions – a face in which features are assembled in a unique manner, a single time; like works, they cannot be substituted for one another. Perhaps we learn about singularity through the contact with works, which would be, if it is true, one way of pursuing the Kantian argument in showing how the experience of the beautiful – and even more to the point, of the sublime – leads us to morality.

But I think that, if one really wants to reflect on the transposition of aesthetic experience into lateral domains, one would have to take into account the two main aspects of the work: its singularity and its communicability, with the particular form of universality that the latter implies. To remain in the ethical domain, I wonder if the work of art, with its conjunction of singularity and communicability, is not a model for thinking the notion of testimony. In what way can one say that, in the realm of extreme moral choices, we find exemplarity and communicability? For example, one would have to explore here the beauty of the grandeur of the soul: there is, it seems to me, a beauty specific to the acts that we admire ethically. I am thinking particularly of the testimony given by exemplary lives, simple lives, but that attest by a sort of short-circuit to the absolute, to the fundamental, without there being any need for them to pass through the interminable degrees of our laborious ascensions; see the beauty of certain devoted, or as we say, consecrated, faces.

In extending this line of comparison with aesthetic experience, one could say that such examples of goodness, compassion or courage, together with what is rare in them, are in the same relation to the situation in which they occur as the painter who is solving the particular problem he is confronting, he and he alone. And from the solitude of the sublime act we are led directly to its communicability by a pre-reflective and immediate grasp of its relation of agreement with the situation: in this given case, here and now, we are certain that *this* is exactly what had to be done, in the same way that we consider a given painting to be a masterpiece because right away we have the feeling that it realizes the perfect adequation of the singularity of the solution to the singularity of the question. Do you remember the men and women whose testimony Marek Halter collected in his film *Tseddek*? What did they all say when they were asked, "Why did you do that? Why did you take the risk of saving the Jews?" They simply answered, "What else could you do? It was the only thing to do in that situation."

In apprehending this relation of agreement between the moral act and the situation, there is an effect of being drawn to follow, which is really the equivalent of the communicability of the work of art. To express this capacity for following after, this exemplarity, German has a word that is lacking in French: *Nachfolge*. If we translate it by "imitation," then this is in the sense in which we speak of the *Imitation of Jesus Christ*. In evangelical morality, but also in the prophets of Israel, where does this effect of emulation come from? Without doubt, lying in the background of their acts there are norms. But it is the exemplarity of the singularity that poses a problem for me. To each of the rich young bourgeois of Assisi, Francis says: "Sell all you have and come." And they follow him! It is not a universal order he addresses to them but an injunction of one singular individual to another singular individual; the effect of following after passes by way of this, just as analogous acts, themselves just as singular, are inspired by it. To return to Kant, we are in the sphere of reflective judgment in which communicability does not lie in applying a rule to a case but in the fact that it is the case that summons its rule; and it calls for the latter, precisely, in rendering itself communicable. Here the case engenders its normativity and not the reverse. And the communicability is itself made possible by the prereflexive apprehension of the agreement of the response to the demands of the situation.

- *Would you extend to other domains the idea that we find in certain moral acts, just as in works of art, an effect of exemplarity, a communicability, quite unlike the universality of an order?*

- This is, in any case, what Hannah Arendt suggests in her *Lectures on Kant's Political Philosophy*.[4] She transposes aesthetic judgment to singular historical events – the French Revolution, for example – which are not prevented by their singularity, quite the opposite, from relating to the general problem of the destination of humanity. But what is most interesting in these analyses, from my viewpoint, is the fact that it is strictly for the "world spectator" and not for the actors themselves that the singularity of the historical event is communicable, that it can occasion a sympathetic judgment. By its singularity, the event stands as testimony relative to the destination of the human species. It is not a matter of constructing a philosophy of history that would permit us to find a *phylum*, as it were, of humankind, obeying a finality analogous to that of animal species; for the cosmopolitan dimension to which the views of Kant, reappropriated by Hannah Arendt, destine humanity is of an entirely different order than the biological dimension – it is regulated by this specific mode of communicability which is that of great historical events, or of people who go beyond the sphere of the ordinary, and which results from their singularity.

● *Does this also hold in the order of evil? Is there in your opinion an exemplarity of evil?*

● I have always resisted the idea that one could make a system of evil, that its manifestations could give rise to a summons. I am always struck, on the contrary, by its character of irruption and by the impossibility of comparing forms or magnitudes. Is it a prejudice to think that good gathers together, that expressions of the good gather *themselves* together, while those of evil scatter *themselves*? I do not believe that, even in its own manner, evil is cumulative and that there is in this order an equivalent of what I called, in connection with the good and the beautiful, a *Nachfolge*. For the transmission of evil, the only model we have is borrowed from biology; we think in terms of *contamination, infection, epidemic*. None of that is of the order of *Nachfolge*, of the communicability by means of extreme singularity; in evil, there is no equivalent to the iconic augmentation performed by the beautiful.

Perhaps this is, allow me to say in passing, the major problem of an attempt like that of Sade or Bataille: to establish in the order of evil an equivalent of iconic augmentation proper to the work of art; perhaps this, finally, is the ultimate impasse of perversion, to wish to allow evil to benefit from what, at very high cost, the good and the beautiful manage to produce.

● *On the other hand, the transposition you make of the experience of the beautiful into the sphere of morality, the immense value you confer on the notion of testimony, does all this not orient your analyses in the direction of the religious?*

● I should not like to sanction a sort of confiscation of the aesthetic in the name of the religious. All that can be put forward is that, in permitting detachment with respect to the strictly utilitarian, with respect to what is manipulable, art opens us to an entire range of feelings among which can appear feelings that could be called religious, such as veneration. Between the aesthetic and the religious, I would say that there is a zone of overlap rather than domains that are coextensive.

● *In speaking of a region of overlap, are you thinking of sacred art, which was long prevalent in the West, in music, painting, and in sculpture?*

● It is certain that art was initially completely infused with the religious. But in the opposite sense, one can also say that the sacred was initially characterized aesthetically, thanks to music, poetry, painting, or sculpture.

It is striking, moreover, to note that Jewish iconoclasm, so radical in the area of visual representations, was not extended to music. The Psalms are full of musical notations – "To the singing master. On stringed instruments. On the octave. Psalm of David"; "To the singing master. On the flutes," and so on – and this music has even been recreated and played.

But one of the richest examples of this overlap of the religious and the aesthetic is, undoubtedly, the Canticle of Canticles. The fact that the same poetry can be interpreted as erotic and as spiritual, as an allegory of the male/female relationship and as an allegory of the marriage between Yahveh and his people, or yet again, between the soul and the Christ, this sets us thinking. The whole scale of values, the entire trajectory *eros*, *philia*, *agapè* can be traversed with a single play of metaphors. And the fact that the body is constantly cast in metaphorical terms – "Your lips are like a thread of purple"; "Your neck is like the tower of David"; "Your two breasts are two fawns, twins of a gazelle" – makes the text open to several readings with, ultimately, a sort of theological audacity: for, in the prophetic tradition, there remains a vertical relation between the human and the divine – man and God are not on the same level. Yet love introduces an element of reciprocity that can imply crossing the threshold between the ethical and the mystical. Where ethics maintains the vertical dimension, mysticism attempts to introduce reciprocity; the lover and the loved occupy equal, reciprocal roles. Reciprocity is introduced into verticality by means of the language of love and thanks to the metaphorical resources of the erotic.

One could believe that it is an extreme irony that the only erotic poem in the Bible has been used to celebrate chastity. But this is because chastity is another kind of nuptial bond, since it accompanies the wedding of the soul and God; there is a form of nuptial that passes through chastity just as it passes through the erotic. The great metaphorical complex of the Canticle of Canticles is what makes this transfer possible.

To be sure, it is because the assembly of Yahveh was given an exclusively spiritual interpretation that the Canticle of Canticles was integrated into the Hebraic canon. And a good thing too! But its equivocalness must absolutely be maintained and any unilateral reading shunned, that of Yabné just as much as that of certain exegetes, in particular positivist Catholics, who battle to reestablish an exclusively erotic sense, as though they were trying to make up for all the time lost in traditional readings. It is more important to note that the presence of the Canticle of Canticles in the canon allows it to benefit from the entire range of meaning of the rest of the book, onto which, in its turn, it overflows with its own erotic values and, in particular, its capacity to introduce tenderness in the ethical relation. Let us leave the scholarly exegetes to their scholarly naivety!

# Notes

Chapter 1 From Valence to Nanterre

1 Marc Sangnier, journalist and political activist, represented the social democratic tendency within French Catholicism. He founded the journal *La Démocratie* and the political movement La Jeune République. (Tr.)

2 John Darby (1800–82), English theologian and Anglican pastor, developed a doctrine, which spread especially throughout the Anglo-Saxon countries and marginally in France, taking the form of a very strict Calvinism stressing predestination and the "ruin of the Church."

3 Roland Dalbiez, *La Méthode psychanalytique et la doctrine freudienne* (Paris: Desclée de Brouwer, 1936).

4 *Honneur aux maîtres*, presented by Marguerite Léna (Paris: Critérion, 1993).

5 Jules Lagneau (1851–94) and Jules Lachelier (1832–1918) embodied the grand reflexive tradition of French philosophy. Lagneau was in particular the teacher of Alain, who never ceased to express his great admiration for him and who published his courses posthumously under the title *Célèbres Leçons et fragments*. On Lachelier, see *Oeuvres* (2 vols, Paris, 1933), vol. 1: *Fondement de l'introduction suivi de Psychologie et métaphysique et de notes sur le pari de Pascal*; vol. 2: *Études sur le syllogisme suivies de l'observation de Platner et de notes sur le Philèbe*.

6 Georges Davy (1883–1976) was, in turn, Dean of the Academy at Rennes (1931), Inspector General (1939), then Professor of Sociology at the Sorbonne (1944–55). See *Des clans aux empires* (Paris, 1922); *La Foi jurée* (Paris, 1922); *Le Droit, l'idéalisme et l'expérience* (Paris, 1922); *Sociologues d'hier et d'aujourd'hui* (Paris, 1931).

7 Ricoeur has frequently mentioned the strong impression made on him as a boy of the arrest and conviction of an innocent man, Seznec, for the crime of murder. Sent to a penal colony, he was later released. (Tr.)

8 The Croix-de-Feu began as a right-wing organization of First World War veterans. It became more politically active under the leadership of Colonel François de La Rocque. With the dissolution of the leagues in 1936, it was replaced by the Parti Social Français (PSF). (Tr.)

9 Z. Sternhell, *Ni droite ni gauche* (Paris: Le Seuil, 1983). For a discussion of

Sternhell's theses, see the study devoted to him by Philippe Burrin in *Histoire des droites en France*, ed. J.-F. Sirinelli (Paris: Gallimard, 1992), vol. 1, ch. 10, "Le fascisme," pp. 603–52.

10 This discussion refers to the split between the Socialist and Communist parties in France, following the Congrès de Tours in 1920. Socialists continued to adhere to the Second International, referred to here as the "old house," while the Communists joined the Third International. At the time of the Popular Front in the mid-1930s, the debate concerned the nationalization of the Bank of France and consequences for the nation's financial policies. The wealth of the nation was alleged to be concentrated in the small circle of privilege known as the two hundred families. (Tr.)

11 The SFIO, Section Française de l'Internationale Ouvrière, a union of several socialist groups, was founded in 1905 and replaced in 1969 by the current Parti Socialiste (PS). (Tr.)

12 Founded in the small village of Uriage, near Grenoble, this was the most famous of the leadership programs established before the war to train officers and the directors of youth groups through several months of physical exercise and ideological debates. It was run by Captain Dunoyer de Segonzac. Proudhon, Mauras, and Péguy were the preferred authors.

13 Paul Ricoeur's French translation of Husserl's *Ideen I* was published in 1950 (Paris: Gallimard) with notes and an introduction. This introduction appears in English translation in Paul Ricoeur, *Husserl: An Analysis of his Phenomenology*, tr. E. G. Ballard and L. Embree (Evanston, Ill.: Northwestern University Press, 1967). An English translation of *Ideas* by W. R. Boyce Gibson had appeared in 1931 (repr. New York: Collier, 1962).

14 Karl Jaspers (1883–1969), Professor at Heidelberg from 1922 to 1937, was stripped of his teaching position by the Nazis in 1937. After the war, disappointed by the behavior of his compatriots in confronting the guilt associated with the crimes of the Nazis, he went into exile in Switzerland. He taught at the University of Basle from 1948 until he retired.

15 Mikel Dufrenne and Paul Ricoeur, *Karl Jaspers et la philosophie de l'existence*, with a preface by Karl Jaspers (Paris: Le Seuil, 1947).

16 Kostas Axelos and Jean Beaufret together translated *Qu'est-ce que la philosophie?* by Heidegger (Paris: Gallimard, 1957); Heidegger was introduced into France almost entirely through Beaufret, to whom Heidegger had addressed the famous *Letter on Humanism* (1947). It was also through the intermediary of Beaufret that, in 1955, Heidegger met René Char.

17 Karl Jaspers, *Strindberg and Van Gogh*, tr. Oskar Grunow and David Woloshin (Tucson: University of Arizona Press, 1977).

18 Eugen Fink (1905–75) and Ludwig Landgrebe (1902–92) were both assistants of Husserl in the 1920s.

19 Emmanuel Mounier (1905–50), strongly influenced by Jacques Maritain and Gabriel Marcel, embodied Christian existentialism. Before the war he published, in particular, *Révolution personnaliste et communautaire* (Paris, 1935); after the war, in addition to his *Traité du caractère* (Paris, 1946), he also published *Introduction aux existentialismes* (1947) and *Qu'est-ce que le personnalisme?* (1947).

20 Paul-Louis Landsberg (1905–44) had left Germany when Hitler came to power. After teaching in Spain from 1934 to 1936, he came to France, where he worked with Mounier on the journal *Esprit*. He was deported to the Oranienburg concentration camp.

21 Jean Nabert (1881–1960) belongs to the French tradition of reflexive philoso- phy. His main works are *L'Expérience intérieure de la liberté* (1924), repub- lished in 1994 with a preface by Paul Ricoeur (Paris: P.U.F., 1994); *Éléments pour une éthique* (1943), republished with a preface by Paul Ricoeur (Paris: Aubier, 1962); *Essai sur le mal* (1955), 2nd edn (Paris: Aubier, 1970).

22 Paul Ricoeur, *Lectures 2. La contrée des philosophes* (Paris: Le Seuil, 1992), pp. 137–48.

23 Reprinted in Maurice Merleau-Ponty, *Signs*, tr. Richard C. McCleary (Evanston, Ill.: Northwestern University Press, 1964), pp. 84–97.

24 Paul Ricoeur, *Lectures 1. Autour du politique* (Paris: Le Seuil, 1991), pp. 368– 97.

25 *Philosophie de la volonté. Finitude et Culpabilité. I. L'homme faillible* (Paris: Aubier, 1960); *Fallible Man*, tr. C. Kelbley (Chicago: Henry Regnery, 1965). *Philosophie de la volonté. Finitude et culpabilité. II. La symbolique du mal* (Paris: Aubier, 1960); *The Symbolism of Evil*, tr. E. Buchanan (New York– Evanston–London: Harper and Row, 1967; Boston: Beacon Press, 1969).

26 Paul Ricoeur, *Freud and Philosophy: An Essay on Interpretation*, tr. D. Savage (New Haven and London: Yale University Press, 1970).

27 *Philosophie de la volonté. I. Le volontaire et l'involontaire* (Paris: Aubier, 1950); *Freedom and Nature: The Voluntary and the Involuntary*, tr. E. V. Kohák (Evanston, Ill.: Northwestern University Press, 1966).

28 Giovanni Pico della Mirandola, known in French as Pic de la Mirondole, was a fifteenth-century Italian scholar known for his vast erudition, in particular for his familiarity with many languages and religious traditions. (Tr.)

29 Mircea Eliade, *Traité d'histoire des religions* (Paris, 1949).

30 This is the title of Gadamer's best known work, published in 1960 in Tübingen under the full title *Wahrheit und Methode. Grunzüge einer philosophischen Hermeneutik*; *Truth and Method* (London: Sheed and Ward; New York: Seabury, 1975).

31 Hans-Georg Gadamer, *Années d'apprentissage philosophique. Une rétrospective* (Paris: Critérion, 1992).

32 It is considered a great honor to be invited to deliver this series of lectures at the University of Edinburgh.

33 René Rémond, *La Règle et le consentement. Gouverner une société* (Paris: Fayard, 1979).

## Chapter 2  France/United States: Two Incomparable Histories

1 The institutions on the other side of the Atlantic where Paul Ricoeur has taught over the past forty years or so are the University of Montreal, the Union Seminary in New York, Yale University, the Department of Comparative Literature of the University of Toronto, the National Humanities Center in North Carolina, and finally the University of Chicago (1967–92).

2 Paul Tillich (1886–1965), philosopher and Protestant theologian of German origin, emigrated to the United States after having published in 1933 one of the first in depth critiques of national socialism (*Sozialistische Entscheidung*). Greatly influenced by Schelling and Bultmann, he attempted to construct a work that takes note of the secularization of contemporary societies and that preserves the sense of transcendence, of the "one thing necessary." He exerted a strong influence on postwar philosophical and theological thought.

3 Professor at the Collège de France from 1951 to 1963, Martial Gueroult (1891–1976) provided the defense and illustration in France of a systematic approach to philosophical doctrines centered on the analysis of methods of investigation, convinced that a philosophical thesis is inseparable from the demonstrative procedures that establish it. He is the author, in particular, of *Descartes selon l'ordre des raisons* (2 vols, Paris, 1953); *Malebranche* (3 vols, Paris, 1956–9); *Spinoza* (2 vols, Paris, 1968–74).

4 Peter Frederick Strawson, *The Bounds of Sense: An Essay on Kant's Critique of Pure Reason* (London: Routledge, Chapman and Hall, 1966). Strawson is also known for his book *Individuals: An Essay in Descriptive Metaphysics* (London: Methuen 1959).

5 John Rawls is the author of *A Theory of Justice*, published in 1971, a key book that has given rise in the United States and throughout the world to a huge amount of discussion.

6 For Michael Sander, see most notably *Liberalism and the Limits of Justice* (London: Oxford University Press, 1982). For Michael Walzer, see in particular *Spheres of Justice: A Defense of Pluralism and Equality* (New York: Basic Books, 1983).

7 Jean-Marc Ferry, *Les Puissances de l'expérience: essai sur l'identité contemporaine* (Paris: Le Cerf, 1986).

8 Michael Walzer, *The Revolution of the Saints* (New York: Atheneum, 1970).

9 Immanuel Kant, "Perpetual Peace," in *On History*, ed. and tr. Louis White Beck (New York: Macmillan, 1963), pp. 102–3.

10 Ibid., p. 103.

11 Ibid.

12 Luc Boltanski and Laurent Thévenot, *De la justification* (Paris: Gallimard, 1991).

### Chapter 3  From Psychoanalysis to the Question of the Self

1 "Le conscient et l'inconscient," in *L'inconscient. VIe Colloque de Bonneval*, ed. H. Ey (Paris: Desclée de Brouwer, 1966); "Consciousness and the Unconscious," tr. W. Domingo, in *The Conflict of Interpretations: Essays in Hermeneutics* (Evanston, Ill.: Northwestern University Press, 1974).

2 Jean Hyppolite (1907–68), Director of the École Normale Supérieure (Ulm), then Professor at the Collège de France, is known for his books on Hegel; he also devoted pioneering works to Freud and his interest in philosophy. See, in particular, his study "Commentaire parlé sur la *Verneinung* de Freud" (1955), in Jean Hyppolite, *Figures de la pensée philosophique*, vol. 1 (Paris: P.U.F., 1971).

3 Elisabeth Roudinesco, *Histoire de la psychanalyse en France* (2 vols, Paris: Fayard 1994).

4 This first appeared in English under the title "The Question of Proof in Freud's Psychoanalytical Writings," *Journal of the American Psychoanalytic Association* 25.4 (1977); it was reprinted in *Hermeneutics and the Human Sciences*, ed. J. B. Thompson (Cambridge: Cambridge University Press, 1981).

5 Heinrich Rickert (1863-1936), Professor of Philosophy at Heidelberg, where he succeeded Windelband; he denied the possibility of formulating general laws of history; cf. *Kulturwissenschaft und Naturwissenschaft* (Tübingen, 1899).

6 For Jean Ladrière, see, in particular: *Discours scientifique et parole de foi* (Paris: Le Cerf, 1970).

7 Claude Lévi-Strauss, *The Naked Man*, tr. J. Weightman and D. Weightman (New York: Harper and Row, 1981); this is vol. 4 of *Introduction to a Science of Mythology*.

8 Foucault is discussed in ch. 10, "Towards a Hermeneutics of Historical Consciousness," of *Time and Narrative*, vol. 3, tr. K. Blamey and D. Pellauer (Chicago: University of Chicago Press, 1988), pp. 217–19.

9 *Time and Narrative*, vol. 1, tr. K. McLaughlin and D. Pellauer (Chicago: University of Chicago Press, 1984); *Time and Narrative*, vol. 2, tr. K. McLaughlin and D. Pellauer (Chicago: University of Chicago Press, 1985); *Time and Narrative*, vol. 3, as in note 8 above.

10 *Oneself as Another*, tr. K. Blamey (Chicago: University of Chicago Press, 1992); translation of *Soi-même comme un autre* (Paris: Le Seuil, 1990).

11 *The Rule of Metaphor*, tr. R. Czerny (Toronto: University of Toronto Press, 1978); translation of *La Métaphore vive* (Paris: Le Seuil, 1975).

12 Max Black's works include, notably, *Models and Metaphors* (Ithaca: Cornell University Press, 1962).

13 *History and Truth*, tr. C. Kelbley (Evanston, Ill.: Northwestern University Press, 1965); translation of *Histoire et vérité* (Paris: Le Seuil, 1955).

14 "Philosophies critiques de l'histoire: Recherche, explication, écriture." in P. Floistad (ed.), *Philosophical Problems Today* (Boston: Dordrecht. London: Kluwer, 1994).

15 Marcel Proust, *Time Regained*: "But to return to my own case, I thought more modestly of my book and it would be inaccurate even to say that I thought of those who would read it as 'my' readers. For it seemed to me that they would not be 'my' readers but the readers of their own selves, my book being merely a sort of magnifying glass like those which the optician at Combray used to offer his customers – it would be my book, but with its help I would furnish them with the means of reading what lay inside themselves"; see *Remembrance of Things Past*, vol. 3, tr. C. K. Scott Moncrieff, Terence Kilmartin, and Andreas Mayor (New York: Random House, 1981) p. 1089.

16 Books by Hans Robert Jauss available in English include *Aesthetic Experience and Literary Hermeneutics*, tr. M. Shaw (Minneapolis: University of Minnesota Press, 1982); *Toward an Aesthetics of Reception*, tr. T. Bahti (Minneapolis: University of Minnesota Press, 1982). He has also devoted a work to Marcel Proust: *Zeit und Erinnerung in Marcel Proust "À la recherche du temps perdu"* (Heidelberg: Carl Winter, 1955).

17 Wolfgang Iser, *The Act of Reading: A Theory of Aesthetic Response* (Baltimore: Johns Hopkins University Press, 1978).

18 Gaston Bachelard, *L'Intuition de l'instant* (Paris: Stock, 1932).

19 Derek Parfit, *Reasons and Persons* (Oxford: Oxford University Press, 1986).

20 Northrop Frye, *The Great Code: the Bible and Literature* (New York: Harcourt Brace Jovanovich, 1982).

21 "Le sujet convoqué. À l'école des récits de vocation prophétique," *Revue de l'Institut Catholique de Paris*, no. 28 (1988). "Phénoménologie de la religion," *Revue de l'Institut Catholique de Paris*, no. 45 (1993); repr. in *Lectures 3. Aux frontières de la philosophie* (Paris: Le Seuil, 1994).

22 For a more detailed discussion of hard cases, see the chapter "Duty of Memory, Duty of Justice."

23 Maurice Halbwachs (1877–1945), elected Professor at the Collège de France a few weeks before being deported to Buchenwald, where he died. For him, social consciousness was manifested by means of a "collective memory," embodied in material traces, rites, traditions, and so on. He was the author, in

particular, of *Cadres sociaux de la mémoire* (Paris: Alcan, 1925), and of *La Mémoire collective* (Paris: P.U.F., 1968).
24 Edmund Husserl, *Cartesian Meditations*, tr. D. Cairns (The Hague: Martinus Nijhoff, 1977), sec. 58.

## Chapter 4   Politics and Totalitarianism

1 "Le paradoxe politique," in *Esprit*, no. 5 (1957).
2 Max Weber, *Economy and Society: An Outline of Interpretive Sociology*, ed. Günther Roth and Claus Wittich, tr. E. Fischoff et al. (New York: Bedminster Press, 1968; repr. Berkeley: University of California Press, 1978).
3 Claude Lefort, born in 1924, has written, notably, *L'Invention démocratique* (Paris: Fayard, 1981) and *À l'épreuve du politique* (Paris: Calmann-Lévy, 1991). Student of Merleau-Ponty, cofounder with Cornelius Castoriadis of the journal *Socialisme ou Barbarie* and, with Pierre Clastres, of the journal *Libre*, he is one of the first in France, on the Left, to have criticized Soviet bureaucracy and totalitarianism.
4 Éric Weil (1904–77), author of *Hegel et l'État* (Paris: Vrin, 1950), and of *Philosophie politique* (Paris: Vrin, 1956). The problem of violence is at the center of his reflection.
5 Isaiah 40 and 55.
6 See Isaiah 44: 28 and 45: 1.
7 Margarete Buber-Neumann was first deported to Siberia; she was then turned over to the Gestapo in 1940 and deported to Ravensbrück. She has recounted her life in two books *Déportée en Sibérie* (Paris: Le Seuil, 1986) and *Déportée à Ravensbrück* (Paris: Le Seuil, 1988). It was in the last camp that she knew Milena Jesenska, Kafka's "fiancée": cf. Margarete Buber-Neumann, *Milena* (Paris: Le Seuil, 1990).
8 See, in particular, Saül Friedländer, *L'Antisémitisme nazi. Histoire d'une psychose collective* (Paris: Le Seuil, 1971) and *Reflets du nazisme* (Paris: Le Seuil, 1982). See also his contribution to the collection *L'Allemagne nazie et le génocide juif* (Paris: Gallimard-Le Seuil, 1985).
9 It was set off in Germany following the "revision" of the historiography of Nazism proposed by the historian Nolte. Documents on this topic were published in France under the title *Devant l'histoire. Les documents de la controverse sur la question de la singularité de l'extermination des juifs par le régime nazi* (Paris: Le Cerf, 1988).
10 Karl Popper, *The Open Society and its Enemies* (London: Routledge and Kegan Paul, 1952).
11 Hermann Cohen (1842–1918), leader of the Marburg neo-Kantian school, developed at the end of his life a systematic philosophy of religion inspired by Judaism. See *Pardès* ("Germanité et judaïté"), no. 5 (1987).
12 Cf. Carl Schmitt, *La Notion de politique*, Fr. trans. (Paris: Calmann-Lévy, 1972).

## Chapter 5   Duty of Memory, Duty of Justice

1 What is called the natural law school grants to human beings, in opposition to the idea of divine right, rights that are held to stem from consideration of human

nature alone, abstracting from its origin.

2 For Ronald Dworkin, see, in particular, *Taking Rights Seriously* (Cambridge, Mass.: Harvard University Press, 1977); *A Matter of Principle* (Oxford: Oxford University Press, 1985).

3 Karl Jaspers, *Die Schuldfrage* (Zurich, 1946); *The Question of German Guilt*, tr. E. B. Ashton (New York: Dial Press, 1947).

4 Raymond Aron, *Introduction à la philosophie de l'histoire* (1938; Paris: Gallimard, 1986).

5 Reinhard Koselleck, born in 1923, professor at the University of Bielefeld, is especially known in France for his book *Kritik und Krise* (1959); *Critique and Crisis: Enlightenment and the Pathogenesis of Modern Society* (Cambridge, Mass.: M.I.T. Press, 1988).

## Chapter 6  Education and Secularism

1 Émile Combes was a French politician whose anticlerical policies resulted in laws banning religious education in the schools (1904) and establishing the separation of church and state (1905). (Tr.)

2 Marcel Gauchet, *Le Désenchantement du monde. Une histoire politique de la religion* (Paris: Gallimard, 1985).

## Chapter 7  Biblical Readings and Meditations

1 Karl Barth (1886–1968), Calvinist theologian from Basle, marked a turning point in Protestant theology, which had previously been dominated by Schleiermacher's hermeneutics (cf. his *Commentary on the Epistle to the Romans*), by breaking with the anthropocentric vision of his time, in the name of a "dialectical" conception stressing negation, the infinite distance that separates man from God, where the only mediation possible is neither experience nor history but the Cross, rejecting any idea of synthesis between world and Church, between man and God.

2 For Paul Beauchamp, see in particular *L'Un et l'Autre Testament. Essai de lecture* (Paris: Le Seuil, 1977) and *Le Récit, la lettre et le corps. Essais bibliques* (Paris: Le Cerf, 1992).

3 Charles Taylor, *Sources of the Self: The Making of the Modern Identity* (Cambridge, Mass.: Harvard University Press, 1989). On his work, cf. James Tully (ed.), *Philosophy in an Age of Pluralism: The Philosophy of Charles Taylor in Question* (Cambridge: Cambridge University Press, 1994).

4 Cf. Paul Ricoeur, *Lectures 3* (Paris: Le Seuil, 1994).

5 Xavier-Léon Dufour, *Lecture de l'Évangile de Jean* (3 vols, Paris: Le Seuil, 1988–93); *Face à la mort. Jésus et Paul* (Paris: Le Seuil, 1979).

6 Cf. Léon Brunschvicg, *La Raison et la religion* (Paris, 1939). On the discussion surrounding the question "Is there a Christian philosophy?" raised in 1927 by Émile Bréhier in vol. 1 of his *Histoire de la philosophie*, cf. Henri Gouhier, *La Philosophie et son histoire*, 2nd edn (Paris, 1948).

7 Jean Delumeau, *La Peur en Occident* (Paris: Fayard, 1981).

8 Cf. Hannah Arendt, *The Human Condition* (Chicago: The University of Chicago Press, 1958), p. 247.

9 *Time and Narrative*, vol. 1, pp. 22ff.

10 Cf. François Marty, *La Naissance de la métaphysique chez Kant. Une étude sur la notion kantienne d'analogie* (Paris: Beauchesne, 1980).
11 Cf. A. N. Whitehead, *Process and Reality* (New York: Free Press, 1978). Whitehead (1861–1947) attempted to construct a natural theology capable of reconciling the notion of God and that of becoming.
12 For Charles Hartshorne, who was Whitehead's collaborator at Harvard, see *Man's Vision of God and the Logic of Theism* (Chicago, 1941).
13 *Le Concept de Dieu après Auschwitz* (Paris: Payot et Rivages, 1994).
14 Jean Nabert, *Éléments pour une éthique* (Paris: P.U.F., 1923); *Essai sur le mal* (1955; 2nd edn, Paris: Aubier, 1970).
15 Franz Rosenzweig (1886–1929), born into a bourgeois Jewish family that was almost completely assimilated, was on the verge of converting to Christianity when he had a mystical experience in a Berlin synagogue in 1913. He then decided to remain Jewish. His great work is *The Star of Redemption*, tr. W. W. Hallo (1921; New York: Holt Reinhart and Winston, 1971).
16 Lucien Febvre, *Un destin. Martin Luther*, 4th edn, rev. (Paris: P.U.F., 1968).
17 Gilles Lipovetsky, *L'Ère du vide* (Paris: Gallimard, 1989).

**Chapter 8 Aesthetic Experience**

1 For Michel Henry, see *L'Essence de la manifestation* (2 vols, Paris: P.U.F., 1968).
2 André Malraux, *The Voices of Silence*, tr. S. Gilbert (Garden City, N.Y.: Doubleday, 1953).
3 Gilles-Gaston Granger, *Essai d'une philosophie du style* (Paris: Armand Colin, 1968).
4 Hannah Arendt, *Lectures on Kant's Political Philosophy* (Chicago: University of Chicago Press, 1982).